Organizational Intelligence

ORGANIZATIONAL INTELLIGENCE

Knowledge and Policy
in Government and Industry

BY

HAROLD L. WILENSKY

Basic Books, Inc., Publishers
New York / London

© 1967 by Harold L. Wilensky
Library of Congress Catalog Card Number: 67-17540
Manufactured in the United States of America

For Steve, Mike, and Dan

Preface

This book explores a classic problem in social science—the ways in which knowledge shapes policy. From Machiavelli and Adam Smith to modern social researchers, social scientists have been policy-oriented. In their "applied" roles or moods, they have addressed themselves to the problems of the ruler; intermittently they have turned their attention to the troubles of less privileged groups among the ruled. Even the most "theoretical" social scientists, however, have been policy-oriented in the broad sense that they have dealt with persistent problems of the human condition—freedom and order, equality and hierarchy, security and efficiency, the causes and consequences of the wealth of nations. Despite centuries of concern with policy, we have little solid understanding of the relation of experts and intellectuals to men of power. Yet the conjunction of two current trends—the knowledge explosion and the organizational revolution—makes such understanding indispensable for the proper conduct of administrative life and the effective pursuit of the public interest.

In governments, business enterprises, political parties, labor unions, the professions, educational institutions, and voluntary associations, and in every other sphere of modern life, the chronic condition is a surfeit of information, useless, poorly integrated, or lost somewhere in the system. Too many critics of the organizational and political sources of our troubles see diabolical plots where there is only drift, a taste for reckless adventure where there is only ignorance of risks, the machinations of a power elite where there is, in William James's phrase, only a "bloomin' buzzin' confusion." The professors among the social critics too often have visions of insidious men of power invading the academy and exploiting scholars for private purposes, when there is only am-

biguity—the invaders possessing interests and values that are unclear, the scholar entering a maze of conflicting expectations if not
a vacuum. Although subversion of scholarship occurs, the problem
is more often that the professors and researchers most available for
sustained consultation are the least independent-minded or the
least able.

The most common polemic about the role of the intellectual
pictures a simple dilemma: intellectuals either stand aside and in-
dulge in pure hostility to power and thereby risk irrelevance, or
they join the establishment as experts and risk the corruption of
their knowledge and sensibilities. The roles they in fact play are
far more varied: by utopian and counter-utopian debunking or by
ideological justification of the status quo, they pose issues; by their
work in the mass media, they distract attention or bring new worlds
to view; by their work in universities, they reformulate and communicate the cultural heritage or build it anew. But whatever stance
they take, wherever they are located, and whatever they do, they
should understand the forces in culture and social structure that set
limits to and present possibilities for the application of reason in
man's affairs. This book was written in the conviction that students
of organizational life can further that understanding by giving
more attention to the intelligence function in complex social
systems. It aims to bring together the scattered literature on organizational intelligence and to develop hypotheses about (1) the
determinants of the uses of intelligence and (2) the structural and
doctrinal roots of intelligence failures; and to infer from these
hypotheses the conditions that facilitate the flow of high-quality
intelligence.

Intelligence denotes the information—questions, insights, hypotheses, evidence—relevant to policy. It includes both scientific
knowledge and political or ideological information, scientific or not.
This definition is broad enough to encompass general pictures of
social and natural order as well as specific messages (significant
sequences of symbols) about immediate issues.

High-quality intelligence designates information that is *clear*
because it is understandable to those who must use it; *timely* because it gets to them when they need it; *reliable* because diverse
observers using the same procedures see it in the same way; *valid*
because it is cast in the form of concepts and measures that capture

reality (the tests include logical consistency, successful prediction, congruence with established knowledge or independent sources); *adequate* because the account is full (the context of the act, event, or life of the person or group is described); and *wide-ranging* because the major policy alternatives promising a high probability of attaining organizational goals are posed or new goals suggested. By an intelligence failure I shall mean the inability to muster the intelligence needed for successful pursuit of organizational goals. When the relevant information is not in the organizational system as a result of the lack of appropriate search procedures, we can speak of an intelligence failure. The appropriate arena of search may be internal or external; for instance, when the State Department deals with diplomatic-military issues, the relevant information system includes intelligence agencies and the academic community—both of which cut across the boundaries of formal organization or political jurisdiction. When competent sources have been explored and high-quality intelligence does reach the decision-maker, but he is not in a position to act upon it because he is clearly constrained by forces beyond his control, we cannot refer to the instance as an intelligence failure. If available technology and personnel do not permit heads of state to monitor an impending attack from an unknown planet, or if they know everything there is to know about such an attack but can do nothing, not intelligence but power is deficient.

The military establishment provides a convenient analogue for understanding problems in the non-military uses of intelligence. Is inaccurate, untimely, or poorly interpreted information costly to every executive? In the military it can be calamitous, as the history of modern warfare attests. Are secrecy, hierarchy, centralization, and inter-agency rivalry major sources of distortion of messages in complex social systems? The military, with its accent on command and security, with its lively inter-service squabbles, exaggerates each of them. Do anti-intellectualism and a narrow empiricism, in odd combination with a demand for scientific prediction, lead to foolish ideas about the proper organization and possibilities of intelligence? Wartime estimates of enemy power and intent dramatize the effects of doctrines of intelligence on its quality. Do hierarchical organizations that are new, rapidly expanding, or crisis-ridden have great difficulty striking a balance between control and the mobilization of expertise, and, therefore, are they prone to innovate in staffing and technology? The strain is especially apparent in the wartime military establishment: on the one hand, great resistance to unconventional careers and ideas; on the other, pioneering innovations—in training, in human engineering (designing machines for optimal human use), in operations research, and in electronic data processing, now widely used in non-military settings. In the routine succession of top leaders, does the need for continuity move new leaders toward established policy? Military elites, despite the necessities of rapid innovation, despite the obsolescence of weapons systems in five or six years, are notorious in their penchant for the strategy of the last war.

To provide a perspective for the study of problems in the organization of the intelligence function common to all complex social systems, I shall apply the military analogy to a wide range of cases in politics, international relations, industry, and welfare.

Combating the rationalistic bias of their predecessors, contemporary sociologists have delighted in the unanticipated effects of purposive social action[1] and the social functions of ignorance.[2] Perfect knowledge, they argue, is not only impossible; it is undesirable. What would happen, they ask, if prospective brides and bridegrooms, employees and employers, consumers and producers, clients and professionals, Negroes and whites, knew everything about one another? What would happen if organizations knew all the hostile schemes devised by their competitors, including schemes abandoned because they were thought illegal or unethical? Chaos would reign. Potential marriage partners would feel betrayed; the marriage rate would drop. Subordinates would be so suspicious of managers, clients so cynical about professionals, and children so mistrustful of parents, that authority would be undermined. Were the foibles of the aged and experienced known, respect for seniority would disappear. Were salaries posted, jealousy over unequal rewards among equals would be disruptive. Were guest lists for social events noised about, resentment would replace cordiality and sociability. Were outcomes of games predictable, adventure would be drained out of them. Were results of all competition calculable,

---

[1] Robert K. Merton, "The Unanticipated Consequences of Purposive Social Action," *American Sociological Review*, I (December, 1936), 894–904.

[2] Wilbert E. Moore and Melvin M. Tumin, "Some Social Functions of Ignorance," *American Sociological Review*, XIV (December, 1949), 787–795.

organizations and individuals slated to lose would give up pre-
maturely. Were stereotypes punctured, no quick orientation to
social life would be possible. Were violations of rules known, no
rule would be sacred. Were the true motives of potential enemies
bared, their businesslike accommodation and cooperation would be
unlikely. In short, we would face a world in which nothing would
be stable, everything would be "up for grabs."

I do not deny the social functions of ignorance. Obviously it is
not always bad for the public interest, or bad for an organization
when an organization, because its leaders are unaware of issues,
does nothing—exerts no pressure, mounts no campaign, makes no
decision. Further, the unconscious impulse, as well as the conscious
calculation, may serve human ends. Finally, rational action does
not presume complete knowledge; men can perform successfully
and logically from the wrong premises or with the right guesses.
Most organizational behavior, however, is purposeful. Whatever the
goals they pursue, administrative leaders everywhere favor the
rational, efficient, and economical action; such action is less likely
when ignorance prevails. I begin with the assumption that high-
quality intelligence is, on balance, desirable. Even if it were not, the
phenomenon of organizational cognition deserves more explicit
attention than it has received in sociological theory—if only to show
its place in a world otherwise shaped by unplanned, unconscious,
non-rational, or wasteful patterns of behavior.

The competent organization of the intelligence function cannot
substitute for political judgment and administrative leadership. Nor
are all failures in judgment related to intelligence failures. What is
important for my purposes is that the direction and effectiveness
of policy—reasonable standards for judging the performance of
administrative leaders—are in some degree affected by the quality
of intelligence and its flow from the source to the user. A man who
knows more is alert to more opportunities and consequences. And
an executive who understands the problem of intelligence, who
grasps the limitations and contributions of men of knowledge, is
more likely to temper power with wisdom.

Begun in the benign climate of the Center for Advanced Study
in the Behavioral Sciences in 1963, this book was completed in the
spirited atmosphere of the Berkeley campus. I am grateful to both
institutions not only for generous support but also for the oppor-

tunity to gain insight into the flow of information under sharply contrasting conditions. I have incorporated an entry on "Organizational Intelligence" written for the *International Encyclopedia of the Social Sciences;* I appreciate the editors' permission to include it here. The Institute of Industrial Relations, University of California, Berkeley, provided indispensable time, encouragement, and assistance; Director Lloyd Ulman and Co-director Margaret S. Gordon have my warm thanks. J. Malcolm Walker, Stephen A. Longstaff, J. Richard Woodworth, and Lillian Rubin supplied valuable research assistance. Philip Selznick and Martin A. Trow, commenting on both first and later drafts, stimulated major revisions in every chapter. For criticism and helpful suggestions, I am also indebted to Joseph Ben-David, Reinhard Bendix, Eugene A. Hammel, Sanford H. Kadish, William Kornhauser, Irving Kristol, Sheldon L. Messinger, Nelson W. Polsby, Albert J. Reiss, Jr., Claire Rosenfield, and Aaron Wildavsky. None of these tough-minded scholars will be quite satisfied with the finished product; all tried to rescue me from those lapses of intelligence that threaten any analysis of intelligence failures. Sins of factual error, taste, or bias are, therefore, mine. My wife, as usual, patiently accepted the demands of the task and kept domestic policy under control.

HAROLD L. WILENSKY

Berkeley, California
December 22, 1966

Contents

Organizational Intelligence

CHAPTER 1

Introduction

Four fundamental problems in the sociology of complex organizations are also urgent problems for the administrative leader. The first is *goal setting*, the problem of organizational purpose and mission. Research questions include the following: How are goals made operational, made guides for choice? How are the multiple goals of various sub-units arranged in a system-wide order of preference? What kinds of goals are most vulnerable to displacement? What kinds of organizations are most vulnerable to drift? The second is *control*, the problem of getting work done and of securing compliance with organizational rules. Under such headings as "leadership," "authority," "coordination," "incentives," "informal work groups," "human relations," and "democracy," more has been written on this topic than any other. The third is *innovation*, the problem of the conditions conducive to change in organizational structure and purpose. That portion of popular sociology that complains of the decline of initiative and the rise of "conformity" and the "organization man" has concentrated here. Some research attention has been devoted to administrative arrangements that hamper or foster individual creativity and organizational change. The fourth is *intelligence*, the problem of gathering, processing, interpreting, and communicating the technical and political information needed in the decision-making process. It is discussed under such labels as "communication," "information theory," and "decision theory." A major sociological research question is: What are the sources and effects of staff-line conflict? The staff and consultants described are heterogeneous, but they are typically men of specialized knowledge and training who function as experts. Many of them are or once were "intellectuals."

The four problems are obviously interdependent: the executive who lacks accurate, relevant, timely information about the selection, supervision, performance, and morale of his employees will suffer difficulties in control and have trouble launching new programs. Further, the possibilities uncovered in the search for intelligence partly determine the choice of goals. Thus, if a businessman lacks information about opportunities for foreign investment because he mistakenly thinks they are not worth exploring (a matter of intelligence), he will block new lines of expansion (a matter of goal setting). But these problems are analytically separable. And among them, the intelligence function has received least explicit and least systematic treatment. Because the available literature is so widely scattered over disciplines and is so often an incidental part of studies of other matters, it is useful to begin by characterizing typical sources.

Manuals on the production of strategic intelligence provide such vacuous homilies as "Patriotic Service Through Timely Truth Well Told" and "Any sound intelligence estimate must recognize the fundamental influence of the Spirit of the People."[1] We have a few more-analytical books by students of military and governmental intelligence, chiefly foreign policy experts trained in history and political science;[2] a few round-by-round accounts of the failures and successes of intelligence in national crises, especially in books on the presidency,[3] on military campaigns,[4] and on military consultants,[5] but very few blow-by-blow accounts.[6]

[1] Washington Platt, *Strategic Intelligence Production: Basic Principles* (New York: Frederick A. Praeger, 1957).

[2] Note especially Roger Hilsman, *Strategic Intelligence and National Defense* (Glencoe: The Free Press, 1956); Sherman Kent, *Strategic Intelligence* (Princeton: Princeton University Press, 1949); Willmoore Kendall, "The Function of Intelligence," *World Politics,* I (July, 1949), 542–552; George S. Pettee, *The Future of American Secret Intelligence* (Washington: Infantry Journal Press, 1946); and Harry Howe Ransom, *Central Intelligence and National Security* (Cambridge: Harvard University Press, 1958).

[3] See Robert E. Sherwood, *Roosevelt and Hopkins,* Bantam edn., revised and enlarged, 2 vols. (New York: Harper & Brothers, 1948); Richard E. Neustadt, *Presidential Power: The Politics of Leadership* (New York: John Wiley & Sons, 1960); Arthur M. Schlesinger, Jr., *A Thousand Days: John F. Kennedy in the White House* (Boston: Houghton Mifflin, 1965); and Theodore C. Sorensen, *Kennedy* (New York: Harper & Row, 1965).

[4] See Barbara Tuchman, *The Guns of August,* Dell paperback edn. (New York: Dell Publishing Co., 1963); and S. L. A. Marshall, *The River and the*

We have many popular articles on intellectuals or experts in non-military settings, much discussion of staff-line relations or decision making in management,[7] endless polemics about the nature, types, plight, or sins of the intellectual in society;[8] but only a handful of systematic-empirical studies of the interplay of men of knowledge and men of power. These include studies of economists and lawyers in government agencies and congressional committees,[9] controllers[10] and scientists in industry,[11] staff experts in

Gauntlet: Defeat of the Eighth Army by the Chinese Communist Forces, November, 1950, in the Battle of the Congchon River, Korea (New York: William Morrow & Co., 1953).

[5] See the excellent analysis of the impact that RAND has had upon policy by Bruce L. R. Smith, "Strategic Expertise and National Security Policy: A Case Study," in *Public Policy,* ed. by John D. Montgomery and Arthur Smithies (Cambridge: Graduate School of Public Administration, Harvard University, 1964), pp. 69–106; and Bruce L. R. Smith, *The RAND Corporation: Case Study of a Nonprofit Advisory Corporation* (Cambridge: Harvard University Press, 1966).

[6] See Richard C. Snyder and Glenn D. Paige, "The United States Decision to Resist Aggression in Korea," in *Foreign Policy Decision-Making: An Approach to the Study of International Politics,* ed. by Richard C. Snyder et al. (New York: The Free Press, 1962), pp. 206–249, for an account of the Korean decision; Ely Devons, *Planning in Practice: Essays in Aircraft Planning in War-time* (Cambridge, Eng.: At the University Press, 1950), for an account of planning in the British Ministry of Aircraft Production; and, by far the most painstaking and analytical, Roberta Wohlstetter, *Pearl Harbor: Warning and Decision* (Stanford: Stanford University Press, 1962), for a discussion of the Pearl Harbor surprise.

[7] See L. Urwick, "Organization as a Technical Problem," in *Papers on the Science of Administration,* ed. by Luther Gulick and L. Urwick (New York: Columbia University, Institute of Public Administration, 1937), pp. 49–88; Herbert A. Simon, Donald W. Smithburg, and Victor A. Thompson, *Public Administration* (New York: Alfred A. Knopf, 1950), pp. 280 ff; Ernest Dale, *Planning and Developing the Company Organization Structure,* Research Report No. 20 (New York: American Management Association, 1952); Peter Drucker, *The Practice of Management* (New York: Harper & Brothers, 1954); Melville Dalton, *Men Who Manage: Fusions of Feeling and Theory in Administration* (New York: John Wiley & Sons, 1959); and James G. March and Herbert A. Simon, *Organizations* (New York: John Wiley & Sons, 1958).

[8] See especially George B. de Huszar, ed., *The Intellectuals: A Controversial Report* (Glencoe: The Free Press, 1960); and Loren Baritz, *The Servants of Power: A History of the Use of Social Science in American Industry* (Middletown: Wesleyan University Press, 1960).

[9] Stephen K. Bailey, *Congress Makes a Law: The Story Behind the Employment Act of 1946* (New York: Columbia University Press, 1950); V. A. Thompson, *The Regulatory Process in OPA Gas Rationing* (New York: Columbia University, King's Crown Press, 1950); and Edward S. Flash, Jr., *Eco-*

labor unions,[12] Washington lobbyists,[13] a variety of experts in the federal budgetary process.[14] There are also a few indirectly relevant studies of experts, politicians, and pressure groups in the making or administration of public policy: on the tariff,[15] on work relief,[16] on the Tennessee Valley Authority,[17] on public housing,[18] on national security,[19] and a few general books on science and the social order which review empirical data.[20] Finally, the American Sociological Association is publishing an extensive treatment of the penetration of social-science data and perspectives in various professions, establishments, conflict situations, and institutional areas,[21] but such books are more programmatic than substantive, more a statement of the promise of applied social research than an analysis of the conditions that shape its actual uses and abuses.

nomic Advice and Presidential Leadership: The Council of Economic Advisers (New York: Columbia University Press, 1965).

[10] Herbert A. Simon et al., Centralization vs. Decentralization in Organizing the Controller's Department (New York: American Book–Stratford Press, 1954).

[11] William Kornhauser, Scientists in Industry: Conflict and Accommodation (Berkeley and Los Angeles: University of California Press, 1962).

[12] Harold L. Wilensky, Intellectuals in Labor Unions: Organizational Pressures on Professional Roles (Glencoe: The Free Press, 1956).

[13] Lester W. Milbrath, The Washington Lobbyists (Chicago: Rand McNally & Company, 1963).

[14] Aaron Wildavsky, The Politics of the Budgetary Process (Boston: Little, Brown, and Company, 1964).

[15] Elmer E. Schattschneider, Politics, Pressures and the Tariff: A Study of Free Private Enterprise in Pressure Politics, as Shown in the 1929–1930 Revision of the Tariff (Englewood Cliffs: Prentice-Hall, 1935); and Raymond A. Bauer, Ithiel de Sola Pool, and Lewis Anthony Dexter, American Business and Public Policy: The Politics of Foreign Trade (New York: Atherton Press of Prentice-Hall, 1963).

[16] Arthur W. Macmahon, John D. Millet, and Gladys Ogden, The Administration of Federal Work Relief (Chicago: Public Administration Service, 1941).

[17] Philip Selznick, TVA and the Grass Roots: A Study in the Sociology of Formal Organization (Berkeley and Los Angeles: University of California Press, 1949).

[18] Martin Meyerson and E. C. Banfield, Politics, Planning, and the Public Interest (Glencoe: The Free Press, 1955).

[19] Warner R. Schilling, Paul Y. Hammond, and Glenn H. Snyder, Strategy, Politics, and Defense Budgets (New York: Columbia University Press, 1962).

[20] Bernard Barber, Science and the Social Order, rev. edn. (New York: Collier Books, 1962).

[21] Paul F. Lazarsfeld, William H. Sewell, and Harold L. Wilensky, eds., The Uses of Sociology (New York: Basic Books, 1967); cf. Alvin W. Gouldner and S. M. Miller, Applied Sociology: Opportunities and Problems (New York: The Free Press, 1965).

Failures in intelligence, which have received so little scholarly attention, can be more fateful than lapses in control, which have preoccupied students in the sociology of organization. The former may bring sudden death; the latter, no more than slow decline. If an auto manufacturer mishandles his labor relations, he merely suffers increased labor turnover or an unnecessary strike; if he miscalculates his consumer market and produces an Edsel, hard upon the heels of a Mercury, a whole division is finished. Many problems of internal administration plagued General Dynamics Corporation in the late 1950's, but its monumental miscalculation of the costs and uses of its Convair 880 and 990 commercial jets put it into near bankruptcy. President Eisenhower's vacillations in the exercise of authority in the Little Rock school crisis of 1957 and again on the question of a balanced budget in 1957–58 meant merely a slow erosion of faith in his skill and will,[22] which was not irretrievable. Khrushchev and Kennedy's overestimation of each other's caution produced an earthshaking missile crisis.

The obvious significance of the intelligence function in government and industry has not resulted in the long bibliographies of solid sociological studies typical of other areas of organizational theory and practice. It is strange that social scientists, who are by profession devoted to the application of reason to man's affairs, have been more impressed by the use and misuse of power than by the use and misuse of knowledge. On the one hand, those who are alert to the social functions of ignorance—or who are eager to show how recalcitrant subordinates complicate the exercise of authority—are not attracted to the study of rational men assessing information. On the other hand, those decision theorists who place the calculating organism at the center of their work do not give sufficient weight to structural and ideological constraints on rationality. This book delineates the institutional threats to the reasoned use of knowledge without abandoning the problem of the competent organization of the intelligence function.

[22] Neustadt.

CHAPTER 2

Varieties of
Organizational Intelligence

The resources an organization devotes to intelligence, the kinds of experts it uses, and the functions these experts serve are a product of several interrelated forces: the availability of intelligence, the relation of the organization to its external and internal environment, the degree of rationalization of that environment, and the organization's structural complexity.

The celebrated knowledge explosion assures increased availability of intelligence. It is seen in the exponential expansion of scientific knowledge, of knowledge-producing professions and industries, of research and development units, of the media of communication, of information services and machines; it is evident in the accent on education, not just in the school but in the home, on the job, in the church, in the armed forces;[1] it is symbolized by the spectacular spread of electronic computers and automatic control systems. In industry and politics, as in the armed forces and the agencies of national security, the greater ease of obtaining and processing information has induced more information-consciousness among executives—they are more willing to use both overt sources of intelligence, such as government data and private surveys, and covert sources, such as electronic snoopers.

Information is more available; so is manpower. By the 1960's the Central Intelligence Agency's invisible personnel nearly matched

[1] Cf. Fritz Machlup, *The Production and Distribution of Knowledge in the United States* (Princeton: Princeton University Press, 1962).

the total employees of the Department of State;[2] the budget of the CIA, less than half that of the intelligence operations of the Defense Department, exceeded the State Department's by more than 50 per cent.[3] The swift growth of the OSS in World War II and its successor, the CIA, of the FBI, of the intelligence units of both the armed forces and the police, of research in every agency of government—a trend common to every rich country—has yielded a pool of potential manpower for industry, labor, political parties, indeed, for every type of organization. Many intelligence specialists in such agencies find their skills transferable; a free labor market facilitates their use. Another growing manpower supply, tapped mainly for covert intelligence, consists of maintenance technicians and engineers, men preferred as undercover operators in industry because they can move about unnoticed.

In short, the opportunity to gather, process, transfer, and deliver information has expanded; suitable manpower is available; and there has been a corresponding increase in information-consciousness among officials and executives.

The availability of information specialists and technology is not enough. That an ex-Signal Corpsman who can install a wiretap is discharged from the Army does not assure his employment in private industry; that an accountant who has been investigating anti-trust violations for the FBI is restive with his salary does not guarantee his shift to a management consulting firm. For there are great variations in the receptivity of organizations to staff services and in the types of experts they use. To explore these variations, I shall delineate types of experts found in all complex organizations[4] and relate their incidence to general propositions about the roots of large budgets for intelligence.

[2] Ransom, p. vi.
[3] Schlesinger, *A Thousand Days,* p. 427.
[4] The functional typology and decision-making analysis in this chapter derive in part from a detailed study of the functions, orientations, and influence of staff experts in labor unions (Wilensky, *Intellectuals,* pp. 33–108, 181–195, 196 ff., and 299 ff.), which I have here applied to the wider context of industry and government.

HOW MUCH AND WHAT KINDS OF INTELLIGENCE

There are four major determinants of the manpower, time, and money that a formal organization allocates to the intelligence function: (1) the degree of conflict or competition with the external environment—typically related to the extent of involvement with and dependence on government; (2) the degree of dependence on internal support and unity; (3) the degree to which internal operations and external environment are believed to be rationalized, that is, characterized by predictable uniformities and therefore subject to planned influence; and, affecting all of these, (4) the size and structure of the organization, its heterogeneity of membership and diversity of goals, its centralization of authority. On all counts we can expect that the typical formal organization in modern society, whatever its products or services, whatever the cultural context, will make increasing use of experts.

The more an organization is in conflict with its social environment or depends on it for the achievement of its central goals, the more resources it will allocate to the intelligence function and the more of those resources will be spent on experts whom we might call "contact men." The contact man supplies political and ideological intelligence the leader needs in order to find his way around modern society; he mediates the relations of the organization and the outside world. His primary concern and skill is with facts about and techniques of changing the thoughts, feelings, and conduct of men through persuasion and manipulation. He is valued for his knowledge of the political and social topography of the containing society—the kind of realistic political intelligence that tells him who can make what decisions or who has what information and how and when to reach him; for his "contacts," which are so well developed that they become nontransferable; and for his skills in exploiting these contacts—skills in private inquiry, consultation, negotiation, mediation. Typical titles include general counsel; lobbyist, Washington representative, legislative representative, or trade association representative; public relations, community relations, or press relations man. The backgrounds of such specialists are heterogeneous: law, politics, journalism, business, religion; most have held jobs in the bureaucracies with which their employers deal. The NLRB Regional Director becomes the union lawyer; the reporter covering a labor beat on a commercial daily takes over the union's press relations job; the military officer in defense procurement becomes the corporation vice-president in charge of sales; the regulatory-agency staff man goes over to the regulated industry. The contacts of these experts are used mainly for keeping information channels open for the speedy transmission of accurate political intelligence, typically between competing staffs.[5] In addition to serving as a listening post, the contact man interprets his employers or clients to important publics, real or imagined, and those publics to the organization he represents.

The contact man is called to service because of the entanglements of diverse private and public bureaucracies defending and promoting special interests. The greater the public impact of these struggles, the more government supervision. The more complicated the entanglements and the wider the scope of government intervention, the more indispensable are the skills of the contact man. We see this among labor unions and public utilities deeply involved with government. When labor disputes in a union's jurisdiction typically invite large-scale federal intervention, as in the railroad brotherhoods, or when a union is heavily dependent on the action of federal agencies for its economic gains, as in textile unions (tariffs and the minimum wage are issues) or unions in maritime, atomic energy, and aerospace firms, we find that the number of experts in relation to the size of the union is large and that contact men and publicists are prominent. Similarly, public utilities must persuade legislators to grant favorable charters, regulatory commissions to set favorable rates, the public to tolerate both; utilities have a long history of skillful, large-scale lobbying. Government agencies themselves must remain in touch with a very fluid and complex environment, both governmental and private; they, too, develop antennae for the reception of operational information.

Actions restricting essential information are a different source of outside intervention that move organizations to use contact men,

[5] Milbrath, pp. 256 ff., 269, 339; Wilensky, *Intellectuals*, pp. 61–79; Wildavsky, *Politics of Budgetary Process;* Bauer, Pool, and Dexter, pp. 324 ff., 346 ff.

especially in covert operations. When the courts limit the use of coercion by police in search, arrest, and interrogation, the police respond by expanding their covert intelligence; secret surveillance proliferates. Sections that rely most heavily on the collection of information through electronic eavesdropping, informers, secret agents, and the like are those charged with enforcing laws against acts of moral "harmfulness"—narcotics use, prostitution, bookmaking, or espionage.[6] In these "crimes without victims" the burdens of discovery, evidence, and complaint fall heavily on the police. Recent court decisions that protect the civil liberties of the accused make it more difficult to conceal the identity of informers in such cases. Concerned more with the control of crime than with due process of law, the police have probably elaborated their intelligence operations—the number and diversity of devices for gathering and protecting information essential to detection and arrest. For an example not entirely hypothetical, a police department depends upon the informer but maintains a double set of records: one set, open to the defense through discovery procedures, makes no mention of informants; the second set contains the full story. A double record system works only as long as defense lawyers do not know of it; it requires perfect security and therefore more men and attention.[7]

In sum: the more an organization is in conflict with outsiders or dependent on them, and the more numerous its lines of potential support in government, law, and public opinion, the more it turns to contact men. The government agency competing for budget money, no less than the private firm competing for markets, is moved to protect its "trade" secrets and ferret out the operations

---

[6] Cf. Jerome Skolnick, *Justice Without Trial* (New York: John Wiley & Sons, 1966), pp. 100–102, 112–138; and Edwin M. Schur, *Crimes Without Victims* (Englewood Cliffs: Prentice-Hall, 1965).

[7] For obvious reasons this example cannot be documented. Another police response to court restrictions on the use of anonymous informants is to erect additional barriers to defense attempts to discover who the unknown man or woman is. Before the court restrictions, the police customarily made a search without a warrant on the tip of the informer; courts generally refused to allow the defense to identify the source of information. Now the police obtain a warrant on the word of the informant; the defense then has a limited time to challenge the warrant, and still may not discover who the informant is if the judge has, in the past, been impressed with his reliability (Skolnick, pp. 134–135). For an analysis of the quality of secret information and its relationship to the ideal of justice, see pp. 66–74 and pp. 133–144 below.

of its rivals. If its major sources of information are restricted by outside parties, an organization will emphasize secret information. Contact men have a special affinity for inside dope; more than other intelligence specialists, they are apt to be impressed with covert intelligence.

A second major force that shapes the use of experts is the problem of internal control—coping with the inner environment. *The more an organization depends on the unity and support of persons, groups, factions, or parties within its membership for the achievement of its central goals, the more resources it will devote to the intelligence function and the more of those resources will be spent on experts whom we might call "internal communications specialists."*

The internal communications specialist supplies political and ideological intelligence the leader needs in order to maintain his authority. He transmits policies downward or reports on membership sentiments and opinion, or both; he helps induct new members and train activists and leaders. His primary concern and skill is with facts about and techniques of changing the thoughts, feelings, and conduct of members through persuasion and manipulation. He is valued for his propaganda and group work skills, his ability to gauge group reactions, and his knowledge of the politics and personalities of the employing organization. Typical titles include editor of the house organ, education, recreation, or training director, personnel or industrial relations officer, safety director, security man. Some auditors or controllers belong in this list. Insofar as director of community relations is a euphemism for trouble-shooter in race relations, he may belong here, too. Backgrounds, while diversified, typically include administrative, ideological, or political jobs that provide a grasp of the organization's internal operations and structure.

Heterogeneous in origin and activity, these men fulfill similar functions: (1) build executives' prestige and facilitate their control over the members; (2) supply information about the performance, politics, and morale of various organizational units; (3) locate and train new leaders; (4) allay minority group pressures when they threaten stability. Occasionally they function to maintain morale in crisis situations. If the crisis is rooted in threats from rival organizations, as in a jurisdictional squabble, strike, secession movement, union organizing drive, or "raid" on personnel, the work of the internal communications specialist shades into that of the contact man.[8]

When organizations that are formally democratic—political parties, unions, voluntary associations—cannot assume member support but must win it, they are especially likely to need assistance in internal communications. Some unions, despite severely limited resources, allocate more staff and time to internal morale problems than their far richer corporate counterparts; a formal democratic constitution, whatever the degree of oligarchy, vastly complicates the problem of internal control. Democratic or not, an organization that keenly competes for member loyalty or requires mass participation will use such staff. A study of industrial relations departments of thirty-four companies found that those faced with strong unions, especially if operating in a tight labor market, gave more authority to their personnel and industrial relations experts.[9] In general, the more directly accountable the leader is to the rank-and-file, the more he needs to know about their state of mind; the more he depends on their compliance with organizational rules and goals, the more he needs to know about their performance.

A third major source of variation in the number and types of experts used is the uneven rationalization of social life. *The more an organization sees its external environment and internal operations as rationalized—that is, as subject to discernible, predictable uniformities in relationships among significant objects—the more resources it will devote to the intelligence function and the more of those resources will be spent on experts whom we might call "facts-and-figures men."* The facts-and-figures man supplies technical economic, legal, or scientific intelligence that helps the leader build his case in dealing with outsiders and members, fend off attacks, and compete with rival organizations for markets, power, and prestige. His primary concern and skill is with data, records, arguments; he is expected to produce quick, simple answers to complex technical questions as well as judgments of the power and intent of competitors and enemies. His human relations skills are

[8] Cf. Wilensky, *Intellectuals,* pp. 80 ff.; Charles A. Myers and John G. Turnbull, "Line and Staff in Industrial Relations," *Harvard Business Review,* XXXIV (July–August, 1956), 113–124; Simon *et al., Centralization vs. Decentralization.*

[9] Myers and Turnbull.

less prominent. Titles encompass director of research, of planning and analysis, of reports and estimates, or, simply, of intelligence; economist, statistician, accountant, actuary, pension and insurance consultant; industrial engineer, human engineer; or the ubiquitous "management consultant." Included here are lawyers confined largely to court litigation, case building for negotiations and arbitration, drafting contracts and briefs, appearances before administrative agencies, and housekeeping operations, and lobbyists who accent "research." The backgrounds of facts-and-figures men are mainly in the law, college teaching, accounting, market and consumer research, operations or systems research, engineering and the physical sciences, and in the social sciences (especially economics, statistics, demography, psychology, industrial relations, and, more recently, sociology). On the average, they have more formal education than other intelligence specialists. They tend to be suspicious of secret sources, more impressed with public data open to independent checks.

Facts-and-figures men function both to supply information and to mobilize support. In internal policy deliberations and decision making generally, they introduce a "rational-responsible" bias—a more conscious examination of alternatives, of relevant factors beyond power, even of "long-range" consequences. In external relations they build pressure on outside parties via the state and the public, imparting a tone of public responsibility to the executives' rhetoric; they persuade and impress legislative committees, executive agencies, and judicial or quasi-judicial boards, promoting an all-around reorientation toward data; they strengthen the morale and conviction of their employers and in turn the members, thus boosting bargaining power with rivals.

The importance of the facts-and-figures man is evident in insurance companies, investment houses, law firms, and corporations and unions that are subject to much government regulation. The brokerage firm operates in a sphere believed to be highly rationalized. Economic intelligence, both rapid and accurate, is nowhere so extensively elaborated. Information technology is sophisticated, the base of research is highly developed, the movements of earnings and prices are closely studied. Similarly, corporations and labor unions whose activities are most strictly regulated by law may not fully embrace the myth of the majesty and certainty of the law, but they know that opposing parties and neutral officials will invoke authoritative precedent and rational argument drawn from a codified set of rules. Executives in such organizations often feel "surrounded by laws," develop "sea lawyer" inclinations of their own, and readily turn to lawyers and economists for help. Responding to this demand, the large law firm or the tax consultant will elaborate cases and calculate likely outcomes so as to reinforce the impression that strategic planning by a variety of specialized facts-and-figures men yields great gains.

We see here a kind of dialectic of expertise, part of a general tendency toward the interpenetration of rational-bureaucratic structures. If the manager sends a lawyer to bargain for him, the union counters with its house counsel. If a congressional committee hires economists to prepare for a hearing on automation, the parties who testify will be attuned to economic data. Facts-and-figures men are preoccupied with rational argument and criteria; their technical competence compels opposing parties to be more careful or honest in the use of information, to match each other expert for expert, fact for fact.

WHEN THE FACTS COUNT

When experts describe their functions as "window dressing" and say they are "there for front, for the show"; when they observe that "really it boils down to public relations," or "supplying slogans," they point to activities common to all experts everywhere—the defense of established policy. Among intelligence specialists, no conviction is stronger than the notion that their main function, whatever their intentions, is "backstopping." And administrative leaders who hire experts tend to derogate technical intelligence and accent the importance of political and executive skills they themselves possess. They throw in their "research" staff ritualistically, much as a tribal leader, embarking on a war, calls on the shaman for supporting incantation.

There is no doubt that much policy is improvised and later, with the help of experts, made to appear planned. Neither is there doubt that all experts, including facts-and-figures men, contribute to the self-esteem of their employers by lending them prestige and "fronting" for them with various publics, "taking the heat" when mistakes are made, and, in general, creating the verbal environment of the organization. But such observations obscure both the conditions under which the "facts" do count and the significance of "mere slogans."

A study of the interplay of technical economic-legal considerations and political-ideological considerations in union decision making[10] found that union staff experts have highest sustained influence in the entire decision-making process on problems in public relations and governmental relations—issues such as taxes, tariffs, welfare legislation, and world politics, which, while objectively important to the members, are seen by top officers as far from the core function of the union. But some problems are so technical that the specialized knowledge of facts-and-figures men becomes overriding even at the core of union functioning and despite the presence of political considerations: (1) complex secondary wage issues such as pensions and insurance, problems of wage structure and wage "inequities," and problems of job content in relation to wage rates; (2) wage bargaining where negative employment effects are clearly involved, and problems of government action which employers say will adversely affect employment or ability to pay; and (3) problems of wage and strike policy or of internal control and rival union relations where government intervention or potential litigation is of crucial importance.

Similarly, a study of governmental budget making, an eminently "political" process, suggests that a good "case" often counts.[11] Although precedent is the major determinant of who gets what the government has to give, and although governmental officials are convinced that what counts is not the technical data supporting their requests, but the cultivation of an active clientele (Congress and the public), the development of confidence among other government officials, and the skills and strategies of contact men, nevertheless substantial departures from previous budgets and new programs with no precedent receive careful scrutiny and have a better chance if accompanied by well-documented arguments. Moreover, the cultivation of political support and official confidence are themselves partly a product of how well the homework is done. For

10 Wilensky, *Intellectuals*, pp. 181–195.
11 Wildavsky, *Politics of Budgetary Process*.

instance, Budget Bureau examiners depend for information on the agency they are assigned to investigate; the agency often converts the examiner into an advocate of particular programs by a sensible, even open flow of information (discounting the risk of disclosing weaknesses). Slippery statistics and grossly inaccurate reports are avoided; the expert from the Budget Bureau is put in touch with agency experts whose data he can trust.[12] If trends in federal budgeting practices of the 1960's continue—if there is a further shift from "ceiling budgets" or "incremental budgeting" based on previous decisions to a "planning-programming budgeting system" (PPBS) based on calculations of the cost effectiveness of alternative program outputs—reliance on technical data will increase.[13]

This story is repeated in industry, where an enterprise may use "share of the market" as an operational guide to simplify its calculations, and yet at the same time be forced to resort to special cost studies, carefully scrutinized, a premium put upon the facts and figures, whenever there is deviation or innovation. And an auditor, investigating the operations of a local plant, can more easily be converted into its advocate at central headquarters if he learns to trust the local sources of his information.[14]

Perhaps the heaviest burden of calculation, hence the greatest urge for systematic appraisal of departures and innovations, appears in industries whose processes and products are unstandardized.[15] The epitome is university education. By the mid-1960's such diverse institutions as the mammoth University of California and the Office of Economic Opportunity—each facing its own demanding wars—were considering the adoption of program budgeting and cost-benefit analysis in decision-making. Modern management techniques will receive their most severe test in such growth industries with hard-to-measure outputs. Whether the swing toward PPBS in government, education, and industry will result in improvements in efficiency or any other value—whether it "vastly overestimates man's limited ability to calculate and grossly underestimates the

[12] *Ibid.,* pp. 3, 13, 39, 56, 62–67, 136, 147, 169.

[13] Charles J. Hitch, *Decision-Making for Defense* (Berkeley and Los Angeles: University of California Press, 1965).

[14] Richard Cyert and James March, *A Behavioral Theory of the Firm* (Englewood Cliffs: Prentice-Hall, 1963), and Simon *et al., Centralization vs. Decentralization.*

[15] Cf. March and Simon, p. 164.

importance of political and technological constraints"[16]—is another matter (see Chapter 8); but the greater prominence of technical data in planning seems assured.

Facts-and-figures men who command technical intelligence obviously are given more discretion where the problems are technical. Less obviously, they also carry more weight when the organization is weak in grass-roots political resources. Among Washington lobbyists, for instance, representatives of small organizations with limited political resources—humanitarian organizations, specialized trade associations—accent research in their lobbying strategy, in contrast to large-membership organizations, such as farm groups, veterans groups, and labor unions, who incline toward grass-roots campaigns and publicity.[17] Again, this emphasis upon research is possible because of the interpenetration of rational-bureaucratic forms: lobbying here has a circular, "intramural" character, involving expert-to-expert contact within the legislature, among staffs of legislators and committees, and between them and agency staffs, all of whom draw on lobbyists for information.[18] Paradoxically, this may give an advantage to the weak, whose case, if strong and technical, can count for something.

THE SIGNIFICANCE OF SLOGANS

Even if technical intelligence never persuades anybody (and we have seen that this assumption is grossly exaggerated), the "window dressing" function goes beyond the rationalization of policy to the creation of the verbal environment of an organization—hardly a trivial matter. In foreign policy, staff experts invent slogans that reinforce policymakers' adherence to a wartime myth of the single enemy, thereby blinding the vision and reducing the number of recognized options. For instance, the image of the "Sino-Soviet bloc" fostered so much rigidity in the State Department and its publics

---

[16] Aaron Wildavsky and Arthur Hammond, "Comprehensive versus Incremental Budgeting in the Department of Agriculture," *Administrative Science Quarterly*, X (December, 1965), 321.

[17] Milbrath, pp. 227 ff., 343, 348.

[18] Milbrath, p. 196; Wildavsky, *Politics of Budgetary Process;* Bailey; Bauer, Pool, and Dexter, Part 4.

in the 1950's and early 1960's that President Kennedy, seeking very minor modifications of our China policy to fit dramatic signs of the Sino-Soviet split, felt himself a captive of both his foreign office and the mass media.[19] Self-righteous Cold War rhetoric, rooted in the facts of past conflicts, served to perpetuate policies long outmoded; indeed, this rhetoric helped make it seem reasonable to both Khrushchev and Kennedy to push the Cuban missile crisis to a nuclear confrontation, risking the destruction of the world. Kennedy invoked the need to defend "international prestige" and to provide proof of "national will and courage"; Khrushchev, the need to close the "missile gap" (a technical slogan easily shifted from the 1960 presidential election to the 1962 debate in the Kremlin); apparently neither was responding to any real shift in the balance of power.[20] The President chose a naval blockade, a contest of wills involving a possible nuclear holocaust. He considered but rejected the following alternative: "Bring diplomatic pressures and warnings to bear upon the Soviets. Possible forms included an appeal to the UN or OAS for an inspection team, or a direct approach to Khrushchev, possibly at a summit conference. The removal of our missile bases in Turkey in exchange for the removal of the Cuban missiles was also listed in our later discussions as a possibility which Khrushchev was likely to suggest if we didn't."[21] Two months earlier the

[19] Schlesinger, *A Thousand Days*, pp. 410–430, 483 ff.

[20] Cf. Schlesinger, *ibid.*; Sorensen, *Kennedy;* Benno Wasserman, "The Failure of Intelligence Prediction," *Political Studies,* VIII (June, 1960), 156–169; John H. Kautsky, "Myth, Self-fulfilling Prophecy, and Symbolic Reassurance in the East-West Conflict," *The Journal of Conflict Resolution,* IX (March, 1965), 1–17; Klaus Knorr, "Failure in National Estimates: The Case of the Cuban Missiles," *World Politics,* XVI (April, 1964), 455–467; Arnold L. Horelick, "The Cuban Missile Crisis: An Analysis of Soviet Calculations and Behavior," *World Politics,* XVI (April, 1964), 363–389; and Elie Abel, *The Missile Crisis,* Bantam edn. (New York: J. B. Lippincott Company, 1966). Sorensen writes that "these Cuban missiles alone, in view of all the other megatonnage the Soviets were capable of unleashing upon us, did not substantially alter the strategic balance *in fact.* . . . But that balance would have been substantially altered *in appearance*" (p. 678). If one side was motivated by a decline in relative military strength, it was the Soviet Union (see Horelick and Abel).

[21] Sorensen, *Kennedy,* p. 682. This and similar proposals received considerable support from some Pentagon advisers; it was advocated as the best alternative by one unidentified regular member of the key group in on the decision (Sorensen, *loc. cit.,* pp. 682—683). Adlai Stevenson advocated the neutralization of Cuba: the removal of Soviet missiles in exchange for a UN presence in Cuba,

Jupiter missile bases in Italy and Turkey, obsolescent and vulnerable, had been ordered removed anyway; both the Secretary of Defense and the Congressional Committee on Atomic Energy had recommended this step in 1961.[22] Even on the basis of the sympathetic accounts of Schlesinger, Sorensen, and Abel, it can be argued that the President's foreign policy for two years reflected the national trauma of the CIA's adventure in the Bay of Pigs; his intense desire to avoid once again giving the impression of weakness made him reluctant in 1962 to adopt the slower, less dramatic, and less dangerous alternative.[23] Customary Cold War rhetoric—the "courage" of "the Free World," "the credibility of our nuclear deterrent,"

---

an American guarantee not to invade, and relinquishment of the Guantánamo base (Schlesinger, *A Thousand Days*, pp. 807–808; Abel, pp. 79–80).

[22] Schlesinger, *ibid.*, p. 807; Sorensen, *ibid.*, pp. 695–696; and Abel, *ibid.*, pp. 169–171.

[23] The argument, a close one, is that the President's choice of the naval blockade—known within the "Executive Committee" as the "slow track" (Abel, p. 49)—was the second-best alternative but that it was far better than the other, more bellicose alternatives seriously considered—an air strike, an invasion, and so on (see p. 76 below). The most persuasive stated arguments against a track slower than the blockade included the following. First, the neutralization of Cuba would have encouraged the Soviet Union to make bolder moves, thereby imposing still greater risks at another time and place. This argument is like repeated-play considerations in insurance company strategy: although it would be cheaper to settle out of court, an insurance company may prefer to bring suit in order to deter other potential nuisance suits. For the duration of his and Kennedy's short tenure, Khrushchev was presumably deterred. Second, anything less than the blockade would have weakened Kennedy's political position at home; domestic "hawks" would have blocked any subsequent move toward *détente*. But there are also persuasive arguments against Kennedy's choice. Whether in the East or the West, bellicose factions on the side that "backs down" acquire new strength—an argument which, however speculative, is the same as the one above; Soviet hawks, smarting from *their* humiliation, could have strengthened their position. Second—and this seems to me the decisive argument for caution in Cuba—the blockade involved a hair-raising risk. If Khrushchev had not backed down, participants report, the United States would have taken direct action against Cuba, inviting Soviet counter-action. Sorensen records that Kennedy later told him that at the time of the decision the odds that the Soviets would go all the way to nuclear war seemed to him " 'somewhere between one out of three and even' " (p. 705). To call this "Kennedy's finest hour," as Abel does, is justified only in the sense that the intelligence assembled was of good quality; the policy, once adopted, was executed with finesse, and the awesome risk taken did not result in catastrophe. In retrospect the President himself had second thoughts; one look down the nuclear gun-barrel apparently persuaded him that such confrontations were intolerable (cf. Sorensen, *ibid.*, pp. 722, 726–727; Schlesinger, *ibid.*, p. 893).

"test of wills," "showdown"—dominated the discussion and played a part in the choice.

During the heady weeks when General MacArthur was chasing a battered North Korean army toward the 38th parallel and assuring President Truman and his speech writers that the Chinese would not intervene, there was an almost imperceptible shift from a modest original objective of restoring the *status quo ante* to a new war aim of a unified, non-Communist Korea. Public rhetoric reflected in private discussions facilitated this shift. "In White House memoranda and in papers for the National Security Council, in intelligence evaluations, and the like, repeated use of such terms as 'the UN objective,' 'the decision of the UN,' 'the UN's purpose to unify,' soon dulled awareness that the new war aim was nothing but a target of opportunity chosen rather casually (and at first provisionally) by the very men who read these words. The tendency of bureaucratic language to create in private the same images presented to the public never should be underrated."[24] In domestic policy surely such bogies as "the balanced budget" have worked similar mischief. Doctrines of economic individualism, activated by phrasemaking, help explain why America, unique among the rich countries, tolerated an unemployment rate of 4 per cent or more from 1954 until 1966[25] and has moved so reluctantly toward a humane welfare state.[26] Francis Bacon's warning that man converts his words into idols that darken his understanding is as pertinent today as it was three centuries ago.

On the positive side, such doctrines as "stable nuclear deterrence" (a surprise attack by one side cannot prevent retaliation by the other), a strategy invented by arms control experts, and "transitional deterrent," an ingenious phrase to make that strategy appeal at once to "doves" who wanted a transition to comprehensive disarmament and to "hawks" who clung to massive retaliation—these symbols moved debate inside the Kennedy administration toward a disarmament policy culminating in the 1963 test-ban treaty.[27] It

[24] Neustadt, p. 139.
[25] Margaret S. Gordon, *Retraining and Labor Market Adjustment in Western Europe*, United States Department of Labor, Manpower Automation Research Monograph, No. 4 (Berkeley: Institute of Industrial Relations, 1965), pp. 8–9.
[26] Harold L. Wilensky and Charles N. Lebeaux, *Industrial Society and Social Welfare*, enl. ed. (New York: The Free Press, 1965).
[27] Schlesinger, *Kennedy*, pp. 470 ff., 889 ff.

can also be argued that however obsolescent the rhetoric of the Cold War for Asia in the 1960's, it fitted the national interest in Western Europe in the late 1940's when a disorganized continent lay under the Soviet gun. American policy from the Marshall Plan to containment, sharpened by appropriate slogans, must be counted a success.[28]

Stereotypes and oversimplifications derived from "backstopping" experts are fateful even in industrial firms, presumably subject to the more tangible tests of the market. Consider the fate of the Edsel, a huge, dazzling, medium-priced automobile styled by the Ford Motor Company in 1955, introduced in 1957, and discontinued in 1959, after a net loss exceeding a third of a billion dollars. Conventional studies of their markets had persuaded top executives that the low-income owners of Fords, Plymouths, and Chevrolets turn in these symbols of poverty as soon as their annual earnings top $5,000 or so and "trade up" to a medium-priced car. (Ford owners unfortunately did not usually trade up to Ford's own medium-priced Mercury.) Based on these preconceptions and a two-year study, a Forward Product Planning Committee in 1954 projected a huge market for large medium-priced cars among a growing mass of upwardly mobile consumers. To appeal to the status consciousness of such consumers, Edsel designers accented heavy ornamentation and gadgetry. Among several sources of failure, stereotypes of their market blinded the company to accelerating sales of small foreign cars, which Detroit contemptuously dismissed as "the teacher trade," and by the time the Edsel hit the road, it was the year of the "compact."[29]

This is not to say that symbols in support of established policy and comfortable prejudice inevitably serve as a substitute for policy deliberations. It is to say that facts, arguments, and propaganda directed at friends and enemies alike, in and out of an organization, can be self-convincing. Executives and politicians often become persuaded that the world of crisis journalism they create and respond to is the real world; many a decision-maker is in this way diverted from things which really happen or which are not happening but should be. Many a leader becomes captive of the rhetoric he custom-

[28] Raymond Aron, *On War* (New York: Doubleday Anchor Books, 1959).
[29] John Brooks, *The Fate of the Edsel and Other Business Adventures* (New York: Harper & Row, 1959).

arily presents or of the media image he projects. Students of modern society have given too little attention to this reverse action of propaganda—the effect on the people who themselves make the news. If supplying the symbols that guide executive action is "window dressing," it is the kind of display that tells what is in the store.

THE POWER OF PRECONCEPTIONS: THE CASE OF STRATEGIC BOMBING

A case that graphically dramatizes the longevity of preconceptions in the face of evidence is the bombing of Germany from 1939 to 1945.[30] Allied scientists, military experts, and statesmen alike held to an extravagant faith in the efficacy of bombing, at various times claiming that it would destroy the enemy's (1) war production, (2) armed forces, and (3) will to fight. Before the war, air force chiefs in Britain and the United States embraced the doctrine that strategic bombing—independent air forces striking at the sources of enemy power—could alone win a war. Until D-Day several dedicated air force specialists clung to the belief that large-scale use of

[30] This section is based on the following sources: Sir Charles Webster and Noble Frankland, *The Strategic Air Offensive Against Germany, 1939–1945*, 4 vols. (London: H.M.S.O., 1961), the best of the British official histories, cited hereafter as *WF*. The somewhat uncritical official history of the USAAF, United States Office of Air Force History, *The Army Air Forces in World War II*, ed. by Wesley F. Craven and James L. Cate, 7 vols. (Chicago: University of Chicago Press, 1948–1958), cited as *USAAF. The United States Strategic Bombing Survey*, 316 vols. (Washington, D.C.: GPO, 1945–1947), cited as *USSBS*. The *USSBS* materials are uneven in quality and diverse in viewpoint. I rely mainly on the reasonably balanced summary reports: *Over-all Report: European War*, cited as *USSBS–OR;* European Report No. 3, *The Effects of Strategic Bombing on the German War Economy*—a splendid treatment of the German economy under attack—cited as *USSBS-3;* Pacific Report No. 53, *The Effects of Strategic Bombing on Japan's War Economy: Appendix ABC*, cited as *USSBS-53;* and Pacific Report No. 55, *The Effects of Air Attack on Japanese Urban Economy: Summary Report*, cited as *USSBS-55*. Among secondary sources, see A. J. P. Taylor, *English History 1914–1945* (New York and Oxford: Oxford University Press, 1965), pp. 390–392, 517–520, 551–553, 570–572, 591–592, a biting but only mildly biased general account, and C. P. Snow, *Science and Government*, Harvard University Godkin Lectures, 1960, rev. with new appendix (New York: New American Library, 1962), pp. 46–49, 104–112, a slashing attack on the scientific believers in bombing, marred by exaggeration of the power of personality.

ground forces would be unnecessary.[31] Many others thought that German industry could be paralyzed before the invasion, and that resistance would be decisively weakened.[32] Political leaders in both the United States and Britain were favorably disposed toward these claims.[33] Scientists articulated disparate views, but the men listened to were those most committed to the doctrine of bombing.[34] Throughout the war, the proponents of strategic bombing exaggerated both the results already achieved and those to be expected.[35]

It is now clear that the U.S. and British bombing offensives, ending in a fury of fire storms, were launched without adequate understanding of either the general nature of the German economy or of its specific parts, and without a sense of the resilience of the social system.[36] When it was all over, teams of social scientists and military experts fanned out over Germany to evaluate the damage, in what may be the most systematic survey ever conducted of the impact of air power. The Strategic Bombing Survey showed that while strategic bombing had killed at least 300,000 German men, women, and children—these estimates run from 305,000 to 593,000 —and injured about 780,000 more, it also killed 155,546 British and American airmen, and the slaughter made little contribution to victory.[37] Despite specific successes in the final year of the war, notably against oil, steel, and transportation targets,[38] the bombing offensive as a whole must be counted an expensive failure.

The British Belief in Area Bombing

A major part of this offensive was "area bombing." Aimed primarily at the working-class districts of German cities, it was based on the premise that the destruction of urban housing, public utili-

[31] *USAAF*, Vol. I, pp. 149, 593; *WF*, Vol. I, p. 372, Vol. III, p. 23.

[32] *USAAF*, Vol. II, pp. 226, 305; *WF*, Vol. I, p. 370, Vol. II, p. 51.

[33] *USAAF*, Vol. I, pp. 115–116, 118, 592, Vol. II, p. 296; *WF*, Vol. I, pp. 155, 355–356.

[34] See e.g., *WF*, Vol. I, pp. 331–336, and Snow.

[35] *WF*, Vol. II, pp. 51, 254.

[36] *USSBS-OR*, p. 31; *WF*, Vol. I, pp. 169, 469–470, 475–477, Vol. II, pp. 215–220, 247–250; *USAAF*, Vol. II, pp. 278, 369, Vol. III, pp. 791, 795, 801.

[37] *USSBS-OR* p. 1; Taylor p. 591.

[38] *USSBS-OR*, pp. 10, 37, 41–45, 61–64, 80–81; *WF*, Vol. III, pp. 34, 40, 182.

ties, and transportation would disrupt the economy: because of the physical damage, the German worker would be unable to work; because of the effects on morale, he would be unwilling to work.[39] Twenty-four per cent of all the bomb tonnage rained on Germany from October, 1939, through May, 1945—almost twice the weight of bombs launched against all manufacturing targets together— was dropped in attacks against large cities.[40]

With the fall of France, bombing seemed to be the one strategy left to the British. Churchill wrote in July, 1940, that only one thing would bring Hitler down: "an absolutely devastating, exterminating attack by very heavy bombers from this country upon the Nazi homeland. We must be able to overwhelm them by this means, without which I do not see a way through."[41] Anxious to demonstrate Britain's capacity to wage offensive war, eager to retaliate for the bombing of Britain, the Prime Minister was receptive to the arguments of the true believers in area bombing and, indeed, encouraged it until 1945.[42] Churchill's stance was heavily influenced by both Lord Cherwell, his closest scientific adviser, and Air-Chief Marshal Harris, Commander-in-Chief, Bomber Command.[43] In March, 1942, when the concept of area bombing was being questioned, enthusiast Cherwell presented to Churchill his estimate of the possibilities:

"If even half of the total load of 10,000 bombers [to be produced by mid-1943] were dropped on the built-up areas of these 58 German towns, the great majority of their inhabitants (about one-third of the German population) would be turned out of house and home. . . . There seems little doubt that this would break the spirit of the people."[44]

Although Churchill did not accept the precise estimates as accurate, he accepted the thesis; Cherwell's position and the timing of his report weighed heavily in the decision to continue area bombing in its hour of crisis.[45]

In December, 1943, after a period during which area bombing

[39] WF, Vol. II, p. 235, Vol. III, p. 44.
[40] USSBS-OR, p. 71.
[41] Winston S. Churchill, Their Finest Hour, Vol. II: The Second World War (Boston: Houghton Mifflin, 1949), p. 643.
[42] WF, Vol. I, pp. 155–162, 168–169, 291, 342, 355, Vol. III, pp. 112–115.
[43] WF, Vol. I, pp. 331–336, Vol. III, pp. 79–80.
[44] As quoted in WF, Vol. I, p. 332.   [45] WF, Vol. I, p. 336.

had achieved no significant success, Air-Chief Harris claimed that the RAF bomber command could " 'produce in Germany by April 1st, 1944, a state of devastation in which surrender is inevitable.' "[46] He never deviated from his faith.[47] Of the attack on Berlin in 1943–44 he wrote: " 'We can wreck Berlin from end to end if the U.S.A.A.F. will come in on it. It will cost us 400–500 aircraft. It will cost Germany the war.' "[48] His belief that the German people could be cowed from the air was partly rooted in a past success: in 1922, the RAF had quelled a revolt in Iraq by bombing tribal villages.[49]

Scientist Cherwell and Officer Harris—forceful men, close to Churchill—steadily articulated a doctrinaire belief in area bombing to which the Prime Minister was already attuned. The weight of Cherwell's opinion was enhanced by Churchill's long-standing respect for his scientific and political advice. The weight of Harris' opinion was enhanced by his prestige among the public and among his own air crews. Churchill thus persisted in area bombing despite the growing evidence of its ineffectiveness, the operational feasibility of other forms of attack, and the declining confidence of the Air Staff; from 1939 to 1945 the British gradually implemented a policy of indiscriminate attack on civilian populations, competing with the Nazis in frightfulness.[50] A pity, for area bombing neither disrupted the German economy in any decisive way nor broke the will of the German people.[51] The fraction of the population driven from house and home was not the predicted one-third by mid-1943, but one-tenth for the entire war.[52] Until the closing months of the war, bombing did not even have a sizable effect on arms produc-

---

[46] As quoted in *WF*, Vol. II, p. 56. [47] *WF*, Vol. II, pp. 54–58, 68.
[48] As quoted in *WF*, Vol. II, p. 190. [49] A. J. P. Taylor, p. 229.
[50] *WF*, Vol. III, pp. 35–37, 53–57, 66–67. I do not imply that Hitler was by comparison a delightful fellow. In the strange morality of war, it might even be argued that Nazi concentration camps, mass extermination, and *Blitzkrieg* tactics justified retaliation by fire storms. But it is difficult to argue that the German attack on the city of Rotterdam, carried out on May 14, 1940, after the capitulation, was worse than the Allied raid on Dresden, carried out by 800 bombers in the closing weeks of the war (February 13–14, 1945). Packed with refugees from the east, Dresden was a target where bombing produced fire storms and at least 60,000 dead bodies (Fred Charles Iklé, *The Social Impact of Bomb Destruction* [Norman: University of Oklahoma Press, 1958], p. 201; Taylor, p. 591).
[51] *WF*, Vol. II, pp. 235–243.
[52] Cf. *USSBS-OR*, p. 72; *WF*, Vol. I, p. 332.

tion.[53] And a good case can be made that in 1942 and 1943, when the crucial Battle of the Atlantic was nearly lost, area bombing diverted aircraft desperately needed to protect shipping and to attack submarines.[54]

The American Belief in Precision Bombing

While the RAF became committed to area bombing, the commanders of the United States Army Air Forces in 1942 believed that selective precision attacks on systems vital to the German economy would be the ultimate weapon—this, in the face of the recent failures of precision bombing offensives by the Luftwaffe and the RAF.[55] Their investment in the idea was heavy. Air Force doctrine prescribed precision bombing, crews had been trained and aircraft designed for such bombing, and the reputation of Air Force chiefs depended on the fulfillment of its promise.[56] Unfortunately, as the official Air Force historians observe, the belief in precision bombing was more "a matter of faith than of knowledge empirically arrived at."[57] The U.S. bombers could not successfully defend themselves against enemy fighters in 1943, and major difficulties were experienced with both target identification and bomb aiming. A succession of targets was attacked without the predicted disruption of the enemy's ability to wage war. Targets were chosen on the basis of inadequate information concerning either the role of a given industry in the German war effort or the extent to which the production and use of a product would be affected by the attack.[58]

Thus, during 1943 and early 1944, despite the destruction or severe damage of 90 per cent of the fighter airframe industry, the front-line strength of the Luftwaffe was not reduced;[59] in fact, production of fighters tripled.[60] Intelligence estimates regarding the location of factories were accurate and immense damage was inflicted, but the Germans dispersed their facilities, introduced improved mass-production methods, and mobilized unused capacity.

An outstanding case of intelligence failure during the selective

53 WF, Vol. IV, p. 54.
54 WF, Vol. I, pp. 326–327, 335, 343; and Captain S. W. Roskill, The War at Sea, 1939–1945 (London: H.M.S.O., 1956), II, 368–371.
55 USAAF, Vol. I, pp. 601–607, Vol. II, p. 305; WF, Vol. I, p. 354.
56 WF, Vol. II, p. 38.
57 USAAF, Vol. II, p. 298.   58 USAAF, Vol. II, pp. 367–368.
59 WF, Vol. II, p. 280.   60 Ibid., p. 277.

bombing offensive is that of the ball-bearings industry, evaluated at the time and even in retrospect as the most rewarding of all the operationally feasible targets.[61] Because bearings were essential to the production of aircraft and many other armaments, it was predicted by intelligence agencies, operational air chiefs—except Harris, who clung to the promise of area bombing—and the U.S. and British Air Staffs that an attack on the bearings industry would block production of aircraft, tanks, artillery, diesel engines—everything dependent on ball bearings.[62] With great ingenuity, intelligence experts located the factories and estimated the contribution of each to total bearings production.[63] This intelligence led to devastating but very costly attacks on the major bearings factories—especially in Schweinfurt, where more than half of total production was concentrated.[64]

Public reaction in the United States to the heavy losses suffered by the Eighth Air Force in the raids of October, 1943, on Schweinfurt evoked a particularly unfortunate public statement from General "Hap" Arnold: "Our attack was the most perfect example in history of accurate distribution of bombs over a target. It was an attack which will not have to be repeated for a very long time if at all."[65] Again, the bold predictions and optimistic assessments were wrong. The effect on armaments production was insignificant for several reasons: the time required to construct new machines was overestimated; the rapid dispersal of production after the first attacks was not foreseen; the possibilities for substituting plain for antifriction bearings in some equipment and for eliminating the use of bearings in other equipment were not recognized. Most important was the ignorance of large stocks at both the bearings and the armament factories—sufficient for more than six months' supply of most implements, and enough to support an expansion of the armaments industry.[66]

Perhaps the difficulties of Allied intelligence in this instance should not surprise us. The Germans themselves thought that the attacks would be disastrous; according to war production chief Speer, they would " 'bring armament production to a standstill.' "[67]

61 *Ibid.*, p. 77. 62 *Ibid.*, pp. 60–64, 220, 269–270.
63 *WF*, Vol. II, pp. 270, 272. 64 *USSBS*, Vol. III, p. 4.
65 As quoted in *WF*, Vol II, p. 63. 66 *Ibid.*, p. 272.
67 As quoted in *ibid.*, p. 276.

Only after the second attack on Schweinfurt in October, 1943, did the Germans discover the large stores of bearings.[68]

Strategic Bombing in a Social and Economic Context

The merits of area versus selective precision bombing were endlessly debated and never resolved. Numerous intelligence units, in two countries, each with its competing services, were bound to produce rival target-systems, adopt different priorities, and make opposing evaluations of progress (see Chapter 3). To justify their own preconceptions, military experts committed to one or the other strategy used faulty intelligence predictions or manipulated intelligence estimates of what had been achieved, and at the same time downgraded or rejected intelligence that supported the rival strategy.[69] The distinction between area and precision raids was often more doctrinal than real: bad weather and poor visibility, weak fighter support, the German air defense, and limitations of bomber range often meant that "precision" bombs were sufficiently wide of the mark to become, in effect, "area" bombs.[70]

That a target here and there would be misidentified or missed, that the enemy's resilience in this or that city or industry would be underestimated, are to be expected. The failure of strategic bombing in Germany, however, was rooted in more than operational troubles and the hazards of guesstimates in a swift-moving war. It reflected an inability to grasp the reality of the German economic and social system. Scientists, military technicians, and Allied statesmen alike were carried away by their doctrines and techniques. Their working models of German society were fallacious; in judging the effects of bombing, they did not adequately analyze the range of relevant variables. Their estimates were based on a tragic combination of ignorance, hatred, and wishful thinking.

Insofar as the strategic bombing offensive was a grand intelligence failure, it was a failure to understand the urban area as a functional system, with consumer-resources ratios of varying elasticity. The degree of elasticity of supply—that is, the ease with

---

68 *WF*, Vol. II, p. 272.
69 *WF*, Vol. I, pp. 312, 346, 475, Vol. II, pp. 254, 256, 265, 270, and Vol. III, p. 80.
70 *USSBS-OR*, pp. 9, 72.

which the supply of goods and services responds to a change in consumer demand—is a function of the level of resources before destruction (e.g., how much "fat" can be drawn on), the divisibility of resources (e.g., how easily dwelling units can be subdivided), and the state of organization (e.g., how easily scarce resources can be shifted to places of greatest need).[71]

Most important in miscalculating the impact of bombing on Germany was a radical misconception that the German economy was stretched to capacity in the early war years.[72] In fact, there was abundant reserve capacity, especially in the consumer goods sector, which was turned to war production, permitting it to increase until mid-1944. Most important in sustaining the belief in area bombing was the failure to anticipate quick recovery of production in apparently devastated cities.[73] The experts and planners simply did not appreciate that the social and economic life of a large city can survive even when its physical structure is severely damaged. By intensive use of remaining resources or by substitution, life goes on. In Germany, housing proved to be a highly elastic resource:[74] bombed-out families doubled up with more fortunate relatives and friends or were reaccommodated in factory dormitories or barracks near their workplaces; schools were converted into dormitories. Although transportation is less elastic than housing, much was done: non-essential travel was restricted, sightseeing buses were diverted into the regular transit system, empty cabs were filled, millions turned to bicycles. Public utilities and intra-urban transportation were quickly restored.[75] Factories and workers alike were relocated; machinery was shifted to intact buildings. Workers were imported or put on second shifts; evacuees were billeted in private homes and employed on new shifts in the industries of receiving areas. Recovery efforts were well organized and energetically effected.

Although they did not usually forecast the outright collapse of German morale,[76] scientific and military experts—ignoring British experience—exaggerated the psychological effects of area bombing and misconstrued the connection between morale and production.

[71] Iklé.
[72] WF, Vol. I, pp. 475–476, Vol. II, p. 247.
[73] USSBS-OR, pp. 71–74.   [74] Iklé, pp. 40–76, 183.
[75] USSBS-OR, p. 73.   [76] WF, Vol. II, p. 247.

They were correct in their assumption that air raids would produce *feelings* of depression, but wrong in their belief that such feelings would determine actual *behavior* under stress; habit, discipline, fear of punishment, and the absence of alternatives meant that the willingness to work remained substantially unaffected.[77]

In any event, neither area nor precision bombing played a major role until the final year of the war. The air offensive of 1940–41 killed more members of the RAF than German civilians.[78] The U.S. daylight offensive was stymied by the end of 1943; in the spring of 1944, the RAF Bomber Command was in danger of defeat.[79] Not until the German fighter force was knocked out in 1944 was there even a possibility of a decisive defeat through air power.[80] By that time, Allied armies were in France and the Russian armies were sweeping across eastern Europe. The most favorable thing that can be said is that the fifth-year success of strategic bombing was "merged with and, to some extent, was even overtaken by, the general victory of all Allied arms operating from all directions."[81]

The Belief in Bombing Today: A Footnote on the Far East

Although the Strategic Bombing Survey is the main source for many books on air power, its more critical findings remain unpublicized. The waste in the bombing of Germany constitutes one of the best-documented and least-known series of intelligence failures in history; the data seem to have had little effect on subsequent use of air power. Area bombing failed in Germany, strengthening the American conviction that precision bombing was superior. Yet, strategic bombing of all kinds continued to fascinate the planners of war, shaping their strategy in such places as Japan, Korea, and Vietnam. In November, 1944, when the United States had already demonstrated decisive superiority over the Japanese on land, sea, and air, when Japanese war production was in a steady decline—a result of the sea-air blockade against an economy already desperately short of raw materials and skilled labor—at this late date, we turned to mass bombing. That offensive was an apparent success: it destroyed over two-fifths—one report says almost half—of the

77 Iklé, pp. 75, 198.   78 A. J. P. Taylor, p. 519.
79 *WF*, Vol. III, p. 123.   80 *USAAF*, Vol. II, p. 730.
81 *WF*, Vol. III, p. 94.

built-up area of 66 cities surveyed;[82] it killed about 330,000 and wounded about 476,000 civilians, exceeding the total combat casualties among Japanese armed forces for the whole war; it induced the migration of millions more.[83]

But the Bombing Survey on the Japanese economy, a summary quite sympathetic to the doctrine of strategic bombing, phrases the impact of this destruction cautiously: "The economic disintegration caused by the blockade was finished by the bombers."[84] Drawing on the same data, the official air force history suggests that "strategic bombardment had less effect on production than did shortages imposed by the blockade."[85] Having succeeded in paralyzing Japan's capacity to wage war without mass bombing, we bombed; having brought the Japanese economy very close to collapse through the combined weight of the blockade and bombing—and weeks after key Japanese leaders had begun moves toward peace[86]—we undertook the atomic obliteration of Hiroshima and Nagasaki. Twenty years later, impressed with the late and limited success of precision bombing in Germany, possessing vivid memories of successful (if unnecessary) devastation of Japanese cities, having failed to "interdict" the Chinese in Korea, again inspired by visions of easy victory by air power, we apply the "lessons" to wholly different cases. We use area bombing against villages in Vietnam, where total devastation is at best self-defeating and where terror from the air strengthens resistance and undermines our own political base more than that of the opposition; we use precision bombing against oil depots and transportation routes, where the oil plays a small part in the economy and where the main modes of transportation—footpaths in jungles and rice paddies, pontoon ferries of boats and bamboo—

---

[82] USSBS-55, p. 9; USSBS-53, p. 2.

[83] USAAF, Vol. V, pp. 754–755. In his autobiography General Curtis LeMay, who initiated the great fire raids on Japan and in 1948 became head of the Strategic Air Command, boasts that "we burned up nearly sixteen square miles of Tokyo," producing more casualties than those of Hiroshima and Nagasaki combined (General Curtis LeMay with M. Kantor, Mission with LeMay [Garden City: Doubleday, 1965], p. 10). LeMay's recollections are expressed with a touch of unseemly zest: "Enemy cities were pulverized or fried to a crisp." Ibid., p. 420. He is not exaggerating.

[84] USSBS-53, p. 2.   [85] USAAF, Vol. V, p. 754.

[86] USAAF, Vol. V, pp. 726 ff., 741; Robert J. C. Butow, Japan's Decision to Surrender (Stanford: Stanford University Press, 1954), pp. 130–135.

either lie beyond the reach of any bomber or when destroyed are quickly replaced.

It is a melancholy story of three decades of rigid doctrine and massive destruction—both of dubious value to any nation's interest.

THE MERGER OF TECHNICAL, SOCIAL, AND POLITICAL INTELLIGENCE

The longevity of the strategic bombing doctrine should not obscure equally impressive successes of intelligence—data and doctrine converging to persuade political leaders of sensible alternatives and possibilities. And all these cases, test bans and bombings alike, illustrate the increasing influence of men who combine technical and political skills.

Both points are evident in the slowly increasing receptivity to advice from the social sciences, both specialized and general, and in the emergence of freewheeling experts who combine training in physical science and some understanding of social and political life.[87] In World War II and in the Cold War, the military made extensive use of mathematicians and physical scientists to answer such questions as "What is the best depth for detonation of a torpedo?" But these physical scientists went far beyond such narrow questions. For instance, the Tizard Committee's decision to back the development of radar and subsequent arrangements for its operational use in Britain in the mid-1930's plainly required not only technical insight but political understanding and courage. Against the passionate opposition of the doctrinaire Lindemann (later Lord Cherwell), this tiny band of researchers and liaison men between science and government laid the foundations for the effective defense of Britain in the Battle of Britain, giving the Spitfires of 1940 time to take off.

[87] A recent study found that judgments concerning the likelihood of a variety of developments in foreign affairs, made by a group of "thirty distinguished social scientists, preponderantly political scientists and psychologists from the academic community," and a group of "policy-makers and scientists from the defense community" with physical science or engineering backgrounds, were very similar. See T. W. Milburn and J. F. Milburn, "Predictions of Threats and Beliefs about How to Meet Them," *American Behavioral Scientist,* IX (March, 1966), 3–7.

For two crucial years, 1935–36, the doctrine that "the bomber will always get through," developed by the Italian General Doughet, preached by the American General Billy Mitchell, and embraced by Prime Minister Baldwin, was questioned. Without the strong push by these skeptical scientists, without the radar they developed and promoted, it is likely that Hitler would have conquered Britain.[88] Social scientists also played their part in breaking through perceptual barriers. The military employed psychologists to devise testing, selection, and training programs, sociologists to analyze the internal organization and morale of the armed forces, anthropologists to tell us about the culture of New Guinea and the Solomons. At the same time the federal government turned to political scientists as experts in public administration, economists to staff the agencies of economic control (WPB, OPA, FEA), and every kind of social scientist to modernize and man our propaganda and intelligence machinery. The Strategic Bombing Survey of 1944–46 itself represented one of the most extensive uses of social research in that period. Although its evidence of the limits of air power did not carry the day in World War II, it may have helped dampen enthusiasm for the unrestrained use of air power in the 1950's and 1960's.[89]

By means of the standing advisory committee, contract research, and the support of semi-autonomous operations research institutes, the government began to tap more generalized advice from the academic community.[90] A model for the non-military uses of such advice can be derived from the best of the military examples: small,

88 Cf. A. J. P. Taylor, p. 392; Snow, pp. 28–38, 83–89.

89 Before the end of the war, the survey group submitted to Washington interim reports on their findings with respect to Germany and suggestions for strategy in Japan. Three of the nine directors of the USSBS later became presidential advisers—George W. Ball, John K. Galbraith, and Paul H. Nitze. Galbraith remained a caustic critic of the illusion of the omnipotence of air power. Ball was the first to argue vigorously against an air strike in the Cuban missile crisis. In 1966, after President Johnson's repeated escalations of the air war in North Vietnam, Ball resigned as Under Secretary of State. Although not known as an enthusiast for bombing, Nitze was one of the early advocates of an air strike against Cuba. Like other members of the Kennedy "Executive Committee," however, during the deliberations he shifted to the more cautious alternative of the blockade. At the time of this writing he remains Assistant Secretary of Defense.

90 Don K. Price, *Government and Science: Their Dynamic Relation in American Democracy* (New York: New York University Press, 1954).

flexible, loosely organized, interdisciplinary groups in RAND, an advisory corporation engaged in systems analysis for the United States Air Force. Especially valuable is an account of research by RAND—from its inception in an Air Force request to its reflection in strategic policy—on the effectiveness and vulnerability of air bases.[91] In May, 1951, the Air Staff commissioned a study of the most efficient selection, construction, and use of overseas air-base facilities for the period 1956–61. The study was undertaken by Albert Wohlstetter, a political scientist of varied background, two economists (one of whom had engineering training), and an aeronautical engineer. RAND colleagues from other disciplines, including electronics, mathematics, and cost analysis, contributed as occasional consultants. Reformulating what appeared to be a routine, logistical study, Wohlstetter came up with a broader range of questions about the vulnerability of the Strategic Air Force to surprise attack and about system-wide costs—both more important than the question of minimum cost for given facilities, the main criterion prevailing among Air Force planners. The research group evaluated four basing systems in terms of their total costs and effectiveness in destroying enemy targets. They concluded that under the existing basing system—reliance on advanced overseas operating bases— almost all the Strategic Air Force could be destroyed while still on the ground by a first-strike surprise attack; the surviving remnants could not mount an effective retaliatory strike. RAND calculated that the least vulnerable and least costly alternative would be a system of domestic operating bases combined with overseas bases for staging and refueling.

The Air Staff adopted RAND's major recommendations three years after the start of the study, and about one year after formal presentation. That the report was not immediately accepted was to be expected: its shattering conclusion required rigorous examination. That it faced skepticism, inertia, and opposition illustrates again the power of preconceptions and the structural barriers to innovation. Acceptance meant big changes in the plans, operating procedures, and responsibilities of many branches of the Air Force. But the relative autonomy of RAND and its reputation for independence and objectivity prevented the study from being associated with in-

[91] Bruce L. R. Smith, "Strategic Expertise."

ternal squabbles and vested interests and permitted it to surmount hierarchical hurdles. In gathering information and in communicating their results, the researchers used informal contacts to enlist the support of numerous officers, from majors to generals; they presented their findings and recommendations to all Air Force groups concerned (Wohlstetter alone gave 92 briefings in 1953); they stimulated key people to rethink the whole problem of deterrence. When faced with delaying tactics, Wohlstetter and a group of RAND executives visited General Thomas S. White, acting chief of staff of the Air Force, thus smoothing the way toward acceptance of their findings.

The original request for a routine study of basing costs resulted in a reappraisal of our deterrence strategy by the RAND group, then by the Air Force, and later by the Department of Defense. Effective deterrence of enemy atomic attack necessitated not only what was then recognized—a powerful U.S. first-strike capacity—but also the maintenance of an invulnerable second-strike force. By forcing a clear recognition of this distinction, RAND's research and political persuasion made a vital contribution to national security. For that brief moment in history, with only two opposing powers in the nuclear club, world peace rested on both sides' belief in the second-strike capability of the other. In the 1950's this belief was a major constraint against a big pre-emptive war or the easy escalation of small wars urged by reckless minorities in the USSR and the United States.[92]

In short, there is an urgent demand for broad policy advice on issues of politics and administration that relies heavily on technical intelligence. In which of ten communities should a new plant be located? What proportion of resources should be put into bombers in comparison with naval vessels, land forces, or missiles? What is the effect of a proposed arms-control agreement on the national defense? To cope with such issues, administrative leaders are turning to a new breed of experts who can interpret the work of separate disciplines, combine the functions of contact men, internal communications specialists, and facts-and-figures men, supply a

[92] In Chapters 3 and 5, I shall return to the structural and doctrinal roots of success in the RAND case. For similar examples from Britain see R. V. Jones, "Scientific Intelligence," *Journal of the Royal United Service Institution*, XCII (August, 1947), 352–369.

blend of technical and ideological intelligence, and, in general, enrich the verbal environment of elites. Needless to say, there is more demand than supply for such experts.

INTELLIGENCE AND STRUCTURAL COMPLEXITY: A SUMMARY

Within a context of increased availability of information and a growing demand for generalized policy advice, an organization in conflict with its environment, especially one deeply involved with or part of government, will turn toward contact men; an organization heavily dependent on internal solidarity will hire internal communications specialists; and an organization that sees its external relations and internal operations as rationalized will depend on facts-and-figures men. These general determinants of the amount and type of resources devoted to the intelligence function are reflected in more familiar attributes of structure. Briefly, the more complex the structure, the more use of experts. The main locus of the managerial revolution is in large organizations with many specialized units to coordinate, great heterogeneity of membership manifested in a diversity of goals, and much centralization. Thus a careful study of the attitudes and actions of American business executives on foreign trade issues in 1953–55 compares the heads of firms in various industries and communities and of contrasting social background and party affiliation. As determinants of their policy stance, it concludes, neither self-interest nor ideology was as important as the institutional structures within which they operated: "In almost all our survey results, the most dramatic statistical differences were . . . between the large, medium, and small firms. . . . Thanks to their competence but even more to their staffs, the big-businessmen read more, know more, and do more, particularly with respect to the external environment."[93] Other things being equal, the larger the size, the greater is the public impact, the more intense is the problem of internal control, and the more resources are available for the intelligence function. The more specialization, the more interdependent are the specialized parts, the greater the cost of

[93] Bauer, Pool, and Dexter, pp. 229, 476.

failure of any one part, and, therefore, the more resources devoted by each to keep track of the others, and the more staff at the center to coordinate the whole. Moreover, greater specialization increases the difficulty of recruitment and training and the amount of effort needed to secure information about morale and performance. Finally, the more heterogeneous the membership or constituents of an organization, the more ambiguous, diffuse, diversified, and numerous its purposes or products; this more complex structure of goals means more variables to consider and a more urgent problem of coordination. In other words, size, specialization, centralization, heterogeneity of membership and goals—all of these attributes of structure generate the need for experts insofar as they (1) increase the number and variety of social units in the environment that must be taken account of, (2) aggravate the problem of internal control, and (3) multiply formal rules and intensify the search for uniformities. It is said that the law for the age of computers is that programmed action drives out the unprogrammed. It is also true that unofficial, informal social groups mobilize in response to the multiplication of formal rules; unprogrammed activity is driven underground, creating still more need for intelligence and surveillance.[94]

Illustrative "proof" of these hypotheses is afforded by the types of organizations that have shown the greatest expenditures on staff experts and consultants: in the economy, firms in the aerospace, oil, and chemical and electrical equipment industries, and modern multi-industrial labor unions; in the polity, the White House, the CIA, the Departments of Defense and State. In the spheres of education, science, aesthetics, and entertainment, consider the major universities and the television and radio networks. They are all large, complex, centralized, and fast-growing; they rest on a modern technological base, engage in keen competition for resources, contracts, and markets (constituents, clients), and are heavily involved with the central government or international politics.

There are upper limits to these generalizations. Regarding the degree of conflict with or dependence on the environment, if, like a religious or political sect, the organization is totally at war with its environment, it will not be moved to hire specialists in accom-

[94] Harold L. Wilensky, "Work as a Social Problem," in *Social Problems*, ed. by Howard Becker (New York: John Wiley & Sons, 1966), pp. 117–166.

modative techniques (although it may need staff for internal control). If it has a monopoly of the relevant resources, it has no need for information about rivals. Finally, leaders in an organization needing experts may not recognize the need, be able to afford experts, or find it possible to hire the right ones.

From area bombing to radar, from the Bay of Pigs to the missile crisis and the test-ban treaty, from Korea to Vietnam, failures and successes alike underscore two themes in my analysis of types and functions of intelligence. First, when the problem is technical, when substantial departures from previous practices occur or unprecedented programs are launched, the facts count; but stereotypes constituting the verbal environment of an organization—captured in felicitous slogans—can for years remain impervious to evidence. Second, there is an increasing use of men who combine technical and political skills to create a more sophisticated imagery of organizations (or nations) and their external and internal environments.

CHAPTER 3

The Quality of Organizational Intelligence

To explain the great expansion in intelligence and major variations in the employment of experts is not to understand how their work is organized. Nor does it tell us much about variations in the quality of intelligence. And to assert the significance of slogans and preconceptions is not to discover the conditions in which sensible doctrine overcomes the less sensible.

The knowledge explosion intensifies an old problem: how to draw good intelligence from a highly compartmentalized body of knowledge and get it into the room where decisions are made. Sources of failure are legion: even if the initial message is accurate, clear, timely, and relevant, it may be translated, condensed, or completely blocked by personnel standing between the sender and the intended receiver; it may get through in distorted form. If the receiver is in a position to use the message, he may screen it out because it does not fit his preconceptions, because it has come through a suspicious or poorly-regarded channel, because it is embedded in piles of inaccurate or useless messages (excessive noise in the channel), or, simply, because too many messages are transmitted to him (information overload).[1]

The disaster at Pearl Harbor is alleged to be an intelligence lesson burned into the minds of general staffs and top planners of national strategy. The failure to take the final crucial step of communicating to commanders the urgent warnings about Japan's in-

[1] When appropriate search procedures have been employed but the relevant message is not in the system, or when the intended receiver is not in a position to act on it (he is clearly constrained by forces beyond his control), we cannot call the instance an intelligence failure. See page ix above.

tentions supplied by Far Eastern code analysts[2] is said to be due to "the lack of a high level joint intelligence group and the absence of a high echelon organization for national estimates and an indications center."[3] Yet, twenty-five years later, after a reorganization of the intelligence function to incorporate these structural changes, two presidents were led into disastrous military adventures based largely on miscalculation by intelligence agencies communicating at the top misleading pictures of the situation in Cuba, the Dominican Republic, and Vietnam. The vast expansion of the intelligence community has not prevented successes in the uses of intelligence—among them the excellent beach studies done for the Pacific campaign and the identification of the guided missile development center at Peenemünde in World War II, the CIA's forewarning of a Communist attempt to supply arms to the government of Guatemala in May, 1954, and the Defense Department's spotting of Soviet missiles in Cuba. Neither has it prevented a string of fateful failures.[4]

Intelligence failures are rooted in structural problems that cannot be fully solved; they express universal dilemmas of organizational life that can, however, be resolved in various ways at varying costs. In all complex social systems, hierarchy, specialization, and centralization are major sources of distortion and blockage of intelligence. The quality of intelligence is also shaped by the prevailing concepts of intelligence, the problems to be confronted, the stages of growth of the organization, and the economic, political, and cultural contexts of decision. To explore problems in the organization of the intelligence function, this chapter will employ a military analogy (see p. ix), developing propositions and using examples with wide application to government and industry.

HIERARCHY

Insofar as the problem of control—coordinating specialists, getting work done, securing compliance—is solved by rewards of status, power, and promotion, the problem of obtaining accurate, critical

2 Wohlstetter, pp. 125 ff., 310 ff., 395.
3 Ransom, p. 58. Cf. *Ibid.*, pp. 41, 54–56, *passim.*
4 For examples see Ransom, pp. 60 ff., and Snyder and Paige.

intelligence is intensified. For information is a resource that symbolizes status, enhances authority, and shapes careers. In reporting at every level, hierarchy is conducive to concealment and misrepresentation. Subordinates are asked to transmit information that can be used to evaluate their performance. Their motive for "making it look good," for "playing it safe," is obvious. A study of 52 middle managers (mean age 37) found a correlation of +.41 ($p < .01$) between upward work-life mobility and holding back "problem" information from the boss; the men on their way up were prone to restrict information about such issues as lack of authority to meet responsibilities, fights with other units, unforeseen costs, rapid changes in production, scheduling or work flow, fruitless progress reports, constant interruptions, insufficient time or budget to train subordinates, insufficient equipment or supplies, and so on.[5] Restriction of such problem information is motivated by the desire not only to please but also to preserve comfortable routines of work: if the subordinate alerts the boss to pending trouble, the former is apt to find himself on a committee to solve the problem. The aphorism "Never volunteer for anything" is not confined to the Army; it is part of folk wisdom.

In addition to motive for holding back and distorting, there must be a corresponding opportunity. Middle-level managers, and even lower-level employees, sometimes have a near monopoly of insight into feasible alternatives. For instance, observers of man-paced factory jobs have noted the ingenuity of machinists who invent and hide cutting tools that do the work more efficiently than the prescribed ways and thereby permit more worker control of the pace. Although automation and centralization may change this, first-line supervisors still have indispensable practical knowledge of both unofficial work behavior and "bugs" in the technical system; and local plant managers in multi-plant systems know the limits of their productive capacities far better than does central headquarters.[6]

[5] See the unpubl. diss. (University of Michigan, 1959) by W. Read, "Factors Affecting Upward Communication at Middle Management Levels in Industrial Organizations."

[6] Cf. William F. Whyte, *Money and Motivation* (New York: Harper & Brothers, 1955); Leonard R. Sayles, *Behavior of Industrial Work Groups: Prediction and Control* (New York: John Wiley & Sons, 1958); Benjamin Ward, *The Socialist Economy: A Study of Organizational Alternatives* (New York: Random House, 1967); and Dalton.

Matching the motive and opportunity of the subordinate to remain silent are the superior's motive and opportunity to close his ears. The common belief that staff experts should be on tap, not on top, functions to maintain line authority and reduce the status of the staff. It acts as a self-fulfilling prophecy: the advice of low-status intelligence specialists, however good, can readily be discounted. In the Pearl Harbor case, on December 5, after weeks of being ignored as mere data collectors, subordinate officers in subordinate intelligence and research units tried to communicate their more urgent interpretations directly to the chiefs of Army and Navy war plans. "But their efforts were unsuccessful because of the poor repute associated with Intelligence, inferior rank, and the province of the specialist, or long-hair."[7]

Thus, if an organization has many ranks and if in its administrative style and symbolism it emphasizes rank, the greatest distortion and blockage will attend the upward flow of information. Organizations vary greatly in the prominence given to status display—through insignia (from the single, thin gold stripe of the cadet to the many wide stripes of the admiral); through office decor (from the gray plastic and metal desks of the stenographer to the spacious custom-made rosewood of the "top dog," from asphalt tile to one-inch pile); through forms of address (from Charlie to Mr., Sir, Your Honor, Your Excellency); and through language (from the regional dialect of the janitor to the special accent of the Oxford don). Status symbols serve to motivate performance, legitimize positions, and facilitate some kinds of communication. Without stable, comfortable, certified ways of talking and writing to one another, without observance of the rules of deference and demeanor, people of different rank or different function do not easily maintain harmony. But the harmony is achieved at the cost of lowering the quality of intelligence channeled to the top; and the symbolism tends to metastasize.[8]

---

[7] Wohlstetter, pp. 102, 312.

[8] Cf. Chester I. Barnard, "Functions and Pathology of Status Systems in Formal Organizations," in *Industry and Society,* ed. by William Foote Whyte (New York: McGraw-Hill Book Co., 1946), pp. 46–83; Delbert C. Miller and William H. Form, *Industrial Sociology: The Sociology of Work Organizations,* 2nd edn. (New York: Harper & Row, 1964), pp. 476 ff.; and Tom Burns and G. M. Stalker, *The Management of Innovation* (London: Tavistock Publications, 1961), pp. 150–154.

Afraid that they are being deceived or kept in the dark, men at the top take action: they emphasize criteria for loyalty in recruitment and promotion, uniform indoctrination, and other efforts to create organization men. These "solutions" in turn complicate the intelligence problem: fewer fresh slants, new ideas, and critical questions will be lodged in the system or work their way to the top. A major reason for the American bank's reputation for hidebound conservatism is a hierarchical structure infused with status symbolism, which attracts and shapes conventional, bureaucratic men whose conformity limits innovation.[9] Hierarchy blocks communication; blockages lead to indoctrination; indoctrination narrows the range of communication.

Of course, information can be introduced into the system at any level; the higher it enters, the less subject it is to the processes that distort. Even the Assistant to the President, however, may have both motive and opportunity to hold back information, the more so if he has himself risen through the ranks.

The shape of the hierarchy—not merely the number of ranks but also the number of personnel at each level—conditions the upward flow of information. Where the pyramid is tall and narrows sharply at the top, providing a long promotion ladder for a few, there are many time servers at lower ranks who have neither information nor the motive for acquiring it. In the middle, among the non-mobile, there are many defensive cliques who restrict information to prevent change, many mutual aid and comfort groups who restrict information because of their resentment of their more ambitious colleagues, and many coalitions of ambitious men who share information among themselves but pass on only the portion that furthers one or more of their careers. For the purposes of intelligence, the optimal shape of the hierarchy would be relatively flat (few ranks permit a speedier diffusion of more accurate information) with a bulge in the middle (more specialists who have information and more potential managers motivated to command it).

Whatever the shape of the hierarchy, however, to extract information from those who have it typically requires the bypassing of

[9] See Chris Argyris, *Organization of a Bank* (New Haven: Labor and Management Center, Yale University, 1954), for description of the "Friendly First Bank."

conventional ranking systems. Efforts to resolve the dilemma of hierarchy vs. intelligence include team or project organization, devices for communicating out of channels, machinery for investigation and inspection, performance checks, and reliance on informed outsiders.

The higher in the hierarchy one goes, the less do problems correspond to the specialized structure of knowledge and the less a decision can be programmed. Only at the lower levels of policy deliberation can the specialized expert tackle a specialized problem with a chance of solving it by the precise methods of science.[10] Further, at any level, the role of the expert is self-changing: if he is successful within his sphere of competence, if his advice is taken on matters where his specialized knowledge is relevant, he is likely to be chosen for tasks outside that sphere of competence, where his specialized knowledge may be irrelevant.[11] This is why there is so urgent a demand for generalized advisers at the top. It is also why an appropriate form of organization for industrial research and development or, more broadly, for the use of experts anywhere, is the task force—a team or project of diverse specialists who are brought together to solve a limited range of problems and then are reassigned when the task is done. Several swiftly growing corporations based on sophisticated technology, such as the IBM Corporation, have adopted this form.[12] The great advantages of the task force are flexibility, informality, the release of individual initiative, and above all the swift diffusion of information both within the team and, as team members are reassigned, throughout the organization. The disadvantage is that teams, exempt from standard rules of procedure, ambiguous in status and authority, are difficult to fit into the hierarchy or into established professional niches—prime reasons for their tendency to transform themselves into permanent specialist groups.[13] It is possible that the task force is best for higher policy deliberations and crisis situations—as in the Cuban missile

[10] Cf. Price, p. 164.   [11] Wilensky, *Intellectuals*, pp. 209 ff.

[12] Cf. Herbert A. Shepard, "Nine Dilemmas in Industrial Research," *Administrative Science Quarterly*, I (December, 1956) 295–309; and Fred H. Goldner, "Demotion in Industrial Management," *American Sociological Review*, XXX (October, 1965), 714–724.

[13] Cf. Kornhauser, pp. 50 ff.; and Burns and Stalker, pp. 88 ff.

crisis—and for policy-oriented research or technical development, whereas other forms of organization are appropriate for basic research.

Additional defenses against the information pathologies of hierarchy are various reporting services and statistical controls. These include the "score card" and "attention-directing" uses of accounting data in business—cost variances of individual departments, trend reports on "invisible" operations (machine performance, consumption of operating supplies), accounting statements for "profit centers"—and special "problem-solving" studies (of alternative processes, equipment, products), again done by teams, drawing on accounting information, engineering estimates, and industrial engineering standards.[14] In interpreting such data, top executives, even in very hierarchical organizations, are not entirely defenseless: they have built up a sense of reasonableness regarding performance reports; they can check submitted data for consistency. Finally, there is a universal performance check in every type of economy: the quality of performance of one organization is known by other organizations that receive its products; the metal fabricator who must work with defective steel in the Soviet Union will complain no less than his counterpart in the United States.[15]

Perhaps the most fruitful and common response to hierarchy is communication out of channels: contact men, on salary or retainer, keep in touch with outsiders who have a detached or critical view of the organization; internal communications specialists, some of whom combine close ties to local leaders and loyalties to central headquarters, report on local performance and morale. A variety of marginal men at points along the organization's boundaries supply supplementary and often crucial intelligence.

Modern military services evidence all of these responses to hierarchy. Like executives everywhere, military elites have moved from coercion and command to persuasion and manipulation: instead of a pyramidal structure, a diamond bulging in the middle; instead of ritualistic close-order drill, an accent on the training mission; instead of a mechanical assimilation of the Army way, a reduction in symbols of rank (less spit and polish, less diversity of dress); in-

14 Simon *et al., Centralization vs. Decentralization.*
15 Cf. Ward.

stead of standing operating procedure (SOP), group command conferences and informal briefings, bypassing normal channels.[16]

SPECIALIZATION AND RIVALRY

As a source of information blockage and distortion, specialization may be more powerful than hierarchy. The organization of the armed forces and industry alike encourages rivalry and restriction of information. Each service, each division, indeed every sub-unit, becomes a guardian of its own mission, standards, and skills; lines of organization become lines of loyalty and secrecy. In industry, the personnel department defends its control over selection and training; accounting, its standards of reporting; production, its schedules of output; sales, its interests in product design and customer service —each restricting information that might advance the competing interests of the others. Top men in each are reluctant to let their subordinates "take on" rivals by asking for information for fear that their unit will betray weakness, invite counter-inquiries, or incur debt. While information can also be used to persuade potential allies and to facilitate accommodation with rivals (see discussion of the "rational-responsible" bias above), it is more commonly hoarded for selective use in less collaborative struggles for power and position.

In the armed forces, intense rivalries between services and within services—among supply and procurement, plans and operations, research and development, intelligence—lead to intelligence failures. Combined with the hierarchical distortions already mentioned, they can be fatal. In 1941, the signals of the pending attack on Pearl Harbor lay scattered in a number of rival agencies; communication lines linked them but essential messages never flowed across the lines, let alone to the top. The Army and Navy presented a picture of cordial, respectful communication, empty of solid substance.[17] In foreign affairs, the history of intelligence failures in the major capitals hints that the foreign office, the military, and

---

[16] Morris Janowitz, *The Professional Soldier: A Social and Political Portrait* (Glencoe: The Free Press, 1960), pp. 38 ff. Cf. Burns and Stalker, pp. 77–96, 118–125.

[17] Wohlstetter, pp. 385–395.

the intelligence agencies seldom if ever form an effective three-way communication network. In the Bay of Pigs fiasco of 1961, for instance, the intelligence branch of the CIA was out of touch with the operations branch, which was planning the adventure; operations was only loosely in touch with the Joint Chiefs, who loosely went along; the CIA kept both President Kennedy and the Cuban exiles uninformed; the President approved a plan on the assumption of two possible outcomes, national revolt or flight to the hills— neither remotely possible; activists in the CIA and the Joint Chiefs rejected the more accurate intelligence of the Department of State (which never pressed it hard), of the British, and of alert newspaper reporters, because that intelligence contradicted the assumptions of the plan they were determined to launch.[18]

Only a decade before, in Korea in the fall of 1950, as General MacArthur raced to the Yalu River, President Truman confidently discounted the military-diplomatic dangers. One reason is that "no one [in Washington] went to Truman [to warn him of the Chinese concentration of forces] because everyone thought someone else should go."[19] On the ground in Korea, intelligence, operations, and supply housed many men who doubted the official assumption that the Chinese would not intervene, but the doubts were not aired where they would count.[20] Punctiliousness about jurisdiction fostered this failure, although it is possible that the Joint Chiefs, who were low-ranking officers when MacArthur was a great general, were also constrained by old habits of deference from countering MacArthur's optimism. France locates a similar case in the particularism of Army branches and the insulation of the General Staff in the decade before World War II.[21]

The dilemma of intelligence vs. specialization is twofold: specialization is essential to the efficient command of knowledge but antithetical to the penetrating interpretation that bears on high policy; specialization and its concomitant, inter-unit rivalry, frequently block the sharing of accurate information, but if problems of upward communication can be solved, rivalry can result in great

[18] Herbert Lionel Matthews, *The Cuban Story* (New York: G. Braziller, 1961); Sorensen, *Kennedy;* Schlesinger, *A Thousand Days.*
[19] Neustadt, p. 145.
[20] Marshall, pp. 6–14.
[21] Stefan T. Possony, "Organized Intelligence: The Problem of the French General Staff," *Social Research,* VIII (May, 1941), 213–237.

gains—the clarification of clashing alternatives and the presentation of opposing cases. The primary cost of specialization in intelligence is parochialism—the production of misleading or irrelevant information, a product of the familiar limitations of the expert.[22] The professionally biased producer of intelligence remains too distant from the intelligence user, too ignorant of policy needs, and is forced to compete with other producers for the support and guidance of the user.[23] No less obvious is the value of efficiency, that is, economy, speed, and accuracy in the performance of a task. A translator of a foreign newspaper may work better in a translation section, an economist expert in the economy of Rumania works better in the company of other social scientists concerned with Eastern Europe. The gain from constructive rivalry is another matter; it depends on administrative styles and structures that expedite the free flow of rival perspectives and solutions to the responsible executives and their general advisers.

To resolve this structural dilemma, especially in organizations dependent on technical intelligence, administrative leaders use the following devices: they recruit managers from professional or scientific staff (e.g., several top executives of the Du Pont Company have experience in their research laboratories); they bind specialists in the field closely and informally to the home staff via rotation, frequent conferences, and career lines that lead from the field to central headquarters; they expose themselves systematically to intelligence by examining multiple sources firsthand and sometimes by stimulating competition between sources.

President Franklin D. Roosevelt, despite his reputation for disorderly administration, was apparently a master of the last two techniques. "The first task of an executive, as he evidently saw it, was to guarantee himself an effective flow of information and ideas. . . . Roosevelt's persistent effort therefore was to check and balance information acquired through official channels by information acquired through a myriad of private informal and unorthodox channels and espionage networks. At times he seemed almost to pit his personal sources against his public sources."[24] He would tell

[22] Harold J. Laski, *The Limitations of the Expert* (London: The Fabian Society, 1931).

[23] Kent, pp. 81, 94 ff.

[24] Arthur M. Schlesinger, Jr., *The Age of Roosevelt*, Vol. II: *The Coming*

his peripatetic wife, Eleanor, " 'Watch the people's faces. Look at the condition of their clothes on the wash line. You can tell a lot from that. Notice their cars.' " Upon her return from a trip, the President would question her carefully.[25] As the war years approached, he worked closely with Hull and Welles but he often communicated directly with ambassadors and ministers, and in a restless search for ideas and expedients turned to a wide range of contacts outside the State Department—Ickes, Hopkins, Wallace, Cox, Baruch, the Pope, a host of friends abroad.[26]

Not only did Roosevelt rely heavily on unofficial channels, but he also fostered competition within: he would use one anonymous informant's information to challenge and check another's, putting both on their toes; he recruited strong personalities and structured their work so that clashes would be certain. "His favorite technique was to keep grants of authority incomplete, jurisdictions uncertain, charters overlapping."[27] In foreign affairs, he gave Moley and Welles tasks that overlapped those of Secretary of State Hull; in conservation and power, he gave Ickes and Wallace identical missions; in welfare, confusing both functions and initials, he assigned PWA to Ickes, WPA to Hopkins; in politics, Farley found himself competing with other political advisers for control over patronage.[28] The effect: the timely advertisement of arguments, with both the experts and the President pressured to consider the main choices as they came boiling up from below. Roosevelt was willing to suffer the cost: a drain on his subordinates' energies as well as his own, and an occasional casualty—a bitter resignation by a lieutenant who had lost the struggle once too often.

That casting a wide intelligence net via internal competition and external contact figured in Roosevelt's policy successes is nowhere more evident than in the first large-scale federal work relief program in American history, the Civil Works Administration

---

of the New Deal (Boston: Houghton Mifflin, 1959), pp. 522–523; cf. Sherwood, I, 62 ff.

25 James MacGregor Burns, Roosevelt: The Lion and the Fox, Harvest paperback edn. (New York: Harcourt, Brace and World, 1956), p. 173.

26 To what extent FDR's foreign policy failures and successes in the late 1930's can be attributed to such a casual variety of intelligence sources is a moot question.

27 Schlesinger, The Age of Roosevelt, p. 528.

28 Burns, pp. 173, 252, 371 ff.; Sherwood, pp. 86 ff.

(later the WPA), headed by his confidant, Harry Hopkins. In October, 1933, with a desperate winter approaching, Roosevelt instructed Hopkins to act fast. Hopkins consulted both his own staff and outside contacts in the welfare and academic communities. The idea of federal work relief emerged from talks with two experts in public administration, Frank Bane, a professor of social welfare at the University of Chicago, and Louis Brownlow, Director of Public Administration Clearing House. They were among the men who supplied facts, figures, and precedents to persuade Roosevelt that a vast federal work relief plan not only was workable and salable but was also more desirable than a state-administered grant-in-aid program.[29]

With the continuing assistance of Bane and Brownlow, Hopkins's staff drafted the CWA program in about two weeks. They abolished the means test as undermining the self-respect of the unemployed. Within sixty days over four million unemployed had been put to work.[30] All this was accomplished with a small staff of dedicated administrators who felt they were waging a holy war against want and were thus willing to put in killing hours. By the end of the first year Hopkins and his 121 civil servants, on a payroll of only $22,000 a month, had helped seventeen million work relief recipients.[31] Total spending for the year was one and a half billion dollars, a sum which in 1966 dollars exceeds the annual cost of the Great Society's entire anti-poverty program. "Boondoggle" and "leaf raking" became classic anti-New Deal epithets, but many men who raked leaves on the relief payroll—and millions of others who built schools, airports, roads, bridges, dams, or playgrounds or were re-employed as artists, writers, actors, or teachers—preferred the dignity of work to breadlines or grocery tickets.

Roosevelt's administrative style is nicely expressed in his approach to this welfare program. When he was convinced by

29 Sherwood, p. 62; Macmahon *et al.*, p. 22. FDR was particularly worried about the objections of labor leaders. Searching for a precedent that might help overcome resistance, Aubrey Williams, one of Hopkins's top aides, contacted a leading labor economist, Professor John R. Commons. Commons dug out of his files a statement made in 1898 by Samuel Gompers favoring a "Day Labor Plan" identical to the proposed CWA. See Sherwood, p. 63; cf. Schlesinger, *The Age of Roosevelt*, p. 269.

30 Schlesinger, *ibid.*, p. 270.   31 Sherwood, p. 59.

Hopkins and others of the need and feasibility of an immediate work relief plan, he quickly transferred almost one billion dollars from Harold Ickes, whose Public Works Administration (PWA) was slow in getting started, to Hopkins, the zealous welfare spender. He told Hopkins to "talk it over" with the irate Ickes, but to get help to the people quickly and have no truck with the politicians. FDR then directed his old friend Frank Walker, later Postmaster General, to keep an unofficial eye on Hopkins and inform him if the CWA was fomenting too much political trouble.[32]

About a year later, improvising again, Roosevelt devised an administrative structure that would baffle any conventional student of public administration. He put Ickes at the head of an Advisory Committee on Allotments, an enormous collection of government agencies and interest groups, and let him retain the PWA as an operating agency in his Department of the Interior; he gave to Hopkins the new Works Project Administration (WPA), with responsibility for millions of persons on relief rolls; he put Walker in charge of the Division of Applications and Information, thus injecting a political lieutenant "squarely in the middle as Chief Accountant, custodian of facts and figures and keeper of the peace between the two jarring New Dealers."[33] By any reasonable standard this was sloppy; by the same standard, it worked.[34]

In fact, it is possible to view the implementation of the CWA work relief program and the subsequent development of permanent welfare legislation from 1933 to 1936 as a series of intelligence successes linked to FDR's unorthodox administrative style. Through both external contacts and internal competition he was able to learn (1) the nature and magnitude of the nation's problems, especially welfare and unemployment problems,[35] (2) the political and other obstacles to quick action, (3) the wide range of program alternatives,[36] and (4) the sources of new personnel likely to carry out welfare programs.

The gains of calculated competition cannot be secured, however,

[32] *Ibid.*, pp. 54–94; and Burns, p. 196.

[33] Sherwood, p. 85.   [34] Cf. Macmahon *et al.*

[35] Burns, p. 174.

[36] Cf. Frances Perkins, *The Roosevelt I Knew* (New York: The Viking Press, 1946), pp. 188 ff.

if top decision-makers insulate themselves from the squabbles of their subordinates and force rival departments urging rival doctrines to settle differences in committee. President Eisenhower, for instance, made the National Security Council "the climax of a ponderous system of boards, staffs and interdepartmental committees through which national security policy was supposed to rise to the top."[37] As a result, the NSC was converted into a forum for intramural negotiations; what Dean Acheson called "agreement by exhaustion" blurred policy discord.[38] An ironic feature of such a system is that men of good will are moved to obfuscate their positions and overstate agreements with their rivals, on behalf of an ultimate consensus—"doves" try to impress "hawks" with their caution and toughness; hardliners sometimes try to show that they, too, are for peace.[39] The Joint Chiefs of Staff has also been more a place for courteous confusion and maneuver than a deliberative forum. When they cannot cope with issues by glittering generalities representing the lowest common denominator of agreement, such supercommittees avoid controversial issues entirely, delay decisions, refer issues to other committees, or engage in logrolling, as when the Navy trades off support for more Air Force wings in return for Air Force support for more Navy carriers.[40] Sharp questions, cogent arguments, minority positions, a clear calculation of gains and costs are lost to view.

A much discussed but little studied problem is the effect on the quality of intelligence of various bases for dividing work. We can speculate that of the typical bases—problem, project, or task (promoting employment opportunity for minorities), purpose or program (vocational rehabilitation), discipline, skill, or process (sociology, community organization, casework), industry branch or clientele (building trades, Negro youth), geography (San Francisco County)—the only one that seems generally weak for the purposes of intelligence is geographical unit. Gaps in service can be rooted

[37] Schlesinger, A Thousand Days, p. 209.
[38] Schlesinger, ibid. Cf. Paul Y. Hammond, Organizing for Defense: The American Military Establishment in the Twentieth Century (Princeton: Princeton University Press, 1961), pp. 357 ff.; and Possony, pp. 226–227.
[39] Cf. Theodore C. Sorensen, Decision-making in the White House (New York: Columbia University Press, 1963), pp. 62–63.
[40] Cf. Samuel P. Huntington, The Common Defense: Strategic Programs in National Politics (New York and London: Columbia University Press, 1961), pp. 162 ff.; Hammond, pp. 336, 357 ff.

in any or all of these grounds for specialization,[41] but intelligence failures are greatest if location is emphasized. The chief limitations of specialization by territory are three. First, good intelligence cuts across arbitrary political boundaries; it is oriented toward problem, program, or discipline. One would expect an economic aid desk, a market research desk, an office of the scientific adviser, to be on the average more analytical than a State Department country desk. The success of the Council of Economic Advisers rests in part on specialization by discipline and problem (see pp. 94–109 below). Second, insofar as efficiency is at issue, territorial specialization overelaborates administrative apparatus and makes transfer of resources and information from one locality to another more difficult. It also spreads scarce technical staff too thin; attempts to duplicate staff services in every jurisdiction encounter manpower shortages.[42] Finally, in systems where the most skilled men tend to move to the top, an accent on locality will leave intelligence in the hands of the less able.

These points are evident in the recurrent subversion of attempts at regional decentralization in the Soviet Union. Whenever regional organizations have been officially made the dominant body, functional administrators in Gosplan and state committees—men concerned with supplies, innovation, investment, construction, strategic industries—were either given great power or were able to reassert their power within a short period.[43] Even in post-World War II Italy—with its highly politicized system of prefectural administration and its relatively meager level of government services—clashes between field directors of specialized state services and the regionally dominant prefects have been more and more resolved in favor of the specialists, particularly in the areas of public health and veterinary medicine.[44]

[41] For examples from the welfare field see Wilensky and Lebeaux, 1965 edn., pp. 248 ff.

[42] The "spreading-thin" argument is also used against the decentralization of intelligence (see pp. 58–59 below). The losses of locality specialization and those of decentralization, while analytically distinct, are nevertheless often closely related in concrete situations.

[43] Ward; P. J. D. Wiles, *The Political Economy of Communism* (Cambridge: Harvard University Press, 1962), pp. 161 ff.; and Alec Nove, *The Soviet Economy* (New York: Frederick A. Praeger, 1961), pp. 67–96, 195–217.

[44] Robert C. Fried, *The Italian Prefects: A Study in Administrative Politics* (New Haven: Yale University Press, 1963), pp. 266 ff.

The weakness of locality as a basis for specialization is also evident in the operations of "intelligence sections" of municipal police departments. In the United States these sections apparently engage in amateur political sleuthing—e.g., collecting photographs and gossip on alleged subversives, such as those who attend a civil rights demonstration—as well as detection of organized crime and vice. O. W. Wilson, who later became the superintendent of the Chicago Police Department, lists the duties of the intelligence officer as gathering facts for the Chief of Police on subversive activities, minority group tensions, industrial and labor tensions, organized crime and racketeering, commercialized vice, corruption in public office, and police integrity.[45] Other sources emphasize the war against organized crime more than political surveillance.[46] Insofar as these intelligence sections remain locally oriented and recruit parochial personnel, their information about either politics or the law is perhaps little better than the primitive prejudices of local vigilantes. There are some hints, however, that intelligence officers may be among the least locally oriented of policemen. In 1956 a national association of law enforcement agencies with one or more full-time intelligence operators, the Law Enforcement Intelligence Unit (LEIU), was formed. By 1965 it had 150 member agencies organized into four zones. Each zone holds meetings, there is a national meeting, and the association emphasizes personal contacts for the exchange of confidential information on people in bookmaking, sports, gambling, narcotics, the Mafia, racketeering, etc.[47] It is apparent that the problems are regional and national; the information flow follows.

The weakness of specialization by territory or locality is less apparent in contexts where program and policy are fluid and local operating conditions are highly varied and unstable—usually at a very early stage in an organization's life cycle. Here external forces

[45] O. W. Wilson, *Police Administration* (New York: McGraw-Hill Book Co., 1958), pp. 404–405.
[46] For example, *Municipal Police Administration*, 5th edn. (Chicago: International City Managers' Association, 1961), pp. 114–116.
[47] *Combatting Organized Crime.* Report of the 1965 Oyster Bay, New York, Conference, Governor, New York State (Albany: Office of the Counsel, 1966), pp. 34 ff.; and Capt. James Hamilton, "LEIU—Its Objects and Operations," *Yearbook* (1961), pp. 119–122 (International Association of Chiefs of Police).

may necessitate considerable decentralization of authority and with it some specialization of intelligence by territory. Typically the support of local populations must be mobilized, as in farm production control programs, or new services sold, as in adult education or the relocation of rural populations. Often the cooperation of officials in local bodies must be enlisted.[48] Above all, the regional chief must have at his command good intelligence on the pattern of local power and influence. This is important both for a sensitive interpretation of high policy in the light of local conditions and for neutralizing local interests that would subvert program goals. Furthermore, successful adaptation of high policy rests to some extent on feedback to central headquarters of information on local performance.[49]

It is paradoxical that in the early stages of organizational growth, when the need for local political intelligence is greatest, the need for centralization of authority—for the definition of goals and the indoctrination of personnel at the top[50]—is also greatest. Reinforced by the high costs of specialization by locality, the imperatives of central control understandably dominate.

In short, the merit of any basis of specialization depends on the mission to be accomplished (see the discussion of the value of "task forces," pp. 46–47 above), but specialization by locality is seldom effective for the purposes of intelligence.

The firmest generalization we can derive from this chapter so far is that the greater the number of ranks and the greater the number of organizational units involved in a decision process, the more the distorting influence of rank and jurisdiction and, consequently, the greater the chance of an intelligence failure. It is likely that staff experts communicate most freely with colleagues in the same specialty, second with colleagues in the same unit of the workplace, then to subordinates, and last—with greatest blockage and distortion—to superiors and rival agencies.

[48] Note, for instance, the TVA's commitment to "grass-roots democracy." Selznick, *TVA*.

[49] Cf. James W. Fesler, "Field Organization" in *Elements of Public Administration*, ed. by Fritz Morstein Marx, 2nd edn. (Englewood Cliffs: Prentice-Hall, 1959), pp. 256–258.

[50] Philip Selznick, *Leadership in Administration: A Sociological Interpretation* (Evanston: Row, Peterson & Co., 1957).

CENTRALIZATION

Related to the information pathologies of hierarchy and specialization is the dilemma of centralization: if intelligence is lodged at the top, too few officials and experts with too little accurate and relevant information are too far out of touch and too overloaded to function effectively; on the other hand, if intelligence is scattered throughout many subordinate units, too many officials and experts with too much specialized information may engage in dysfunctional competition, may delay decisions while they warily consult each other, and may distort information as they pass it up.[51] More simply, plans are manageable only if we delegate; plans are coordinated in relation to organizational goals only if we centralize.

Central intelligence (e.g., a CIA) presents the same dangers as specialized intelligence: it keeps data collection too far from its outlet in useful policy; it encourages agreed-on estimates that conceal strong disagreement and the weights of diverse opinions (only partly offset by devices that themselves result from horsetrading and logrolling—e.g., the dissenting footnote); and it competes with its own subsidiaries for scarce personnel and documentation facilities.[52] Centralization contributes one additional danger peculiar to itself: the acquisition of unnecessary responsibility ("empire building") is always accompanied by cries of duplication and inefficiency among the units to be absorbed or eliminated. After administrative reform, a more unified, centralized intelligence agency, producing a unified consensual judgment, then fosters the illusion of security, of reliable intelligence, which, as the Bay of Pigs invasion illustrates, can conceal fantasies at the highest level.

In the minds of political, military, and industrial elites the advantages of centralized intelligence have apparently tended to outweigh these dangers. Most executives have been less concerned about preserving the independence and objectivity of their experts than about controlling them. For their part, the experts, seeing a chance for greater influence, have not been loath to secure guidance from the top. And in the reorganization of national strategic in-

[51] Cf. Wiles, pp. 141 ff.; Ward; and Kent, p. 81.
[52] Cf. Ransom, pp. 81, 94, 197 ff.

telligence, the image of Pearl Harbor—the signals scattered, no central interpretive agency alert to them—has been commanding. This debate about departmental or local vs. central or national intelligence has obscured two fundamental points. First, there is need for interpretive skills at every point where important decisions are taken; the ideal is the close integration of data collection and evaluation in every department and division, and, within the limits of budget and personnel, at every level.[53] Second, various degrees and kinds of decentralization are appropriate for various purposes and measures of effectiveness and types of intelligence. If the pathologies of hierarchy and specialization can be minimized, decentralization of intelligence can be effective, but the one decisive argument against it is usually the costs. Staff experts such as scientists, statisticians, economists, accountants, and lawyers are expensive; the supply is limited. This typically dictates a concentration of intelligence at headquarters.

In single-purpose organizations where operating conditions at the local level are roughly uniform, and where the intelligence flow tends to involve technical communication between like-minded specialists or professionals, centralization of intelligence presents few serious problems. A study of the administrative structure of the United States Forest Service indicates an almost complete concentration of intelligence in Washington, where field-unit budgetary allocations are decided, business with other government agencies carried on, and major and minor policy changes conceived.[54] Centrifugal tendencies, reflecting somewhat varying field conditions, exist. But a tight administrative structure and smooth flow of information are maintained by recruitment, indoctrination, and rotation —the same devices used to cope with the costs of specialization (see p. 50). Only men with an ardent love of the outdoors, uniform professional training in forestry, and a strong commitment to a career in the Forest Service are recruited and survive the basic training period. Nine in ten of the approximately 4,000 employees of the Service are graduates of forestry schools; when in college, many held summer jobs in the forests. They share a common lore, similar technical knowledge, and identification even before em-

53 Cf. Wasserman; and Kent, p. 81.
54 Herbert Kaufman, *The Forest Ranger: A Study in Administrative Behavior* (Baltimore: Johns Hopkins Press, 1960), pp. 68, 114, 209.

barking on ranger training.[55] When they become rangers, they find themselves moving about from post to post, not necessarily upward; in fact, horizontal transfers, while not compulsory, are generally a prerequisite for advancement.[56] Both rotation and the inculcation of the values of the Forest Service facilitate communication between headquarters and the field by keeping loyalties and career interests centrally directed.[57] Rotation and indoctrination also keep the foresters independent of private interests in the regions or communities in which they serve; the training shared at every level fosters communication of problem information up the line.[58] The classic intelligence problem of branch plant or field unit "covering up" (i.e., rigging performance figures or hiding local problems) is minimized. Infused with professionalism, imbued with *esprit de corps,* the Forest Service is able to centralize intelligence resources, yet do without close supervision and elaborate enforcement and inspection machinery.

Sears, Roebuck and Company is said to present a similar case. Its goals are clear: it has a long tradition of central buying of good-quality merchandise to be sold to the middle majority at a competitive price. Its organizational processes are reminiscent of those of the Forest Service: self-selection and recruitment of homogeneous personnel, rotation, promotion from within, and the like. For these reasons, as one observer notes, "Sears can afford to decentralize; everyone thinks alike anyway."[59]

Other organizations with more diffuse or diversified goals are not so fortunate. Where field or branch products and local operating conditions vary, surveillance machinery proliferates. Such machinery is often ineffectual—especially where the local people must submit to inspection either by those outside their profession or specialty (headquarters accountants checking factory production managers) or by those of different ideological persuasion (politically ap-

[55] *Ibid.,* pp. 162 ff.

[56] *Ibid.,* pp. 162 ff. The Federal Bureau of Investigation (FBI) displays similar administrative processes: for its agents it prefers lawyers and accountants; it accents strong prior commitment, heavy indoctrination, and frequent rotation.

[57] *Ibid.,* pp. 165, 175, 197, 214 ff.   [58] *Ibid.,* pp. 75, 176, 215–217.

[59] See the unpubl. diss. (University of Chicago, 1954) by David G. Moore, "Managerial Strategies and Organization Dynamics in Sears Retailing."

pointed vocational training directors of particular states confronting educational reformers from the U.S. Office of Education). Where the social and doctrinal distance between inspectors and local operators is great, the resulting information blockage may imperil top leaders' awareness of and accommodation to local problems as well as their ability to communicate new goals to local units.

That the appropriate degree and kind of decentralization depend on the intelligence mission is best shown in a study of the controller's department in seven multi-plant companies, a study that also provides leads for solutions to the dilemmas of centralization.[60] It found that while all the controller's departments aimed to provide high-quality information services at minimum cost and, incidentally, to facilitate the training of accounting and operating executives, the effectiveness of decentralization depended on the type of information to be provided. If the primary aim is to keep score ("Are we doing well or badly?") and to direct attention ("What problems should we look into?"), then it is best to hire competent professional men who look to the controller's department for promotion, attach them to local factories and district offices, and put them under the factory manager. The formula is much geographical decentralization, some decentralization of formal authority, but very limited decentralization of loyalty. For the purpose of keeping score, the decentralization of location and authority makes it easier to gain access to resource documents and to know the reliability of source records. The accountant is close to the operating situation where the data originate. For the purpose of directing attention, such decentralization gives operating executives direct and active contact with accounting people, and thus more confidence in the operating standards and performance reports going to the boss (e.g., factory managers can negotiate standards of local performance and explain off-standard performance). For the purpose of preserving the quality of data available to central headquarters for special studies and big policy ("Shall we purchase new equipment, close this plant, develop this product?"), it is equally important to encourage loyalty to the controller's department through recruitment of professionally committed men who look there for promotion. With rare exceptions these men felt a conflict

[60] Simon et al., *Centralization vs. Decentralization.*

between maintaining accounting standards and getting along with factory management by not reporting unpleasant facts. But even in the most decentralized company (Eastman Kodak) they adhered to company-wide, professionally set accounting procedures. The formal organization put them close enough to the situation to be accepted by factory management and to obtain roughly accurate information; at the same time, career-line loyalty and professional identification provided enough social support for them to apply standards.

In short, there is a balance to be struck among various kinds of decentralization—of records, of location, of authority, of loyalty, and of channels of communication—an optimal or at least "workable" set of gains and losses depending upon the purposes to be pursued. This is an area where research has barely begun.

DOCTRINES OF INTELLIGENCE

Concepts of the intelligence function—"facts" vs. "evaluated facts," "information" vs. "operations," "secret" vs. "open" sources, "estimates" or "predictions" vs. "analysis" or "interpretation"—deeply affect the organization of intelligence, the recruitment base, and hence the quality of intelligence. Administrative leaders often evince anti-intellectualism, narrow empiricism, and a demand for secrecy in odd combination with a demand for scientific prediction and quantitative estimates. The combination leads to foolish ideas about the proper organization and possibilities of intelligence.

"All the Facts"

If users of intelligence think of it as "facts," not "evaluated facts," if they are imbued with the notion that more raw "information" to "fill in gaps" is their great need, they are likely to make intelligence a distinct, subordinate function, to separate sharply collection of data from interpretation, and to exclude experts from policy deliberations. They will attract either crude empiricists or conformists content to "backstop" the preconceptions of policymakers. Thus, intelligence administrators in government and in the military have typically been lawyers or soldiers trained in school and in practice as empiricists—suspicious of plans and predictions, hostile to generalizations and abstractions. Similarly, intelligence staffs have been comprised mainly of historians, lawyers, journalists, and soldiers.[61] And the most influential Washington lobbyists and union staff experts have been lawyers.[62] The background and outlook of the intelligence producer often match those of his boss; both sometimes display a pervasive anti-intellectualism—a compound of antagonism toward ideology or theory (i.e., new ideas, unfamiliar questions), resentment toward the outsider, and an exaggerated belief in practical experience. In response, students of intelligence, like the writers of introductory textbooks in social science, still tend to belabor the point that the facts never speak for themselves, that information must be gathered in relation to questions and categories for analysis. Some observers claim that the professors, scientists, and lawyers in the OSS in World War II were more imaginative problem definers, but the main question remains open: "What types of experts, with what background and training, make the best interpreters, and what concepts and organization of intelligence attract and motivate them?"

The common distinction between "intelligence" (information gathering) and "operations" (clandestine action) also has consequences for recruitment. While fact gathering appeals to naive realists whose interpretative capacities are limited, the excitement of operations attracts the kind of adventurers and activists who guided the American government into the Bay of Pigs.

"Intelligence Estimates"

Two related concepts of intelligence further complicate the problem of organization and reduce the quality of information services: the accent on short-run prediction ("intelligence estimates"), reflected in a pressure for direct, simple answers to immediate questions; and the accent on secrecy, reflected in loyalty-security

---

[61] Kendall, pp. 550–551; Hilsman, pp. 81, 96; Max F. Millikan, "Inquiry and Policy: The Relation of Knowledge to Action," in *The Human Meaning of the Social Sciences,* ed. by Daniel Lerner (New York: World Publishing Company, 1959), p. 163; and Wasserman.

[62] Wilensky, *Intellectuals,* pp. 230 ff.; and Milbrath, p. 157.

systems and, as government illustrates, in the segregation of clandestine operations from research. Not only do administrative leaders exaggerate the importance of the blind collection of facts, they also expect the experts to do things with the facts that cannot be done. The experts, in turn, fall into the habit of supplying predictions of future events, which, however appropriate in estimating the deployment and order of battle of armies at war, is useless, even dangerous, when the identity of the enemies is unclear; the aims, ambiguous or conflicting; the policy alternatives, poorly defined.[63] Since executives and experts alike seldom keep score on the success or failure of their short-run predictions, we do not know much about the problems for which predictions are valid or the conditions that might improve forecasts of various types. There is little feedback on the quality of intelligence estimates.

Prediction in social science is not impossible; but it is the most risky and least important function of intelligence. The sources of difficulty are well known: scientific generalizations are conditional (if A, B, and C hold, then X is probable); planners and predictors lack control over the environment (the nation does not control the foreign sector, the corporation, its market, the farmer, the weather); all organizations face unanticipated crises and breakdowns rooted in war, business cycles, sudden changes in taste or fashion, failures in supply, natural calamities; and prophecies are self-fulfilling (predictions of inflation are inflationary, predictions of impending success can affect the zeal of the participants). Thus, even without the distortions of hierarchy and rivalry, intelligence estimates, like stock market forecasts, are heavily hedged: "There is a serious possibility that Red China will intervene, but there are some grounds for optimism."[64]

[63] Cf. Kendall.

[64] The London *Daily Express* in 1945 provided the following burlesque of our efforts to explain away intelligence failures in the Battle of the Bulge: "While it cannot be said that Runstedt's offensive achieved its object of changing the Allied time-table, it has undoubtedly made some alteration necessary in that time-table.

"It has rather postponed than delayed an offensive, and in that sense alone, may be said to have lengthened, but not prolonged, the war. The Allies were not surprised, because they knew the possibility of a surprise attack. What surprised them was that the Germans thought it worthwhile to make a surprise attack in spite of the fact that such an attack, though deemed possible, was not deemed probable, in view of the fact that we knew they would try to surprise us." (Platt, pp. 69–70.)

Administrative leaders will of course continue to ask such questions as "Will they send in troops?" "Will Western intervention stop Communist expansionism?" "What are the effects of various strategies of intervention—counter-insurgency operations, occupation by American troops, disengagement, multilateral or unilateral economic aid?" and so on. But where there is great uncertainty—the chronic condition for deliberation on great issues—it makes sense to spend greater intelligence resources on questions and analysis that provide more general orientation: In Southeast Asia, which are the enduring and which the ephemeral sources of cleavage? To what extent can local nationalism be harnessed as a force for neutralization, for independence, for the containment of China? What are the social requisites of political stability at various levels of economic development? When do military elites foster political stability, economic progress, and freedom; when do they subvert such values? What are the possibilities and effects of various patterns of land reform?

We may not be able to predict with greater accuracy than the flip of a coin what Red China will do next month or next year in response to the next American move. We can, however, with sufficient thought and resources, discover what social and political forces can and should be encouraged in that part of the world. In other words, questions that stimulate the imagination, give shape to major policy alternatives, point to general directions and long-run goals are more important than Delphic forecasts of coming events.

Intelligence users and operators, incongruously demanding from researchers "all" the "facts" and short, speedy, journalistic estimates of future developments, use the inevitable hedging and the frequent failures of prediction to justify their anti-intellectualism, their naïve separation of "facts" from "know-how," and their denigration of research ("I wouldn't ask these geniuses to tell me how many pints there are in a quart"). Faced with repeated disconfirmation of short-run predictions, they are susceptible to the "cry-wolf syndrome," discounting all predictions, all warnings.[65]

[65] Cf. Wohlstetter, p. 52. The most urgent demand for simple summaries and short-run predictions comes from executives with passive styles of administration. Sherman Adams, Eisenhower's chief of staff for six years, writes: "Eisenhower was not much of a reader. He was impatient with the endless

Secret Sources

Reinforcing the doctrine that "research" should be separate from "policymaking" and "operations" is the notion that secret sources are intrinsically superior: an emphasis on secrecy means that few experts can be allowed to participate. Students of intelligence agree that while secret (covert or "black") intelligence, like overt intelligence, has expanded in every sphere of modern life,[66] policymakers grossly exaggerate its importance and reliability. As President Kennedy, reflecting upon his experience with the CIA in 1961, ruefully observed, "'You always assume that the military and intelligence people have some secret skill not available to ordinary mortals.'"[67] There is also general agreement that the accent on secrecy, together with its organizational correlates—loyalty-security systems, the segregation of clandestine operations from the rest of intelligence—impairs critical judgment in the production and interpretation of intelligence and dulls the sense of relevance. At the same time, secrecy blinds the executive to increasingly available open sources, as is dramatically evident in the Bay of Pigs affair: the Operations branch of the CIA kept its plans to itself; the Intelligence branch was never officially apprised of the Cuban expedition; the "CIA's elaborate national estimates procedure was never directed to the question whether an invasion would trigger other uprisings. . . . The men on the Cuban desk [in the State Department], who received the daily flow of information from the island, were not asked to comment on the feasibility of the venture. The 'need-to-know' standard—i.e., that no one should be told about a project unless it becomes operationally

paperwork of the Presidency and always tried to get his staff to digest long documents into one page summaries." Adams also reports that "Eisenhower disliked talking business on the phone," so others filled in the gap, speaking for him in matters that really required personal attention. (Sherman Adams, *Firsthand Report* [New York: Popular Library, 1962], p. 82.)

66 *Invasions of Privacy.* Subcommittee on Administrative Practice and Procedure of the Committee on the Judiciary, United States Senate (Washington: Government Printing Office, 1965). Part I: February 18, 23, 24, and March 2, 3, 1965; part II: April 13, 27, 28, 29, and May 5, 6, and June 7, 1965; part III: July 13, 14, 15, 19, 20, 21, 27, and August 9, 1965; and Richard Austin Smith, "Business Espionage," *Fortune,* LIII (May, 1956), 118–121, 190, 192, 194.

67 Schlesinger, *A Thousand Days,* p. 258.

necessary—thus had the idiotic effect of excluding much of the expertise of government at a time when every alert newspaperman knew something was afoot."[68] In Kent's words, the clandestine group is "free to steer its own course behind the fog of its own security regulations."[69]

The distorting effects of secrecy are felt both in the type of personnel attracted to secret operations and in the peculiar conditions for intellectual work that secrecy imposes. The more secrecy, the smaller the intelligent audience, the less systematic the distribution and indexing of research, the greater the anonymity of authorship, and the more intolerant the attitude toward deviant views and styles of life.[70] Such a restrictive atmosphere reduces the incentive for top scholars, whose ways of life and thought are not always orthodox and who work best with critical appraisal and acclaim and with wide-open access to the best sources. Security regulations, loyalty investigations, and a civil-service mentality are all anathema to independent-minded intellectuals. That is why in the United States during the McCarthy era, cautious mediocrities, dedicated to the most impoverished clichés of the Cold War, rose to the top of the foreign service, leaving a legacy of ignorance that has plagued every subsequent President.[71] The preoccupation of totalitarian regimes with loyalty intensifies their problem of securing high-quality intelligence. Insofar as democratic nations become fascinated by secrecy, they suffer similar recruitment difficulties (see pp. 144 ff. below).

If we consider the motives of secret agents, informers, stool pigeons, and other spies, as well as the stigma under which they labor, the limitations of covert intelligence become obvious. In order to protect their sources, clandestine agencies want complete control of data collection and operations; they therefore have a natural penchant for compliant people, good "security risks." The motives of such people have been noted by students of police work, of military intelligence, of foreign affairs: fear, insecurity, revenge,

[68] *Ibid.,* p. 248.

[69] Kent, p. 168.

[70] Cf. Bruce L. R. Smith, "Strategic Expertise," p. 78; and Robert K. Merton, "Priorities in Scientific Discovery," in *The Sociology of Science,* ed. by Bernard Barber and Walter Hirsch (New York: The Free Press, 1962), pp. 447–485.

[71] Cf. Schlesinger, *A Thousand Days,* p. 411; Kent, pp. 69, 74, 146–147; Ransom, p. 178.

envy, remorse, money.[72] The vice-control squad drums up trade among bookmakers, dope addicts, and prostitutes who, because of fear of the law or fear of fellow sinners, are moved to inform on one another.[73] The businessman suffering from competition gives an anonymous tip to a regulating agency, alleging an illegal practice by his competitor. The rejected applicant or jealous lover spreads gossip, perhaps partly true, for revenge. The Peeping Tom may see something worth reporting. The paranoid keeps tabs on the behavior of suspected plotters. The true-believing Communist, converted to another faith, turns on his former colleagues to demonstrate his political virtue. The émigré group, the exile organization —friendless, moneyless, jobless in a strange land, often wholly dependent on the secret agent—tells the story the agency most wants to hear, the story of imminent revolt in the homeland.

Not only do the motives of the secret agent or the informer add to the fallibility of clandestine information, but also the home office, knowing that in sensitive areas the enemy always leaks false information, is likely either to discount accurate information or to fall for fabrication. "During World War II, the British by an artfully devised and minutely planned scheme managed deliberately to mislead the Germans in a *ruse de guerre* of spectacular success. After the battle for Tunisia, the Allies decided that the next step would be the invasion of Italy via Sicily. By causing to be washed ashore in Spain the body of a fictitious Royal Marine carrying letters containing 'secret' military planning information, the Allies tricked the Germans (who were promptly informed by the Spanish) into spreading their defense across Europe, even to the extent of removing warships from the Sicily area. This ruse paved the way for a relatively easy invasion of Sicily."[74] The case was dramatized in a stranger-than-fiction film, *The Man Who Never Was.*

On the other hand, the most clever agent with the best access to the most secret sources may not be able to convince the home office that his information is anything but an enemy deception. In World War II, the valet of the British ambassador at Ankara

---

[72] Malachi L. Harney and John C. Cross, *The Informer in Law Enforcement* (Springfield: Charles C Thomas, 1960), pp. 33–39; Eleanor Bontecou, *The Federal Loyalty-Security Program* (Ithaca: Cornell University Press, 1953), pp. 131–135; Hilsman, pp. 21 ff.; Schlesinger, *ibid.*, pp. 230 ff.

[73] Skolnick.

[74] Ransom, pp. 168–169.

hired himself out to the Germans as a secret agent with the code name Cicero. His accurate reports of Allied plans were so astonishing that Ribbentrop, the Nazi Foreign Minister, refused to believe that they were not Allied fabrications or the reports of a double agent.[75] Inter-agency rivalries, however, in this instance may have been even more fateful than the possibilities of deception; Ribbentrop's Foreign Office was locked in a power struggle with Kaltenbrunner's Reich Security Office.[76] Ribbentrop also hated von Papen, German ambassador to Turkey.[77] Since Cicero reported to German attaché Moyzisch, who was employed by the Reich Security Office and attached to the staff of von Papen, Ribbentrop had every reason to denigrate Cicero's material.

The pressures generated by secrecy and by the clash of rival agencies were, of course, added to the usual pressures to screen out unpleasant information. Berlin was far more interested in that portion of Cicero's stolen documents reporting intra-Allied squabbles than it was in the central theme—the vigor of the coming Allied offensive.

That blocks to the flow of useful information may be most severe where secrecy is combined with inter-agency rivalry is also evident in the departmentalized metropolitan police. Information supplied by informers to the burglary detail about robbery is typically withheld from the robbery detail; not only are the men of the two sections rivals for promotion and budget money, but the standard payoff for the thief-informer is the dropping of charges for his own crimes, a payoff that can be guaranteed only by the police to whom he reports.

Given the limitations of secrecy, modern intelligence agencies spend far more time on overt sources with far better results. This is not merely the consensus of students of intelligence; it is consistent with data on the performance of analysts relying on open sources. During World War II the Analysis Division of the Foreign Broadcast Intelligence Service branch of the Federal Communications Commission (FCC) was asked to interpret the intentions,

[75] L. C. Moyzisch, *Operation Cicero* (New York: Coward-McCann, 1950), pp. 84–100.
[76] Paul Seabury, *The Wilhelmstrasse: A Study of German Diplomats under the Nazi Regime* (Berkeley and Los Angeles: University of California Press, 1954), pp. 130–131.
[77] Moyzisch, pp. 16, 97–98.

strategy, and calculations behind enemy propaganda. Working exclusively with enemy radio-press materials, the FCC analysts made thousands of inferences and predictions about (1) the enemy elites' major strategic moves, (2) enemy anticipation of Allied moves, and (3) changes in situational factors impinging on enemy strategy.[78] After the war a study designed to ascertain the extent of FCC accuracy systematically checked a sample of 1,120 FCC inferences about Nazi propaganda (made over a two-month period in 1943) against German war documents and interviews conducted with Nazi leaders. Of the 119 inferences which could be verified by an adequate historical record, 85 per cent could be scored as "accurate." Further spot checking of the output of a twenty-three-month period (1942–44) showed a success rate of three in four.[79] The analysts did best on matters related to civilian morale; all of the sampled inferences in these areas were accurate. They did least well in deciphering German diplomatic initiatives and relations with Axis partners with 67 per cent accuracy.[80]

Three success stories convey the flavor of these complex estimates.

A possible German offensive against Russia in 1943. After the German disaster at Stalingrad in January 1943, the question was, would Hitler order another attack on the Russian front or go on the defensive to prepare for forthcoming Allied invasions? In May 1943, Washington informed General Eisenhower that the Allies could expect a massive German offensive against Russia in the summer, and expressed confidence that Russia would turn back the Germans and exact heavy casualties. This was comforting to Allied invasion strategists, but the FCC demurred. Fully aware of the effect of Stalingrad on German civilian morale, one analyst had noted that despite the need for a propaganda lift, there was a subtle shift in Nazi domestic propaganda away from the popular line extolling the virtues of German offensive initiative toward the unpopular praise of prudent defense (General Ditmar, for instance, spoke of the "elegance" of defensive strategy). The FCC estimated that the Nazis planned no major offensive in the East that summer. German documents later showed this inference to be correct while the intelligence transmitted to Eisenhower, presumably

[78] Alexander L. George, *Propaganda Analysis: A Study of Inferences Made from Nazi Propaganda in World War II* (Evanston: Row, Peterson & Co., 1959).

[79] *Ibid.*, pp. 260–265.

[80] *Ibid.*, p. 265.

based on the best secret sources, "grossly exaggerated the scope of German offensive plans."[81]

German expectations about the possible defection of Italy as an ally. Did the Nazis anticipate Mussolini's resignation on July 25, 1943, and the Italian surrender on September 8? If so, what countermeasures were they prepared to take? Having noted the Nazis' repeated expressions of confidence in their Italian ally, FCC experts were impressed by the slow, awkward response of Nazi propaganda when news of Mussolini's downfall broke. They correctly inferred that the Germans were not prepared for the loss of their ally and had no well-organized retaliatory strategy.[82]

German estimates of the effectiveness of their submarine warfare. The introduction of the Allies' anti-U-boat measures early in 1943 created a need for intelligence on the German response. Nazi belief in ultimate victory through naval power was a standard domestic propaganda theme. But after improved Allied detection and evasion and other defensive action, there was a marked shift in the tone of Nazi domestic reports on sea battles. Propaganda analysts noted an extraordinary emphasis on the handicaps of weather, unprecedented admissions of Allied successes, and, later, the deletion of all hopeful talk of new German weapons and tactics. Several lines of reasoning led the FCC to conclude that the Nazis were troubled about a drop in U-boat sinkings; that they could do little to counteract Allied defenses for the present; and that despite the return of U-boats to the North Atlantic in September 1943, they did not anticipate a resumption of heavy sinkings.[83]

The study concludes that the FCC's performance was based not only on educated guesses and gifted intuition, but also on methods of inference which can be articulated and codified to an appreciable degree. The sustained validity of their interpretations suggests that the FCC's propaganda analysts went beyond isolated, hit-or-miss successes.[84]

Propaganda or not, none of an adversary's public statements or recorded actions is beyond systematic analysis. To discover that Chinese Communist interest in an offshore island results from the need for fertilizer to prop up faltering agricultural production

[81] *Ibid.*, p. 156. [82] *Ibid.*, pp. 209–214.
[83] *Ibid.*, pp. 242–249. [84] *Ibid.*, p. 269.

rather than from strategic considerations, look to Chinese books and periodicals.[85] To discover the seriousness of a labor union's bargaining demands, compare the tone in its current house organ with that of comparable years, examine its contracts relative to those of rival unions, note the staff it devotes to local contacts, look at its treasury and the state of the labor market. In the end, the most reliable intelligence sources for competing organizations are open; the best data, seldom secret, are the actions of the other party.

Yet, at the very time that open sources multiply and communications technology speeds the processing and flow of information, we may be elevating the position of the spy. Since the onset of World War II and the beginnings of what Lasswell[86] calls the "garrison state," the reservations of diplomats and administrative leaders about spying have weakened[87] and the budgets and influence of spies have expanded. In internal surveillance, modern totalitarian governments naturally bend an ear toward informers and spies; in external relations, they see diplomacy as indivisible from espionage. Pluralist democracies, intermittently inspired by fantasies of conspiracy and by an urge toward more unitary loyalty, display increasing fascination with secret information.[88] Government use of electronic snoopers is widespread, industrial spying is apparently increasing, especially in the automobile, chemical, and oil industries.[89] In Japan there is now a school for industrial spies; in the United States, a professional association, "The American Society of Industrial Security." And much modern popular fiction, unlike the fiction of previous generations, treats spies unequivocally as heroes, bigger, stronger, better than life. The pointed irony directed by Joseph Conrad against Verlor in *The Secret Agent* or the moral

[85] Robert Ellsworth Elder, *The Policy Machine: The Department of State and American Foreign Policy* (Syracuse: University Press, 1960), p. 52.

[86] Harold D. Lasswell, "The Garrison State," *American Journal of Sociology,* XLVI (January, 1941), 455–468.

[87] Cf. Alfred Vagts, *Defense and Diplomacy: The Soldier and the Conduct of Foreign Relations* (New York: King's Crown Press, 1956), pp. 65, 70–71.

[88] Cf. Edward A. Shils, *The Torment of Secrecy: The Background and Consequences of American Security Policies* (Glencoe: The Free Press, 1956); Francis E. Rourke, *Secrecy and Publicity: Dilemmas of Democracy* (Baltimore: Johns Hopkins Press, 1961).

[89] Richard A. Smith; and U.S. Senate, *Invasions of Privacy.*

onus under which Razumov labors in *Under Western Eyes* would be impossible in the glamorous, efficient world of James Bond.

An emphasis on secret information not only threatens individual privacy; it can demoralize an organization. Prying into the personal lives of employees to fend off the efforts of rivals to obtain secret information, conducting disguised surveys to uncover pro-union sentiment, can build resentment, provoke strikes, increase labor turnover, or reduce efficiency. Several labor disputes of the 1960's were triggered by management efforts to spy on employees or subject them to closer overt surveillance.[90] The effect on the quality of intelligence is more certain: the demand for secret prediction evokes a flood of doubtful inside dope.

This area is rife with sensationalism; systematic research is rare. The conditions that would give substance to an Orwellian nightmare are only dimly understood. If secret surveillance is one half of that nightmare, the Ministry of Truth is the other half. One can readily envision a society in which elites have reasonably good secret intelligence both about one another and about the underlying population but use it to terrorize their opposition and to manipulate public opinion. Happily, the balance between what is open

[90] A 1964 UAW-AFL-CIO Convention resolution, "Infringement on Workers' Privacy," noted that one automobile manufacturer, who had already engaged in electronic eavesdropping, threatened to install closed-circuit television cameras to observe workers on the job, and was stopped by the union. "Another manufacturer was caught eavesdropping on a union meeting room during negotiations and spying on workers in locker rooms and cafeterias." The resolution records the UAW's "unaltering hostility . . . to surveillance, whether by machine recording device, motion picture camera, listening device, closed circuit television or otherwise, of workers in and around the factories and during relief and rest periods, and of union representatives in plant meeting rooms." It also opposes the use of polygraph machines. (*Proceedings of the Nineteenth Constitutional Convention, March 20–27, 1964,* Atlantic City, New Jersey. International Union, United Automobile, Aerospace and Agricultural Implement Workers of America, pp. 323–324. Cf. U.S. Senate, *Invasions of Privacy,* especially the statement of President Beirne of the Communications Workers of America, AFL-CIO, on eavesdropping by phone companies, part II, pp. 966–972; and J. Dale on TV surveillance by Chevrolet in Baltimore and GM's Delco Radio Division in Kokomo, Indiana, and the use of peep holes for observation by Ford.) The phone companies' defense—surveillance of employees improves service to customers—is more persuasive than the FBI's argument that its illegal wiretaps and mail interceptions improve criminal prosecution. (Cf. Fred J. Cook, *The FBI Nobody Knows* [New York: Pyramid Publications, 1965].) There may still be enough commitment to privacy and enough awareness of the problem of means and ends, however, to make the American public suspicious of either justification.

and what is hidden, the balance that yields the best intelligence, may also enhance individual freedom and justice. After further analyzing the quality of intelligence in Chapters 4, 5, and 6, I shall return to the problem of relating intelligence to democratic values, giving special attention to the tension between secrecy and publicity.

CHAPTER 4

Organizational Processes

Any analysis of the determinants of the quality of intelligence must take into account the problems to be solved, the stages of decision-making, stages of growth of the organization, and the processes of leadership succession; it must be sensitive to the flow of time and talent.

THE NATURE OF THE DECISION

The nature of an executive decision itself shapes the uses and quality of intelligence because it affects the number, kinds, and organization of experts called to serve. To illustrate, I shall state a few plausible hypotheses using the variables of urgency, cost, innovation, certainty, and technicality.

At first glance, one might think that if the decision were urgent and time were short, there would be few participants, each carrying heavy weight; less search for information and alternatives; and more bias toward preconceptions, especially where the decision activates the core values of elites. A detailed study of President Truman's decision to intervene in Korea in 1950 seems to confirm this. The vacuum existing during the initial crisis was filled by five men from the upper echelons of the Defense and State Departments (including Dean Rusk, at the time Assistant Secretary for Far Eastern Affairs) who happened to be in town; Secretary of State Acheson then assumed the initiative, drafted recommendations, specified the relevant values, and formulated alternative

strategies; eight or nine top decision makers, at most fourteen,
were involved; their communication was highly informal; they
acted with remarkable speed; they considered few alternatives because they were guided by the overriding desire to preserve the
collective security system built up since World War II and especially by preconceptions derived from the 1930's. The decision to
resist Communist aggression, whatever its merits, was based partly
on wishful thinking—overestimates of South Korean strength,
underestimates of North Korean strength.[1]

It is equally plausible, however, to argue that, when the decision
is urgent, the distortions of hierarchy, specialization, centralization,
and doctrine are minimized. Ironically, a "hasty" decision made
under pressure may on average be better than a less urgent one.
The rapid decision to intervene in Korea, with the modest objective
of restoring the *status quo ante* and preserving Allied unity, was
clearly more sensible than the later series of more leisurely decisions
culminating in a new war aim of a unified non-Communist Korea,
which provoked Chinese intervention.[2]

Similarly, compare the two Cuban crises that dominated the
Kennedy years. In the Bay of Pigs affair, planning, begun in the
Eisenhower administration, was lengthy; the august figures of the
Departments of State and Defense, and the Joint Chiefs, each
speaking of the "hard realities," with the full weight of their
agencies and institutions behind them, had a rhetorical advantage;
the White House staff was intimidated; the President, overwhelmed.
Hierarchy, seniority, and official representation—described by one
participant as "bureaucratic momentum"—were major ingredients
of the fantasies that guided the decision to invade.[3] This intelligence
failure may be compared with the Cuban missile crisis, in which
deliberation involved only fifteen individuals and lasted only ninety-
six hours—in urgency not very different from the early Korean
case. In the Bay of Pigs crisis, discussion was rank-oriented; the
range of serious exploration of alternatives and consequences,
limited; and the outcome, disastrous. In the more urgent missile
crisis, discussion was egalitarian; protocol, seniority, and rank

[1] Snyder and Paige.
[2] Cf. Neustadt, p. 139.
[3] Cf. Schlesinger, *A Thousand Days*, pp. 255–258, 289, 293, 297; Sorensen,
Kennedy, pp. 294–309; Matthews.

counted for little; a wide range of alternatives was explored in depth;[4] and, by the standards of the Bay of Pigs, the decisions, in both process and consequence, were superior. Urgency functioned to overcome many information pathologies.

March and Simon[5] suggest an opposite hypothesis: if decision processes are slow and deliberate, all relevant information in the system is likely to be noticed. If organizational theory begins with the nature of human cognitive faculties—with March and Simon's assumption that "the basic features of organization structure and function derive from the characteristics of human problem-solving processes and rational human choice"[6]—it will tend to overrate the payoff from "slow deliberation" and underestimate the effect of attributes of structure and culture that transcend individual psychology—hierarchy, specialization, centralization, occupational ideology, and other barriers to communication. Of course, there is a type of organization in which urgency is sickness and deliberation is health. Where the end is knowledge, as in the scientific community,[7] time serves intelligence; where the end is something else—as in practically every organization but those devoted entirely to scholarship—time subverts intelligence, since, in the long run, the central institutionalized structures and aims (the maintenance of authority, the accommodation of departmental rivalries, the service of established doctrine) will prevail.

Profound national crisis, finally, conditions the efficacy of urgency for intelligence. A major war not only moves top decision makers to specify the issues more precisely and to query the system more efficiently; it also permits mobilization of superior intellectual resources. If scientists and scholars are deeply committed to the values asserted by the war, they flood into applied research and enthusiastically lend themselves to the cause. Thus Allied intelligence achievements in World War II (see pp. 35, 42, 69–72) partly reflected the strength of anti-totalitarian sentiments in the academic community.

4 Sorensen, *ibid.*, pp. 679 ff.
5 March and Simon, p. 169.
6 *Ibid.*, p. 169.
7 Thomas S. Kuhn, *The Structure of Scientific Revolutions*, 1st Phoenix edn. (Chicago: University of Chicago Press, 1962); Warren O. Hagstrom, *The Scientific Community* (New York: Basic Books, 1965).

Related to the question of urgency are the questions of cost, innovation, and uncertainty. The greater the costs and risks or uncertainty and the more significant the changes in method and goals involved, the more intense is the search for information. But the stronger, too, is the weight of established policy and vested interests. Decisions involving many people, much money, great uncertainty or vast risks, and major innovations evoke action and advice from every specialized unit at every level of the hierarchy, thereby increasing the dangers of overload, distortion, or blockage of communication and of paralyzing delays. At the extreme, a costly decision that fails can activate an energetic search for evidence to confirm the mistaken policy. Organizational theory often assumes that where an existing policy satisfies organizational goals there is little search for alternatives but that when policy fails search is intensified.[8] This assumption underestimates man's capacity for clinging to prophecies already proven wrong. The failure of a prediction lays waste actions taken in preparation for its fulfillment. Thus, men use a variety of ingenious defenses to protect cherished convictions under the onslaught of devastating attack. The believers may convince themselves that only the date of the promised millennium is wrong; they may try to find alternative explanations that are reasonable. For instance, in 1648, Sabbatai Zevi proclaimed himself the Messiah who would lead the Jews back to the Holy Land, and many prepared for the promised events, neglecting their work and their business. When Turkish officials arrested Sabbatai and nothing happened, his followers for a long time argued that the very fact that he was still alive proved that he was the Messiah —some hardy souls persisting even after the Turks converted Sabbatai to Islam.[9] Similarly, the disciples of William Miller, a New England farmer who asserted that the Second Coming would occur in 1843, clung to their faith long after the non-event; the Millerite movement did not collapse until two or three further failures of prediction over a period of eighteen months. In fact, when confronted with undeniable disconfirmation men do not merely defend their convictions; under some conditions—when their belief is strong, when they have committed themselves with

[8] Cyert and March, p. 113; March and Simon, pp. 174–175.
[9] Leon Festinger, Henry W. Riecken, and Stanley Schachter, *When Prophecy Fails* (New York: Harper & Row, 1956), p. 11.

some important act which is difficult to disavow, and when they have social support in their denial of reality—they do so with reborn fervor, seeking new converts. A study of a modern group that predicted the destruction of the world by a flood from Lake Michigan showed that attack on their beliefs strengthened faith and increased proselytizing. When the flood failed to flow, the group devised an elegant explanation. The cataclysm, they explained, had been called off; the band of visionaries "had spread so much light that God had saved the world from destruction."[10] Where the believers had flatly refused to have anything to do with the press before the Apocalypse, the period following the "unending" of the world provided a vivid contrast; the leaders sought the press and broadcast their beliefs. Where earlier there had been selective proselytizing directed at those who were "chosen" for membership, subsequent efforts to reach out to converts were frantically indiscriminate. If more and more people could be persuaded that the system of belief was authentic, then, despite all, it must be. The phenomenon is not confined to pitiful bands of millennial or messianic sectarians. Political and military leaders whose prophecies of imminent victory in war fail are a bit like the Millerites of the nineteenth century; when the deliverance does not come according to schedule, they set new dates.

We have seen that technical intelligence has become more indispensable in every sphere of modern life. Does its quality warrant such multiplication? Have scientists and other facts-and-figures men won such excessive deference that in crises involving problems beyond their competence their judgment is substituted for executive judgment? Two forces make this unlikely as a general rule. First, the self-changing nature of their role gives experts competence matching that of their bosses, who in turn accumulate some sophistication about technical matters: there is an interaction of expertise. For instance, an economist in a union acquires some political skill; labor leaders learn a good deal about pension and insurance programs. Second, the receptivity to immoderate claims by experts varies according to type of expert, type of executive, and the nature of their encounter. Civilian chiefs of state may be more intimidated by the esoteric knowledge of military officers, secret agents, and physical scientists than by other advice. Furthermore, when scien-

10 *Ibid.*, p. 169.

tists are closeted in secret session with administrative leaders without the constraints of their scientific colleagues, they may oversell their products. Although the unchecked expert presents a danger to democracy and efficiency, the danger can be contained by the training of executives, the use of adversary safeguards and similar administrative devices, and the force of an enlightened public opinion (see Chapter 7). On balance, even in the "Expert Society" the denigration of intellect, rather than its deification, is the more common problem.

Finally, when the executive is overwhelmed by uncertainty, in order to reduce his huge burden of calculation, he relies not on the expert but on precedent[11] and on trial and error, the short-run reaction to short-run feedback[12]—except where the decisions are so clearly technical and the problems or programs so clearly new that precedent provides a poor guide[13] and expert planning promises much. When a decision is considered nontechnical and the outcome very uncertain (e.g., estimates of the diplomatic-political risks of bombing Hanoi, of the effects of diverse treatment strategies in prisons, hospitals, and juvenile institutions), dependence on nonexpert staff increases; here the generalizing expert functions as any other participant, his influence depending upon personal propinquity, persuasiveness, and the like. An Air Force expert minimizing the political risks may be given as much weight as a diplomat nervous about a wider war. Expert influence, if strong, is broad.

When a decision is thought to be technical and specialists dominate (e.g., psychiatrists in mental hospitals, caseworkers in family agencies), professional ideologies prevail and occasionally technicism flourishes. Intelligence may be substituted for organizational goals; operations may be designed for the convenience of professional practitioners more than for official purposes.[14] Expert influence, resting on a shaky base, is nonetheless broad. (See pp. 155–164.)

11 Wildavsky, *The Politics of the Budgetary Process*, p. 138.
12 Cyert and March, pp. 113 ff.
13 Wilensky, *Intellectuals*, pp. 181 ff.
14 Cf. Erving Goffman, *Asylums: Essays on the Social Situation of Mental Patients and Other Inmates* (New York: Doubleday Anchor Books, 1961); David Street, Robert D. Vinter, and Charles Perrow, *Organization for Treatment* (Glencoe: The Free Press, 1966).

Where technical knowledge is well developed—as in calculations of the relative advantages of two widely used automatic machines in a manufacturing process—expert influence is typically strong but narrow. On the whole, however, the structural and doctrinal determinants of the uses and quality of intelligence may be more important than the nature of the problem.

Perhaps the soundest hypothesis we can derive from these diverse considerations is that only the big (costly, risky, innovative) policy decisions that are also very urgent are likely to activate high-quality intelligence, because deliberation then moves out of channels toward men of generalized wisdom, executives and experts alike, communicating informally and effectively at the top. While such propositions are obviously speculative, they are far from trivial. The emergency atmosphere of World War II generated heavy time pressures and a void for experts to fill.[15] Is the impact of routine crises today in everyday organizational life very different? Clearly, "small" wars in a context of a big Cold War, combined with the clash of powerful interest groups in a society whose parts are increasingly interdependent, assure plentiful crises, generating a heavy press of work and the need for speedy decision. Even crises, however, may become institutionalized and whole societies become crisis-oriented. Then the effects of urgency on intelligence may be modified. If there are too many turning points, too many critical junctures, the weight of established structures and doctrines can inhibit the fresh response to the extraordinary event—the cutting of new channels of intelligence.

STAGES OF DECISION

So often are accurate intelligence estimates ignored—whether in the field or in the file of some subordinate department—that we might infer a general rule: the further we go from data collection to policy decision, the less knowledge and the more error—and, indeed, standard treatments of intelligence imply some deterioration by stages. Contradicting this notion is a study of the influence of staff experts on decisions bearing on 167 problems in the head-

[15] Bruce L. R. Smith, "Strategic Expertise," pp. 75–76.

quarters of 26 labor unions; it shows that the influence of men of knowledge typically increases as one proceeds from the emergence of the problem to policy, to selection of means of implementation through execution. What is most striking in contrasting stages of decision-making is the low proportion of problems which experts originate (pose the initial issue) and the high proportion of problems where they have substantial influence on decisions regarding means and execution.[16]

The contradiction is easily resolved. First, the standard concept of the decision-making process—raw data collection, evaluation, interpretation, communication—ignores the crucial importance of problem formulation, that is, the range and quality of questions posed before data are collected.[17] Such a concept also discounts the many opportunities experts have to influence "policy" at times and in ways far removed from formal or informal policy deliberations: they can "crystallize" the policy when the policy is loose, sharpen the definition of the problem when its specificity is low, fill the vacuum when the boss is busy or time is short, use official policy pronouncements as a lever. Finally, as we have seen, urgency can overcome structural obstacles to the flow of good intelligence.

INSTITUTIONALIZATION AND GROWTH

Because little is known about the growth of organizations, and there is hence no agreement on "stages" of growth, if any, we cannot relate the problem of intelligence systematically to processes of structural change. The literature provides contradictory clues. There is some suggestive evidence of a cycle of staff growth: early in the history of organizations, during the first six to ten years, staff functions (expert advice, support, help) grow geometrically as the line (making and selling a product) grows linearly, but later this relationship tapers off to parallel growth. In other words, the intelligence function looms largest when the organization, still

16 Wilensky, *Intellectuals,* pp. 177–181.
17 Cf. Bruce L. R. Smith, "Strategic Expertise," pp. 159 ff; March and Simon, pp. 174, 199.

forming its character, faces severe problems of coordination and planning.[18] March and Simon suggest that, in a stable environment, organizations that have institutionalized the innovative process have a high rate of innovation;[19] yet these authors also affirm the common idea that a new organization charged with innovation, because its personnel are full of zeal, will at first display a spurt of inventiveness; later, when excitement wanes and programmed activity takes command, it becomes bound by precedent. In short, daily routine, presumably prominent in mature, stable organizations, tends to drive out expert planning.

Applying our scheme for the analysis of intelligence failures, we can hypothesize that stages of growth will affect the quality of intelligence because they affect the types of experts hired and the problems they confront, the doctrines of intelligence, and the salience of structural distortions of intelligence. Given these premises, quality should be higher early rather than late.

Let us assume a new, swiftly growing organization in a rapidly-changing environment. Its problems—unroutinized, unprecedented —are mainly those of internal control and external competition and conflict. It must build a social base (members, employees, customers, clients, constituents); it must select and shape a core of top personnel committed to its mission.[20] In function, its experts tend to be internal communications specialists and contact men; in orientation, they are ambitious, entrepreneurial careerists or dedi-

[18] Mason Haire, "Biological Models and Empirical Histories of the Growth of Organizations," in *Modern Organization Theory*, ed. by Mason Haire (New York: John Wiley & Sons, 1959), pp. 292–293. In the four industrial firms Haire studied, the proportion of staff employees to supervisors stabilized at a fairly early point in the growth curve. The staff was also more resistant to cutbacks than the line—possibly because specialists are in scarce supply and, as men who plan and design the layoffs, they are reluctant to plan themselves out. The methods and theory of this study have been criticized with special reference to the limited utility of a biological model of growth. See Jean Draper and George Strother, "Testing a Model for Organizational Growth," *Human Organization*, XXII (Summer, 1963), 180–194; and W. H. McWhinney, "On the Geometry of Organizations," *Administrative Science Quarterly*, X (December, 1965), 347–363. But the findings regarding staff vs. line growth stand up well.
[19] March and Simon, pp. 185–187. Cf. Joseph A. Schumpeter, *Capitalism, Socialism and Democracy*, 2nd edn. (New York: Harper & Brothers, 1947), pp. 132 ff.
[20] Cf. Selznick, *Leadership in Administration*.

cated "missionaries."[21] Although high degrees of centralization may prevail, it is more certain that hierarchy and specialization will be de-emphasized. And while secrecy may be demanded in intelligence doctrine as in everything else, urgency will shape many decisions, freeing the flow of information, secret or not. In short, information pathologies are minimized. So aggressive, expansionist organizations in touch with a fluid environment apparently have the best intelligence systems.[22]

Suppose that the organization becomes institutionalized ("established") at a slow rate of growth and that it negotiates many stable arrangements with its environment that reduce uncertainty— Cyert and March list plans, standing operating procedures, industry tradition, and contracts with unions, suppliers, etc.[23] The shift in problems and personnel is not simply from innovation to execution, idea men to orderly bureaucrats.[24] In personnel it is a more complicated shift from careerists and missionaries to professionals, some of whom are bureaucratic in mentality but others of whom are program-minded innovators. And, depending on the type of organization, a scattering of old missionaries may persist. Chart 1 specifies hypotheses about the roots of the major variations in the role orientations of executive and professional personnel.

There are two main qualifications to the idea that institutionalization brings bureaucratic professionalism. First, there is the presence of some missionaries in roles created as end products of social movements—for instance, education directors of unions, welfare executives in social agencies (see Chart 1). Second, professional orientations themselves are diverse: beyond the professional service orientation described in Chart 1, scattered throughout the bureaucratic machinery of modern society we find what I have elsewhere labeled the "program professional"—the specialist in depth (e.g., experts in social insurance, rehabilitation, public

21 Wilensky, *Intellectuals*, Part III.

22 Ransom, p. 46. Burns and Stalker describe effective efforts to overcome communications barriers among British firms entering new markets with new products where rates of technical change are accelerating. *Op. cit.*, pp. 77–96, 140–144, 231, 252–253.

23 Cyert and March, p. 119. Cf. Burns and Stalker, pp. 79 ff.

24 March and Simon, p. 187; Paul F. Lazarsfeld, "Reflections on Business," *American Journal of Sociology*, LXV (July, 1959), 22.

assistance, public finance, urban planning, housing, race relations, labor disputes settlement) whose professional competence and devotion are beyond question, but whose commitment to particular programs and policies (e.g., health insurance) is just as strong. By virtue of his technical prowess, he makes himself indispensable as a policy adviser. In his job moves—between government and

CHART 1

Organizational Structure, Life History, and Role Orientation*

TYPE OF ROLE ORIENTATION	ROOTS IN STRUCTURE	ROOTS IN BIOGRAPHY
Professional service (or discipline). Highly identified with profession; oriented toward outside colleague group; wants to give competent, objective, technical service of which outside colleagues would approve; accents full use of skills.	Role is technical, demands formal graduate training. Structure is managed by men with professional training and job histories. Organization's interests impinge on large number of outside groups, organization is public relations–sensitive, so it hires specialists in accommodative techniques who can deal with government agencies and others professionally staffed.	Origins: high-status categories—e.g., upper middle class, Protestant. Education: many years of college—especially professional or graduate school built on undergraduate liberal arts degree. Orderly career. Participates in professional affairs.
Careerist ("Organization Man"). Highly identified with incumbent leadership of his organization; oriented toward career within workplace hierarchy. No ideological commitments, no dilemma-producing non-organizational goals; little professional identification. Wants chance for social mobility, rewards recognized in local community—money, promotions, security.	Role carries prestige in community. Structure provides opportunity for much job progression; career climb associated with residential mobility.**	Origins: middle mass; medium to low status ethnic-religious groups (especially Catholics). Education: college dropout or four-year graduate with low exposure to liberal arts; weak graduate training, if any. Less orderly career (e.g., several tries before got on present ladder). Little participation in professional affairs, more in local community.

CHART 1 (*continued*)

TYPE OF ROLE ORIENTATION	ROOTS IN STRUCTURE	ROOTS IN BIOGRAPHY
Missionary. Oriented toward some abstract concept of a social movement; highly identified with an outside political or religious-political group. Sees organization as vehicle for social change fitting private goals—goals derived from past or present participation in social movement.	Role created as end product of social movement (e.g., labor movement —→ staff of unions; good-government movement—→ city managers; political movements—→ staff of parties, government agencies; humanitarian reform movement—→ welfare occupations, correctional officers, nurses. Role not clearly defined (new because organization is new, new unit in established organization, or organization has diffuse purposes), provides chance for innovator.	Origins: marginal (e.g., minority groups such as Jews and Negroes; families often entrepreneurial, broken, or unusually intellectual). Education: broad (via favored colleges, big-city colleges, or self-teaching). Career: includes "ideological occupations" (e.g., journalism or administrative or organizational work in reform administration, political party, or little magazines; campus radical). Participation: professional and social action.

* Hypotheses derived from Wilensky, *Intellectuals*, pp. 111–174, 313–317.
** Harold L. Wilensky, "Work, Careers, and Social Integration," *International Social Science Journal*, XII (Fall, 1960), 555–556.

private agencies, civic organizations, foundations, universities—he follows the programs to which both his skills and his social philosophy are bound. Both types of policy-minded staff experts —missionaries and program professionals—play an important innovating role in established organizations (see the discussion of the Council of Economic Advisers, pp. 97–109 below). However, these orientations are not typical of top men in established organizations.

In problems confronted, institutionalization means a shift from ideological intelligence emphasizing problems in the strategy of conflict, to technical intelligence emphasizing problems of negotiation and administration; from less routinized to more routinized problems; from most urgency to least. Organizational (or national) myths become more fixed, the counter stereotyping activities of intellectuals more difficult. Hierarchy and specialization become prominent. Insofar as there is also a shift away from secrecy, information pathologies may be reduced, but all the other changes listed would seem to reduce the accuracy, relevance, and timeliness of intelligence.

SUCCESSION

Bound to the growth of organizations is the process of succession. If new, swiftly growing organizations in a fluid environment lean on charismatic leaders, or if they in some sense recruit superior executives, while older, larger, more stable organizations routinize succession, the movement of information will vary accordingly. In the succession crises characteristic of rapidly changing organizations, there may be greater play for policy-oriented intellectuals. In the routine succession characteristic of large stable organizations, there may be a strong bias in favor of established policy and official prejudice: the new man, like his predecessor, strongly desires continuity; he must avoid frightening key incumbents and potential supporters below; the outgoing official wishes to avoid being discredited. Moreover, the new man requires briefing, which both the outgoing administration and the holdover experts are glad to give.

Sheer frequency of succession exerts an influence apart from the mechanism of turnover. Other things being equal, high turnover of administrative leaders discourages the expression of critical opinion in the short run; the newcomers tend to keep quiet until they learn the "lay of the land," build confidence among superiors and subordinates, acquire a political base, or solidify their position in other ways. Frequent, institutionalized succession is one reason for the reluctance of the United States government to liquidate error in such places as Cuba and Vietnam—a striking continuity of policy through a succession of men as different in viewpoint and style as Eisenhower, Kennedy, and Johnson.

A severe limitation of this analysis of process is that we cannot assume a straight-line trend—an inevitable slowing down of growth rates, increasing stability of the environment, a decline in urgency, a reduction in succession crises, and the like. Until we have a diversified analysis of typical growth curves and their correlates, research in this area will remain primitive.

BANKS, BROKERS, WAREHOUSES, AND
SALAD OIL

How uncritical settled organizations become in the uses of information can be seen in the "Great Salad Oil Swindle" perpetrated by Anthony (Tino) De Angelis from 1957 to 1963.[25] Despite public knowledge of his shady past—bankruptcy, cheating on government contracts, indictment on a perjury charge, closure of two bank accounts on suspicion of kiting checks, designation by a senator as a "disreputable" businessman—for six years De Angelis obtained warehouse receipts for nonexistent oil from a subsidiary of an old, established firm, the American Express Company. Using the receipts as collateral, he secured loans from export firms, brokers, and even from American Express itself. (Exporters and brokers, in turn, used the receipts to borrow from banks.) With these loans and a modest supply of real oil, De Angelis became the nation's biggest dealer in vegetable oils. Only in 1963, when his Allied Crude Vegetable Oil Refining Corporation went bankrupt, did American Express and some fifty other firms involved discover shortages of almost 1.9 billion pounds of oil worth $175 million.

Ruling in one of the many cases which followed Allied's bankruptcy, Justice Charles A. Loretto declared the swindle to be "one of the marvels of our time."[26] The true marvel would seem to be that such swindles do not occur more often in commodity trading.

Commodity markets require rapid communication of information about prices, supply and demand, the making of fast deals on short notice, and the ready availability of funds to finance these deals. The markets are characterized by a high degree of organization, stable patterns of operation, traditional procedures, and mutual trust; the men in control are "professionals who pride themselves on their ability to maneuver profitably in complicated deals."[27] Much of the trading depends on "warehouse receipts" issued by a warehousing

25 My interpretation is based on the events described by Norman C. Miller of the *Wall Street Journal* in his book *The Great Salad Oil Swindle* (New York: Coward-McCann, 1965).

26 *Ibid.*, p. 230.

27 *Ibid.*, p. 47.

firm; they certify that a trader owns given stocks of commodities. These commodities are stored either in a public warehouse used by many companies or in a "field warehouse" set up by the warehousing firm on the trader's own property. The field warehouse, typically part of the trader's plant, is supervised by the warehousing firm; sometimes the warehouse hires the storage customer's own employees to guard the operation—discounting the hazards of conflicting loyalties by means of promotional talk about "strict inspection procedures" and the record of reliable storage. In any case —whether the trader polices himself or is policed by independent inspectors—he uses the receipts to secure loans which enable him to purchase additional commodities. Although it is obviously a desirable practice for the lenders themselves to verify that the goods are actually in the warehouse, they usually rely on the warehousing firm and avoid the expense of direct inspection. Similarly, firms that want not borrowers but actual deliveries of commodities do not always check on the physical basis of promises to deliver. As one export company executive said in later court testimony, " 'You must realize that when we deal with another company our business is very much institutionalized. . . . We depend on the warehouseman.' "[28] Tino De Angelis prospered in this environment.

De Angelis's success depended on the American Express warehousing subsidiary's failure to inspect adequately the contents of Allied's oil tanks at Bayonne, New Jersey. There were many reasons to suspect that most of the oil claimed to be in the tanks simply did not exist: rumors of trickery and phony inspections circulated among oil dealers and in the taverns of Bayonne; the warehousing firm received anonymous telephone calls, general warnings from firms in the trade, and specific evidence of malpractice, including attempted bribery of a representative of an independent surveying company; and it was known that Allied paid all its employees disproportionately high salaries (employee Lillian Pascarelli, Tino's "social hostess," in five years received some $180,000). When investigations revealed some irregularities, De Angelis's "explanations" were accepted as true.

Casual inspections of the tanks failed to uncover the fact that there was more salt water than oil at the Bayonne plant. At first American Express Field Warehousing (AEFW) hired De Angelis's

[28] *Ibid.*, p. 101.

guards as custodians of the tanks and the inspection unit of its head
office made periodic checks. According to AEFW President Donald
K. Miller, his chief of inspection could "'smell if anything was
wrong, just by walking into a place and looking around.' "[29] In fact,
instead of taking physical inventory, the inspectors relied on Allied's
(i.e., De Angelis's) employees to tell them what was in the tanks. In
1960 the warehousing firm replaced De Angelis's custodians with
men of its own. Unfortunately, the AEFW men either joined the
swindlers or permitted Allied employees to climb up on top of the
42-foot tanks and call out fake findings, which the inspectors from
American duly recorded. At various times, inspectors dipped into
small false compartments within the big tanks; the oil-filled compartments hid vast stores of water below. If more zealous inspectors
appeared, De Angelis's men, using a network of pipes, transferred
oil from one tank to another ahead of the inspectors.

After an initial inspection in 1957 Miller himself never visited
Allied, although it was his biggest customer. American Express
auditors sent to check Allied's accounts were no match for De
Angelis; his paper inventories of oil convinced them that "sound
accounting practices are being followed."[30] As late as five months
before the crash Miller stated that "Allied has never misrepresented
facts to us";[31] even later, Senior Vice-President Norman F. Page of
American Express described De Angelis as a "sharp but honest
operator."[32] By this time Tino was actually forging warehouse
receipts.

The fifty-one companies involved in financing De Angelis
included some of the nation's best-established firms: respected
brokerage houses, among them Ira Haupt and Company and J. R.
Williston and Beane; eminent banks such as Chase Manhattan,
Bank of America, and Manufacturers Hanover Trust; and major
export firms—Continental Grain Company, Bunge Corporation,
and Scarborough Company. With the exception of Ira Haupt, all
were accustomed to operating in commodity markets. The few that
conducted their own investigations at Bayonne were no more successful than American Express, and were just as uncritical about
De Angelis's explanations of irregularities. Most accepted the warehouse receipts as proof that the phantom oil existed. The reputation

29 *Ibid.*, p. 74.   30 *Ibid.*, p. 139.
31 *Ibid.*, p. 106.   32 *Ibid.*, p. 135.

of American Express—buttressed in the case of the banks by long association in the travelers' check business—usually was enough. Said one banker: " 'We figured with American Express issuing the receipts we couldn't go wrong.' "[33] If not discouraged by De Angelis's business history, rumors of shortages, and in some cases direct evidence of fraud, they still might have been alerted by his extraordinary activities in the vegetable-oils market: he bought oils at the highest prices, sold at the lowest; he "possessed" at one time more vegetable oil than, according to the Census Bureau, existed in the whole country. And in 1963 he made frenzied purchases of vegetable-oil futures—pledging to buy high-priced oil he did not need to fill orders, creating artificially high prices at a time when demand for oils was low and falling. Initially, he may have aimed to corner the market. Whatever his intent, however, when the prices of futures fell, brokers got restive, stopped his credit, and forced him into bankruptcy. Until that final burst of speculation, nothing inhibited the continued support of De Angelis.

The Department of Agriculture, which approves government-financed exports under the "Food for Peace" program, was as careless as the private firms; it continued to permit De Angelis to participate in the program despite knowledge of fraud in some of his export deals (rancid oil, leaky containers, unauthorized shipments). In 1963, the Department's Commodity Exchange Authority, while understaffed and severely limited in its power to intervene anyway, could have shared information about De Angelis's speculation with the exchanges and dealers. Not until the November climax did it launch a serious investigation at Bayonne.

This is not to say that no one of the hundreds of honest people drawn into the swindle had doubts about it. Two assistant inspectors in AEFW—one in 1958, the other in 1960—voiced suspicions; but these men were low in the firm's hierarchy and their advice was discounted higher up. Only late in the game did top executives of American Express question the Allied contract. At one time or another men in several firms raised questions, but they accepted De Angelis's reassurances. For my argument, it is significant that the locus of greatest skepticism, the brokerage house of Haupt and Company, was the only firm in the entire system that might be de-

[33] *Ibid.*, p. 90.

scribed as highly "aggressive, expansionist, innovative" rather than highly "institutionalized"; it had vigorous new leadership at the top (twelve of the fifteen partners had joined the firm since 1959) and it was engaged in swift expansion into both new locations and new lines of business. Although Haupt, like several firms with more established leadership, was eventually drawn into ruin, its executives had turned down Allied's business in 1962 and it took a long time to convert them to the bankers' faith in De Angelis's reliability. More important, in the entire weird tale, the strongest sustained opposition to dealing with De Angelis came from a partner of that firm, Fred Barton.

From beginning to end, however, the general picture was one of trust in conventional arrangements—a great reluctance to question verbal claims and written records. Almost all the brokers, exporters, and bankers failed to institute their own system of surveillance; indeed, they were unwilling even to conceive of a swindle by a fellow dealer.[34] Like all highly institutionalized organizations whose structure and tolerable success block any urge to innovate, they came to believe in their routine pieces of paper.

It is impossible to judge the relative weight of faith in traditional practices, on the one hand, and the "lust for profit" emphasized by the *Wall Street Journal* reporter who covered the story, on the other hand, since they reinforce one another.[35] All parties were making handsome profits from accepting De Angelis's fictional world; further, if Allied went bankrupt, AEFW believed it could collect the oil at Bayonne; the brokers and exporters thought they could look to Bayonne or to AEFW; the banks, of course, thought they could collect from everyone. In the background stood American Express, symbol of probity, a comfortable guarantee. For their part, the planners at American Express had set a rather arbitrary minimum annual profit for their warehousing subsidiary (a practice common among established firms, less common among new

[34] Cf. *ibid.*, pp. 58 ff.

[35] It is possible that, as in the GE price-fixing case, some of the executives involved were deceived while others were deceivers, in collusion with the swindler. After he went to prison, De Angelis claimed that the president of one of the exporting firms, Bunge Corporation, and four of its officials knew as early as September, 1962, that the oil was "missing." "New Food-Oil Inquiry Is Linked to Data Supplied by De Angelis," *The New York Times,* November 1, 1966, p. 53.

firms willing to assume initial losses to develop new markets or penetrate old ones). This short-run profit requirement was a powerful motive for AEFW executives to seek affirmation of the trustworthiness of De Angelis and to screen out the signs of fraud.[36]

Perhaps they were also influenced by the same thoughts as Judge Reynier J. Wortendyke, who, on May 28, 1965, when sentencing the master swindler to jail, spoke of Tino's rise from humble beginnings to business eminence as heartening evidence that in our democratic free enterprise system a man can still go far " 'with only a little backing or influence, by courage and vision.' "[37]

While the salad-oil case illustrates the vulnerability of highly institutionalized organizations to information pathologies, it does not tell us how much expenditure on what kind of search and surveillance procedures would be justified to make such failures impossible or almost impossible. Even a large budget for a slight increase in the quality of intelligence, however, might be justified where an organization's central goals are involved. Surely, the unwitting partners to De Angelis's warehouse receipt racket—especially the biggest losers (American Express, brokers, exporters)—could have benefited from a much greater investment in scrutiny of the men and tanks at Bayonne. Indeed, only a small part of the formidable intelligence apparatus banks routinely devote to an ordinary low-risk applicant for a $10,000 mortgage might have been enough.

[36] Commodity markets are also vulnerable to the pathologies of secrecy (see pp. 66–74 above), which is central to the operations of dealers. Export contracts, for instance, "are won or lost by the narrowest of margins and the company that obtains key items of information which its competitors lack may well find its intelligence has given it the upper hand in bidding on a contract. All the exporters maintain elaborate communication networks to swap information with their domestic and foreign offices; expenses of $500,000 a year for intra-company telecommunications are not unusual. The companies are careful to protect their intelligence from outsiders; at Cargill's headquarters outside Minneapolis recorded music fills the air, not to soothe frazzled nerves, but to drown out the conversations of traders discussing business by telephone with Cargill men in distant offices." (Norman Miller, p. 58.)

[37] *Ibid.*, p. 243.

CHAPTER 5

The Council of
Economic Advisers:
An Illustrative Summary[1]

No intelligence operation in recent American history exemplifies the themes of this book so well as the Council of Economic Advisers (CEA), established by the Employment Act of 1946 to give the President and Congress independent expert advice on general economic policy. The CEA epitomizes organizational defenses against information pathologies; it has done much to overcome structural and doctrinal barriers to the use of knowledge in framing national economic policy. Its successes—for instance, its role in the tax cut of 1964—are not as spectacular as the intelligence failures and successes in international relations described above, but they are no less significant as guides for an improved organization of the intelligence function. In fact, our foreign policy troubles might be

[1] This chapter is based on three studies of presidential economics—Flash; Seymour E. Harris, *Economics of the Kennedy Years* (New York: Harper & Row, 1964); and Corinne Silverman, *The President's Economic Advisers,* Interuniversity Case Program Case Series, No. 48 (Alabama: University of Alabama Press, 1959)—and on a symposium on the federal government's economic program, Fritz Morstein Marx, ed., "Formulating the Federal Government's Economic Program: A Symposium," *The American Political Science Review,* XLII (April, 1948), 272–336, especially Edwin G. Nourse and Bertram M. Gross, "The Role of the Council of Economic Advisers," *ibid.,* pp. 283–295, and Harold W. Davey, "The Experience of Other Countries," *ibid.,* pp. 295–307. I have interpreted these studies in light of conversations with economists at Chicago, Michigan, Berkeley, and Harvard who have had firsthand contact with the Council's work.

reduced if we used the CEA as a structural model for tapping knowledge in the social sciences.

With the specter of 1929 hovering over congressional debate, with the expectation of an imminent depression widely shared, the Employment Act of 1946 became the first official acknowledgment of the federal government's responsibility to "promote maximum employment, production, and purchasing power." Although laissez-faire ideology produced a good many legislative compromises—including the phrase that government should act "in a manner calculated to foster and promote free competitive enterprise" as well as the general welfare—the Employment Act committed government to some kind of economic planning and action.[2] Above all, the law was quite clear about the administrative machinery to be used.

The law specified that the new council would render professional economic advice directly to top policymakers in the White House and Congress. The advice would go beyond specific economic issues to over-all economic policy. It would be independent of partisan politics and of those government agencies—especially the Budget Bureau, the Treasury Department, and the Federal Reserve Board—which had been prone to parochial views of public policy.[3] Under the Employment Act, the President transmits to Congress at the beginning of each regular session an economic report containing an analysis of economic conditions and trends; desirable goals for employment, production, and purchasing power; and programs, long-run and short-run, for reaching these goals. The CEA prepares the President's reports and provides continuing economic advice; the Joint Economic Committee in Congress, comprised of seven members of each house, evaluates the report and advises Congress on

[2] All modern democratic countries had long groped for a realistic balance between public and private enterprise in a mixed economy; all had moved toward planning for full employment as a central goal. Before the end of World War II, Britain, Canada, Australia, and Sweden, among other nations, had formally acknowledged government responsibility for maintaining a healthy economy. (See Davey, p. 296.) By 1960 "Keynesian" fiscal and monetary principles had diffused so widely among academic economists that one could speak of the "post-Keynesian, neo-classical synthesis."

[3] More than administrative wisdom, this move reflected the desire to avoid the choice between the Budget Bureau and the Treasury, neither of which wanted the other to have the general policy role.

broad economic policy—an arrangement unique in the American government.

The position of the Council in the structure of government is crucial. The three-man Council is directly responsible to the President, independent of the regular government bureaucracy, uncommitted to the outside constituencies and special viewpoints of the departments, yet able to draw on the work of a growing number of highly qualified career economists in the departments. There is a natural tendency for the major government agencies, each with their own experts, to evaluate economic policy in the light of their own institutional restraints and clientele—Treasury to be concerned with government financing, Federal Reserve Board with credit and monetary policy, Agriculture with farm production and income, Commerce with business incentives, Labor with employment and wages, and so on. How difficult it is to develop a government-wide perspective from a position in one of these operating departments is nicely expressed by Seymour E. Harris, himself a Keynesian economist, commenting about his role as a Treasury adviser: "It was . . . an embarrassing position. Since my views were much closer to the Council's than to those of the Treasury, which tended to support orthodox positions, more than once when there was a conflict of views, members of the Council and their staff criticized me for repudiation of principles. The Council did not seem to realize that the Treasury could not move ahead as rapidly as the Council; nor that, as the department primarily responsible for the financing of the government and the preservation of the value of the dollar abroad, the Treasury had to retain some confidence of the financial community."[4] The CEA has, in fact, become a small group of elite advisers—three members, never more than twenty staff aides at any one time, and a varying number of outside consultants—with access both to the data and arguments of government agencies and to the President. It combines the flexibility and informality of a task force with a sustained, institutionalized involvement in presidential policy and leadership. Its broad-ranging contacts in and out of government supplement its own staff research. It also represents a fruitful combination of decentralized intelligence, generated by the cabinet officers' experts and interest-group clientele, and centralized intelligence, generated by the Council. The Council works hard to keep

[4] Harris, pp. 21–22.

channels open to these special groups, but asserts a national perspective at the top. In short, the CEA has gone far in minimizing the pathologies of hierarchy, specialization, and centralization in the communication of economic data and advice.

The formal position of the Council accounts in part for its success. Equally important is the interplay of professional independence and strong ties to the academic community, which facilitates the recruitment of high-quality staff. This was the first time an academic discipline was given status as a separate agency within the President's staff. But before the Council's reputation in the government and among academic economists could be established and its independence given substance, it had to attract good staff with no strong personal or institutional ties to vested interests in or out of the government. By the mid-fifties the task was accomplished.[5] No doubt this professionalization of the Council reflected some of the academic closed-shop spirit; nor is there doubt that Chairman Burns, on leave from his position as Professor of Economics at Columbia and Director of Research of the National Bureau of Economic Research, consciously set out to improve the professional reputation of the Council. He established a pattern of recruitment that has persisted under subsequent chairmen, Raymond J. Saulnier (1956–61), Walter W. Heller (1961–64), and now Gardner Ackley, accenting

[5] Before Arthur F. Burns became chairman in 1953, the Council was in some disrepute in the economics fraternity. The reasons: Chairman Edwin G. Nourse and Vice-Chairman Leon H. Keyserling differed sharply and publicly on a number of issues from 1946 to 1949; most members of the staff under Nourse and Keyserling were career government employees, some not economists; and Keyserling, chairman from 1950 to 1953—a Harvard Law School product (LLB, 1931), experienced in liberal Democratic politics and staff work—was from the viewpoint of the academy not only untrained in economics but worse, became identified with the promotion of an expansionist policy under all conditions. Published analyses of the CEA tend to exaggerate the differences in professionalism between the Nourse and Keyserling Councils and later ones. Some of the staff members of the 1940's (e.g., Gerhard Colm) had better academic reputations than their successors of the 1950's; the most publicized Council Chairman, Walter W. Heller, while unusual in his grasp of the interplay of theory and policy, was not renowned as a leading theorist or academic technician; and some observers claim that the CEA, like other White House units, has recently had trouble recruiting outstanding people because of the hostility of the academic community to the administrative style and/or foreign policy of President Johnson. However, the general direction in the Council, as in the operating departments, has been toward the employment of an increasing number of well-trained, academically respectable economists. The same trend is evident in industry.

ability over partisanship, looking toward academicians (teachers, researchers, consultants with permanent roots in or around universities) for whom the Council experience was a temporary assignment. Serving as consultants or staff members, part-time or full-time, these energetic scholars have moved in and out of Washington, fitting the needs of both their own academic schedules and the Council's special projects and report-writing seasons. Council members themselves sustain a brisk traffic between universities, foundations, research institutes, and the government. Nothing could be better calculated to inject fresh slants and solid data into White House policy deliberations. Not only does the turnover of men with an outside base assure independent advice; it means a diffusion of Council contacts and friendships throughout the academic community—an informal alumni association to help in recruitment. Given the Council's functions, the cost of recruitment from universities—high turnover of men who return to the campus just as they begin to "learn the score"—is perhaps worth paying. Influential defense advisory corporations such as RAND (Air Force) and the Institute for Defense Analyses (Office of the Secretary of Defense) similarly augment their staff by borrowing professors, although their reliance on permanent senior scientists is greater than that of the CEA.

In addition to a rising level of expertise, there is an impressive test of the CEA's professionalism—a surprising degree of policy continuity through drastically different administrations. Plainly the various Councils reflected presidential ideologies. Perhaps the greatest contrast was between the Eisenhower desire to control inflation through reduced spending, risking slower growth and higher unemployment, and the Truman-Kennedy-Johnson desire to achieve higher economic growth and full employment, denying or minimizing the risk of inflation.[6] And from the viewpoint of the participants

[6] These were matters of ideology; different Presidents and economists gave different priority to such goals as full employment, economic growth, economic equality, and price stability wherever these goals were in conflict. The actual performance shows low growth rates under Eisenhower, but the trend in unemployment continued to worsen under both Eisenhower and Kennedy. For six years under Truman (1947–52), we had an average annual growth in real GNP of 4.0%, and an unemployment rate of 3.9%; for eight years under Eisenhower, an average growth in GNP of 2.6%, average unemployment of 4.7%; for Kennedy an average growth in GNP of 3.9%, average unemployment

in the daily infighting at higher policy levels, the differences in Council composition and personalities, in approach to economic analysis, in administrative style, all appear commanding. The studies of presidential economics tend to accent such differences. We see the Keyserling Council, directed by a career New Dealer, part of an active, decisive presidency ("the buck stops here"), aggressively accenting full employment; the Burns Council, under a leading student of business cycles, committed to professional objectivity and the avoidance of deep depression, serving a passive administration, hostile to intellectuals, dominated in its economics by Treasury Secretary Humphrey (who wondered about Hemingway's *The Old Man and the Sea,* "Why would anybody be interested in some old man who was a failure?"), accenting economic stability and a narrow interpretation of the Council's mission; and the Heller Council, led by a "worldly and whirlwind academician," an operator like the other pragmatists of the New Frontier, full member of the inner circle, serving a president whose celebrated style combined caution, a contempt for dogma, and an urge to "get the country moving again."

Yet, while these differences in priorities and emphasis are real, the continuities in Council functions and even policies are striking, and, as evidence of an emerging tradition of high-quality economic analysis, more significant. All these Councils used the analytical techniques of Burns, the close study of the economic indicators series, while Burns used the others' techniques of projecting Gross National Product. (There were differences in emphasis: for short-range forecasts, Burns gave greater weight to leading indicators analysis, Heller and Ackley relied more on neo-Keynesian growth theory and econometric model building.) All used the Economic Report as an educational and promotional device; all contributed to an increased acceptance of economic planning, giving some rationale and coherence to diverse economic aims and programs. Most important, the Council has been the center for the high-level merger of laissez-faire and the new economics. Within the confines of Eisenhower's passivity and Humphrey's rigid orthodoxy, Burns

---

of 6.0%. Budget deficits appeared in four of the Truman years, all of the Kennedy years, and five of the Eisenhower years. Eisenhower, in addition to slowing down the growth rate, set a record for the largest peacetime budgetary deficit in history—over $12 billion in 1959.

pressed hard to strengthen the administration's acceptance of limited counter-cyclical responsibilities; he correctly analyzed economic trends before and during the recession of 1953–54, contributing to a climate of opinion in Congress and the administration favorable to remedial action. Burns's commitment to rigorous economic analysis, his on-the-job training as CEA advocate within government, and the liberalism of much of his staff combined to make him less anti-Keynesian when he left the Council than he was upon arrival. If Burns prodded the Republicans into some recession-dampening action, the Council chairmen under the Democrats never questioned the primacy of private enterprise. In short, the preconceptions of Council members were tempered by exposure to White House politics while presidential politics were tempered by economics. The general direction was toward the education of presidents in modern economics.

Professionalism has not meant arid neutrality. Because of its small size, location in government, professional independence, connections with universities, and broad mission (aggregative analysis of the national economy), the Council of Economic Advisers has avoided the false separation of "facts" from interpretation, of data gathering from problems for analysis. Because of its character as a personal staff to the President, it has not been able to avoid advocacy. An early dispute between Keyserling, who favored an active public role, and Nourse, who wanted to keep advice to the President private as much as possible in order to avoid self-inflicted political constraints on policy advocacy, was resolved on the side of promotion. Since then, in speeches, articles, and congressional testimony—and in contacts with agencies—Council members have pursued their educational mission. Public advocacy, however, has its costs and can sometimes be downright embarrassing. For instance, in the mid-1960's the Council engaged in tortured attempts to sell the wage-price guideposts. The effort to "enforce" these guidelines took much of the Council's time and may have impaired its efficiency as an intelligence source, as well as its reputation in the academic community (economists are generally cynical about exhortation as a means of wage and price constraint). On balance, though, the Council has not allowed presidential demand for shortrun forecasts or for political justification to impede general orienting analysis and the encouragement of long-range policy research—

e.g., on national economic budgets, counter-cyclical policies, the improvement of economic statistics.

As all experts do, CEA members and staff have often reformulated problems that come to them loosely stated, and have broadened the scope of alternatives that had been conceived. Necessarily concerned with the effect of any given policy on over-all economic conditions, they have improved the quality and range of questions asked by the White House. If experts in the Department of Commerce estimate that a $50 million expenditure on area redevelopment, most of it for highway construction, will create 10,000 jobs, the Council asks whether an equivalent expenditure on moving allowances and subsidies to facilitate movement of workers and resources away from chronically depressed areas might not be more effective in reducing unemployment. When the Bureau of the Budget recommends a given distribution of government funds, the Council asks that the employment effects of each kind of outlay be considered in the final decision. All the Council chairmen, whatever their leaders' politics, have served to sensitize the Executive branch to economic realities. While they supplied ideological justification for administration policy, all had a primarily liberalizing influence on their presidents—during the 1940's and 1950's, in recurrent periods of unemployment, typically sounding a healthy "yes" to offset the Budget Bureau's "no."

By 1961, fifteen years after its beginnings, the CEA had become an established part of presidential leadership, a major purveyor of economic knowledge in the government. Its advocacy of concepts and principles of economics and its analysis of economic possibilities and problems have been accorded legitimacy by presidents, Congress, economists, and other relevant publics. Its pattern of recruitment reflects close ties to the academic discipline and a rising level of expertise. Even its contacts with operating agencies have begun to go beyond the accidents of personal propinquity and personality; the lines of communication to operating departments are sufficiently stabilized so that each chairman does not have to start from scratch. Of course, the Council, like all advisory groups, must carve out channels of communication in the White House staff and struggle for allies in policy disputes. That struggle is rendered easier, however, by its formal position, and by the diffusion of economic intelligence throughout government (one sign of the latter is that the last two Budget Directors, Charles Schultze and Kermit Gordon, are CEA alumni). While economic policy is pervasive, a component of every major public issue, while powerful operating departments and congressional committees are involved in it and the White House staff rides herd on it, and while the Council cannot do its job without the excellent social statistics of the Bureau of Labor Statistics, the Census Bureau, the Federal Reserve Board, and the Office of Business Economics—the CEA has successfully established itself as a general interpreter of the big picture. In interaction with the Director of the Bureau of the Budget, and with the secretaries of the departments, especially Treasury, the Council chairman acts as a catalyst and guide, reflecting and shaping a presidential perspective. The Council has also raised the level of public debate about economic issues.

In short, like the scientists who sold radar to the British in the 1930's, like RAND economists and engineers who transformed American military strategy in the 1950's, the Council provides a fertile blend of technical and political intelligence, of data and doctrine. It has enriched the verbal environment of the White House, often breaking through prevailing stereotypes and slogans.

This is not to say that the Council has known no failures. Economists point to Keyserling's slow recognition of the onset of the 1948–49 recession, Burns's underestimate of the drop in defense spending in 1954, Saulnier's protracted preoccupation with inflation in the late 1950's, Heller's overly optimistic prediction of the GNP for 1962, Ackley's underestimate of the increase in both GNP and the price level in 1966 (in part a reflection of presidential secrecy and/or confusion about the high cost of the Vietnam war). Neither is it to say that the Council is independent of presidential politics. When giving objective private advice to the President the Council is constrained even more than other agencies from issuing pessimistic public predictions about the state of the economy. It is to say that in the face of gaps in economic knowledge and the hazards of forecasting, the CEA's batting average has been high, both in short-run estimates and long-run education.

The role of the Council in overcoming the power of preconceptions is best revealed in the progress of the economic policy of the Kennedy administration, culminating in the tax cut of February, 1964. When John F. Kennedy was elected President, his understanding of economics was not much better than that of President Franklin D. Roosevelt in 1932. Although as Congressman and Senator (1946–60), Kennedy had frequent contact with such sophisticated economists as Tobin, Samuelson, Harris, and Galbraith, he was more interested in mitigating the effects of industrial migration from New England (e.g., through unemployment insurance and high tariffs on textiles) than in broad economic policy. He remained essentially conventional in his views of fiscal and monetary tools: increases in welfare spending were to be avoided because of the political liability of unbalanced budgets; tax cuts were bad for the same reason; emphasis on the balanced budget and on the primacy of the stable dollar, even at a time of slow growth and high unemployment, would retard charges of "fiscal irresponsibility." Kennedy carried the additional rhetorical burden of his Inaugural Address: the spirit of sacrifice ("Ask not what your country can do for you—ask what you can do for your country") was hardly conducive to the promotion of expansionist spending and tax policies. Less than two years after he entered the White house, however, the President was saying that economic orthodoxy should not determine government policy:

What we need is not labels and clichés but more basic discussion of the sophisticated and technical questions involved in keeping a great economic machinery moving ahead. . . . I am suggesting that the problems of fiscal and monetary policies in the sixties as opposed to the kinds of problems we faced in the thirties demand subtle challenges for which technical answers, not political answers, must be provided. . . . They cannot be solved by incantations from the forgotten past, but the example of Western Europe shows that they are capable of solution—that governments, and many of them are conservative governments, prepared to face technical problems without ideological preconceptions, can coordinate the elements of a national economy and bring about growth and prosperity—a decade of it. (Commencement Address at Yale University, June 11, 1962.)

What had intervened was an extensive education in economics.

As President-elect, Kennedy had commissioned a task force on depressed areas, headed by Senator Paul Douglas, former University of Chicago professor of economics; another on tax reform, headed by Harvard tax lawyer Stanley S. Surrey; and a third on the state of the economy, headed by one of the nation's top economists,

Paul Samuelson of M.I.T. Their reports helped shape the administration's economic program, without, however, reversing its emphasis on budget balancing and inflation avoidance.

The President's long-time advisers—Tobin, Harris, Galbraith—continued to influence his thinking. Their insistence on the use of fiscal and monetary policy to stimulate economic expansion was reinforced by the contributions of economists and tax experts from colleges, universities, and research organizations who participated in the 1961–62 tax reform proposals, together with Secretaries Wirtz of Labor, Hodges of Commerce, and Dillon of Treasury, and experts from a variety of government departments and agencies. All of these groups contributed to the later emergence of a consensus in favor of a tax cut. But the main publicly-visible role was that of the Council, led by Walter W. Heller, on leave from his position as Chairman of the Department of Economics of the University of Minnesota.

That the Council endorsed an active economic policy for government, the full employment concept of the Employment Act, and an emphasis on fiscal rather than monetary policy—all implying priority for expansion rather than balanced budgets—is not surprising. These "Keynesian" principles, accepted by a majority of economists, constitute the rationale for the tax cut. That the advocacy of this tax cut can be described as "revolutionary," "an advanced fiscal approach," is explained by the specific economic circumstances. The country was neither in nor threatened by a recession. Either might have justified counter-cyclical fiscal policy, but both output and employment were rising after the mild recession of 1960–61. The problem instead was to promote faster growth, to narrow the gap between actual and potential GNP, and to reduce unemployment.

What we needed, the CEA argued, was the stimulation of aggregate demand. The current tax structure caused tax revenues to rise faster than expenditures during periods of recovery, thus inhibiting growth. A tax cut would raise private consumption and investment expenditures, increase aggregate demand and production, and reduce unemployment. The Council prescribed a tax cut despite the existence of a budget deficit. This medicine meant not only giving up the orthodox idea that the budget should be balanced each year but also abandoning the more advanced concept that surpluses in good years should offset deficits in bad. In short, the Council said that we

should run a deficit even in a period of expansion when it is necessary to stimulate aggregate demand in order to reach or maintain
full employment.

The tax cut was successful. Private investment and consumption
increased substantially in 1964 and 1965. Real GNP rose by 5 per
cent in 1964; by 5.4 per cent in 1965. Unemployment fell from 5.7
per cent in 1963 to 4.6 per cent in 1965 and continued to decline
in 1966. At the same time, there was very little rise in consumer
prices and none in wholesale prices—until the full influence of the
Vietnam war was felt in late 1965. After mid-1961 the American
economy experienced the longest period of sustained expansion since
World War II. Liberal economists could cogently argue that desperately needed investment in the public civilian sector—in health,
education, and welfare services, in rebuilding the urban environment
—would have been a desirable alternative to the tax cut. That
strategy was unrealistic, however, given the Kennedy Congress. The
Council compromise reflected the President's and Heller's assessment of the political constraints on economic policy: the business
community and their friends in government embraced the budgetary
heresy in exchange for restrictions on government spending. In any
case, no one denies the economic efficacy of the steps taken, whatever the effect on equality and the quality of civilization.

Plainly, the economic intelligence available to the President
makes a difference in policy. Compare two activist presidents as they
confronted increasingly hostile Congresses and tried to educate
themselves, the Congress, and the public in elementary economics—
Franklin D. Roosevelt, who failed to extricate himself from the recession of 1937–38; John F. Kennedy, who succeeded in overcoming
the sluggishness of the economy in the early 1960's. FDR's unsystematic improvisation, his use of internal rivalry and external
contact, got him plenty of economic advice, good and bad, and made
him aware of a great range of alternatives; but it also let his prejudices run free and, as the recession deepened, left him flounder-
ing. There had been no lack of exposure to opposing memoranda from economists in and out of government. Indeed, FDR had
corresponded with John Maynard Keynes himself, had talked with
him in 1934, and in February, 1938, received a long and eloquent
letter from him pleading for massive deficit spending.[7] FDR's sus-

[7] James MacGregor Burns, pp. 331–332.

picion of academic "theory" this time did not serve him well. He remained a captive of his preconceptions and ritual statements about the balanced budget. Entering the recession in 1937, he cut public spending, sided with such orthodox budget balancers as Secretary of the Treasury Henry Morgenthau. When the slump deepened as a result, he pursued only halfway measures—halfway even within the limits imposed by rising congressional opposition. The 1930's ended with eight or nine million people still unemployed. President Kennedy—also suspicious of dogma, perhaps no better educated in economics than Roosevelt (although he may have been more intellectual)—was the beneficiary not merely of the greater consensus among leading academic and business economists regarding significant issues of economic policy, but of the institutionalization of that knowledge in the Council.

The contrast suggests that studies of presidential economics that accent the importance of personality—Heller was an "excellent and articulate" teacher,[8] Kennedy was "a remarkably receptive and educable President"[9]—miss the main story. The upgrading of intelligence in an appropriate structural form means that strong presidents, when they appear, have a source of knowledge; and strong advisers, an effective channel of influence. Nor can the Council's success be attributed to any major shift in American values between 1950 and 1966. Public ambivalence about the welfare state remained strong;[10] the interests pressing for restrictive policies, active; the budget-balancing fetish, unflagging. In their activism and pragmatism, in their mental agility and voracious grasp of details, Roosevelt in 1938 and Kennedy in 1962 were alike; the crucial difference for economic success was the superior economic knowledge available to the latter.

As an example of success in the application of reason to public affairs, economics stands alone among the social sciences. In the rigor of its theory and methodology and in the average level of competence of its practitioners, economics has an edge over the disciplines of sociology, psychology, political science, and anthropology. But that edge is not so great that we cannot use economics as a more general model. It is possible that the makers of foreign policy in the

8 Harris, p. 258.
9 Flash, p. 273.
10 Wilensky and Lebeaux, *Industrial Society*.

United States could profit from an analogue to the Council of Economic Advisers—a small top-level group of free-floating, highly trained, academically oriented, general advisers, operating outside Defense, State, or the CIA, relatively free of bureaucratic rivalry, responsible to the President and the Senate Committee on Foreign Affairs, and assigned to tap social science and history for a comprehensive, long-run interpretation of problems and prospects abroad. Existing agencies are structurally weak for this mission: the Joint Chiefs of Staff and the National Security Council—comprised of the President, the Vice-President, the Secretaries of State and Defense, the Director of the Office of Civil and Defense Mobilization, advised by the Chairman of the Joint Chiefs and the Director of the CIA, all augmented by anyone the President chooses to add (e.g., under Eisenhower the Secretary of the Treasury, the Director of the Budget, and the Chairman of the Atomic Energy Committee and several special assistants)—epitomize the resolution of conflicting advice by a ponderous super-committee. Within the Executive Office of the President, there is the White House staff. But they are non-expert political lieutenants who pull together the recommendations of experts, often recasting them in a form acceptable to the President. If they are assigned to foreign affairs and draw on social sciences and history, they do so only sporadically; they lack the time and the sustained intensity of focus of advisers sufficiently independent of the daily struggle. The Bureau of the Budget has a synoptic view; it must balance military and non-military, foreign and domestic needs. But it does so with the special perspective of a controller responsible for cutting total costs for the operations of hundreds of branch plants and occupational groups. Like the CEA, the White House staff and the Budget Bureau do not have their main roots in the large operating departments; unlike the CEA their ties to the academic community are weak.

The Central Intelligence Agency and the State Department alike have ties to universities. But the former accents secret sources, loyalty-security clearances, and alienates most of the academic community; the latter looks to universities more for support of prevailing doctrine than for intelligence. Both are big and bureaucratic. Rarely is either able to recruit top scholars for staff positions in the manner of the CEA.

The closest counterparts to the CEA for international relations are the research arms of the military, some of them similar in structure and operation, and all much better financed. The Air Force, leader in the use of non-profit advisory corporations, has its RAND (Research ANd Development); the Navy has the Center for Naval Analysis, with several component organizations; the Army looks to RAC (Research Analysis Corporation), HumRRO (Human Relations Research Office), the Special Operations Research Office (SORO), as well as contract research groups supplied by the Stanford Research Institute (SRI) and Technical Operations, Inc.; the Office of the Secretary of Defense has developed parallel advisory institutions, notably the Institute for Defense Analyses.[11] But these agencies add to an accent on concealment the fatal flaw of a narrow mission: their market of ideas reflects competition to create more efficient means to inflict damage on our enemies; their independence is not used primarily to discover other ways to pursue the national interest—e.g., assess the merits of diverse arms control or international aid strategies.[12] If the State Department, the Agency for

[11] Bruce L. R. Smith, *The RAND Corporation*, pp. 1–6.

[12] The spectacular failure of "Project Camelot" is no argument against the desirability of analogues to the Council of Economic Advisers. Camelot was a multi-million-dollar, nonclassified, social-science research project conceived in late 1963 by the Army and activated in late 1964 by the Special Operations Research Office (SORO), a unit of American University that functions under contract with the Department of the Army. The project provoked such revulsion in Chile, bitterness in the State Department, and dismay in the U.S. Senate that it was abruptly terminated in July, 1965, by order of Defense Secretary McNamara in consultation with President Johnson. The accompanying public furor featured attacks by Senators Fulbright and Morse on military sponsorship of social research conducted overseas. For the service of sensible foreign policy, Camelot, it is safe to say, was the wrong kind of social science with the wrong kind of staff in the wrong place. First, it was an overblown research project with the loosest academic and professional controls. Second, although described by SORO's Director as "an outgrowth of continuing interest in the government in fostering orderly growth and development in the newer countries," Camelot was subject to close supervision by the Army and was therefore vulnerable to the narrow counter-insurgency posture of the military; the project emphasized the need to identify and measure the causes and reduction of "internal war potential." The questions "What are the conditions under which the United States could benefit from a revolution in a poor country?" or "Where do revolutions express the values of freedom, equality, and economic progress and where do they defeat these values?"—such questions are unlikely to dominate a research project firmly embedded in an operating agency of the military (even if the project had been able to recruit outstanding staff). It may be fortunate that Camelot never got beyond a preliminary research design. For diverse interpretations of the meaning of Camelot see *Congressional Record,*

International Development, the Arms Control and Disarmament Agency had counterparts to RAND devoted to research and debate on broad policy issues; if the President had a Council of Foreign Affairs comparable to the Council of Economic Advisers, the information pathologies described in this book might be reduced (see Chart 2), and the strength of preconceptions, on occasion, overcome.

Proceedings and Debates of the 89th Congress, Vol. CXI, No. 157, August 25, 1965, pp. 20905–20907; Irving Louis Horowitz, "The Life and Death of Project Camelot," *Trans-action*, III (November–December, 1965), 3–7, 44–49; and Robert A. Nisbet, "Project Camelot: An Autopsy," *The Public Interest*, No. 5 (Fall, 1966), pp. 45–69. The issues posed by the Camelot affair— the appropriate functions and structures for social research on foreign policy sponsored by operating agencies of government—are distinct from the question of general government support for the social sciences in universities. The problem in the present context, again, is to mobilize intelligence resources for peaceful civilian purposes comparable to those of the military.

CHAPTER 6

Economic, Political, and Cultural Contexts

The remaining corner of the picture is the most impressionistic. Although my analysis has been cast in general terms applicable to complex organizations in every modern state, cultural-ideological contexts obviously condition the uses and influence of intellectuals and experts as well as the quality of intelligence. But no comparative studies show how. Moreover, some of these national "cultural" variations turn out to be themselves the structural variations already discussed. For instance, organizational defenses against information pathologies transcend culture. Stalin, like FDR, used overlapping delegation of functions to assure that issues would be brought into the open at the highest level; administrative leaders in every country employ the strategy of calculated competition for the purposes of both control and intelligence.

The main distinctions for our purposes are between command and market economies and between totalitarian and pluralist polities. First, economic and political contexts affect the balance among types of intelligence used. If organizations deeply involved with government in a market economy must rely on the ideological-political intelligence of contact men, major industrial firms in a command economy are even more dependent on such information. In a Soviet-type economy, "planners' tension"—the pressure generated when administratively ordered output exceeds capacity output—necessitates an immense apparatus for communicating and enforcing orders and a complicated system of unofficial expediters and fixers who try to circumvent the orders so that goals may be met (which creates a demand for more planners to keep track of what's going on). In a brilliant dissection of the command economy Wiles describes pro-plan fixers in action: "As the output targets are always the most important part of the plan, and the director's bonus depends mainly on his fulfillment of them, he is always violating the rest of the plan for their sake. Black markets, or rather black bilateral transactions, occur in raw materials and labour, and firms secretly barter services among each other (you repair my furnace, I'll lend you some aluminium until next quarter)." Since all expenditures are tightly controlled, "these activities mean squaring the accountant and probably also the auditors, and in reply the authorities constantly reshuffle directors and accountants before they get to know each other." Directors also hire permanent agents, "tolkachi" who are supposed to know whom to talk to, which forms to use, etc., to reduce the plan targets and expedite or increase supplies.[1] In such an economy, there are numerous agencies engaged in negotiating standards of value and performance which in market economies are determined by fewer, private parties or by the test of the market.

That planners' tension is not primarily a cultural or political phenomenon, but a matter of economic organization, is evident in wartime planning in areas where the government is the only consumer—even in pluralist societies. A penetrating study of the British Ministry of Aircraft Production (M.A.P.) in World War II suggests that a prime root of this tension is the flow of information to producers about what is really going on. Rather than use realistic planning, the British government wanted to use "target" or "carrot" planning—that is, set aircraft production goals somewhat beyond the estimated capacities of the firm in order to maximize incentives and production. The M.A.P. would give the armed forces a minimum realistic guarantee so that the latter could plan for manpower and airfield requirements; at the same time they would give the firms the higher target to shoot at. The fatal obstacle was the wide diffusion of information—the visible performance of builders of hangars, trainers of pilots, and so on (see p. 47). In so complex an

---

[1] Wiles, pp. 132–135. Cf. Joseph S. Berliner, *Factory and Manager in the U.S.S.R.* (Cambridge: Harvard University Press, 1957); and Robert A. Dahl and Charles E. Lindblom, *Politics, Economics, and Welfare* (New York: Harper & Brothers, 1953).

operation, involving so many organizational units, the guarantee (the real production expectation) could not be kept secret from the production directors in the ministry and aircraft firms. And when the production people learned of the lower expectations, they tended to treat the target program as a worthless scrap of paper. Ignorance here would have been salutary; knowledge made the ideal dual program impracticable. Although there was a gradual move toward realistic planning, in keeping with the information spread, the planners in fact never resolved the dilemma.[2] Insofar as market mechanisms are displaced by central planning, planners' tension prevails and contact men who mediate between planners and performers become indispensable.

More generally, totalitarian states, with their penchant for ideological indoctrination, allocate a larger share of all intelligence resources to the political intelligence of both contact men and internal communications specialists (see pp. 10–14 above). And finally they tend to obliterate the distinction between internal and external intelligence; for instance, where the problem of internal control looms large and external conflict is intense, "foreign" intelligence is combined with domestic counter-intelligence and both are suffused with an anxious concern for loyalty and security. Similarly the industries in the United States that spy on competitors are likely to be the ones that keep their own employees under close surveillance; a method used successfully for one problem spreads to others.[3] Perhaps this is why the American automobile industry, long addicted to cloak-and-dagger operations designed to uncover next year's styles of competitors, has been so ready to use industrial spies, closed-circuit television, and electronic eavesdropping to keep in touch with their workers.[4]

Second, economic and political contexts shape the quality of technical-economic-legal data generated, reported, or both. Command economies and totalitarian political systems strengthen the structural roots of intelligence distortion. Hierarchy, of course, is more prominent, so the temptation and opportunity to conceal, misreport,

[2] Devons, pp. 29 ff., 36–37.
[3] The major limit on this combination of internal and external intelligence is secrecy, which implies a segregation of clandestine operations in different fields.
[4] See p. 73 above; Richard A. Smith; and U.S. Senate, *Invasions of Privacy.*

and mishandle data are infinite.[5] Moreover, if central planning is emphasized, information processing costs soar, uncertainty is great, and problems of data collection and interpretation are often insoluble. In Poland and the U.S.S.R., for instance, planners have not yet been able to integrate input-output tables into their planning schemes because of the great expense of revamping the information system. Among many difficulties, the structure of the control apparatus determines the kind of data available; the partitioning into more or less autonomous administrative units such as firms and ministries cuts across the commodity lines required for the construction of input-output tables.[6]

Rooted in intelligence failures, the urge to reorganize and reorganize again in order to make direct physical controls effective, the yearning for merely statistical success—these are conspicuous in Soviet-type economies. Thus, there is merit in the claim of economists that a competitive system of markets and prices, whatever its imperfections, simplifies problems of rational calculation. Prices are a common denominator of values; they summarize a great store of information about consumer preferences, physical and cost efficiency, and so on. They provide better intelligence for economic decisions than that provided by central planners in a command economy.[7]

Secrecy, too, is more prominent and the information pathologies associated with it more highly developed in totalitarian states. The national variations here are considerable. It is said that Russian regimes, whether Czarist or Communist, have shown a passion for secrecy not found in the West. One has the impression, however,

[5] Cf. Wiles, pp. 222 ff.; Dahl and Lindblom, pp. 254–271.

[6] Cf. Ward, chapter 6; and Vladimir G. Treml, "Input-Output Analysis and Soviet Planning," in *Mathematical Techniques and Soviet Planning* (McLean, Va.: Research Analysis Corporation, 1965, mimeo.), pp. 37–38.

[7] Obvious limitations of market price systems for the solution of problems of allocation include the prohibitive cost of some goods to any one individual or group in the market (national defense, sanitation, education); inadequate rewards to attract indispensable labor (a price system cannot recruit millions of men for the armed forces in wartime); the need to accommodate other pre-eminent social goals (eminent domain, zoning, conservation, the control of pollution, income redistribution policies such as subsidies to the aged, the sick, the poor). Because of these shortcomings, all modern societies combine indirect and direct controls with pricing systems. Cf. Dahl and Lindblom, pp. 385 ff. In recent years, however, "socialist" societies have relied a bit less on direct controls and more on market mechanisms, moving closer to the "mixed" economies of Western Europe and the United States—a tendency stimulated partly by the failure of economic intelligence.

that no governments have ever been more obsessed by fear of espionage or more organized to protect secrets than totalitarian systems based on modern technology—Hitler's Germany, Stalin's Russia. Further, when the Nazis wanted to elicit information or obedience, they used the Nazi Party to infiltrate and spy on political and industrial bureaucracies. Stalin used the CP in the same way. In both countries, of course, party agents did not always dutifully check on management performance; they often entered into collusion with the managers, serving as another source of distortion in the upward flow of information.

Information pathologies perhaps reached their climactic expression in these two regimes. Both allocated great resources to experts and developed a huge intelligence machinery at home and abroad; both displayed intense inter-agency rivalries, an accent on hierarchy, command, secrecy, and loyalty, and an anti-intellectual fervor— exacerbated in the Nazi case by a racist ideology, and in the Soviet case by the myth of proletarian sublimity. These forces combined to create social systems dominated by grotesque intrigues and ultimately by paranoid delusions. They also produced some spectacular intelligence failures—among them, Hitler's strategy for World War II. Hitler neither planned nor prepared for a long war. He contemplated a series of separate thrusts and quick victories over enemies even less prepared than Germany, short military operations on the model of the Polish and French campaigns; he did not expect to fight a prolonged war against a combination of major world powers. He grossly underestimated Russian strength —even ordering a large reduction of armaments production three months after he began the Russian campaign. In 1943, solemn declarations about the need for a Spartan life were accompanied by almost undiminished production of civilian goods. Hitler's plans suffered fatally from his imperviousness to ideas in conflict with his own—for instance, the argument that the *Blitzkrieg* strategy was too limited.[8]

That structural and ideological roots of intelligence failure were strong in Nazi Germany is also suggested by comparing Britain's approach to the challenge of radar with that of Germany. Both countries possessed the necessary resources and research and production skills. In Britain, as we have seen (pp. 34–35), the Tizard

[8] *USSBS-3,* pp. 6–7, 16–25. See also pp. 28–31 above.

Committee, acting as liaison between science and government, argued for the feasibility of radar and promoted its operational development in the mid-thirties. Subsequent administrative arrangements for pressing through the work of centimetric radar were carried on by a research and development team in 1939–40. Administration was marked by close relationships between the designers in the Telecommunications Research Establishment (TRE) and the users in the Royal Air Force and in the Air Ministry—an "intimate joining of operational needs with technical possibilities in an immediate, personal, informal way."[9] Among other means for improving communication, the Superintendent of TRE instituted the "Sunday Soviets," open meetings to which everyone interested in a particular type of equipment or operational problem was invited, whatever his affiliation or rank.[10]

Contrast the German approach. Radar development had taken place before the war and some advanced equipment was in production by 1939, but development work was then virtually stopped, again on the assumption of a short war. What was crucial in the subsequent lag in German radar development was a highly bureaucratic arrangement:

When the Germans did start up again, they established a Plenipotentiary for High Frequency Techniques. This official established a chain of new research institutions. He also introduced a system of logging all the available laboratory effort not only in his own institutions but in all the industrial firms, universities, and technical colleges in the country. He then established contact with an official in the Air Ministry corresponding to himself. The Air Ministry official defined specifications of what the Air Force wanted, and these went to the Plenipotentiary for High Frequency Techniques. The latter would then consult his list and see which laboratories were unemployed, and then post off the specification to one of them. The laboratory would thereupon make an equipment designed without any real knowledge of the operational needs and therefore, in many cases, not meeting them adequately. But much more important than these deficiencies was the fact that most of the possibilities were not realized anyway, because the operational people could not envisage the potentialities of the techniques available,

[9] Tom Burns and G. M. Stalker, *The Management of Innovation* (London: Tavistock Publications, 1961), p. 40.
[10] *Ibid.*, p. 40.

nor could the technical people appreciate the problems of the men who were flying machines.[11]

Beginning with much the same resources and know-how, Britain maintained a lead over Germany in radar development throughout the war.

The structural sources of Hitler and Stalin's pictures of their world—intrinsic to modern totalitarian polities with command economies—can be found, in lesser measure, in other nations of the East and West, in most and least democratic societies, in public and private organizations, and in war and peace. By considering impressionistically some variations among modern pluralist societies, we may be able to locate leads for understanding what is uniquely "cultural" about national responses to intelligence problems. The variations, while easily exaggerated, are apparent in patterns of secrecy and publicity; in the ethnocentrism and time perspectives of elites; in the interplay of interest groups and government; and in administrative devices for finding truth and for defending citizens against the abuse of government power.

One could argue that among free societies the distorting effects of secrecy are felt least in the United States, most in parliamentary democracies with aristocratic traditions, such as Great Britain. In the decentralized federalism of the United States, emphasizing the separation of powers, officials and experts can act out parochial loyalties by "leaking" secret information to the press, by conducting investigations or encouraging exposés of rivals; the publicity consciousness of the American public combines with easygoing libel laws to free newspapermen from normal constraints. Secrets cannot be kept for long. In contrast, administrative or scientific subordinates in Britain owe their main allegiance to the Cabinet and hardly anything justifies public deviation from its policies, let alone the use of restricted information as a weapon in the struggle for power; French officials also enjoy extensive privileges of secrecy.[12]

Unfortunately, the bright light of publicity in the United States on balance may not improve the reliability, relevance, and timeliness of intelligence. The pressure of publicity evokes a counterpressure for the safeguarding of secrecy. The opportunity and desire to expose political enemies and their secrets are forces for extrem-

11 *Ibid.*, p. 41.
12 Price, pp. 138–139; and Rourke, pp. 25–26.

ism in which the truth is assassinated together with the characters of the men who seek it. Edward Shils has given us a sensitive analysis of secrecy-fearing extremism, institutionalized in the loyalty-security programs of the 1950's.[13] He locates its ideological roots in hyperpatriotism, xenophobia, isolationism, fundamentalism, populism, and the fear of revolution. He sees its structural roots (1) in the exposed position of the legislator, who, insecure in status and tenure, must appear as a man of the people and compete vigorously for the scattered attentions of an increasingly massified public, and (2) in the cleavages between Congress and the executive, politician and intellectual, reflected in the baiting of bureaucrats, scientists, and professors and in the estrangement of the intellectual from politics.

The favorable publicity accorded the secret activities of the Federal Bureau of Investigation (FBI) reflects America's ambivalent love-and-fear of secrecy. There is no indication that secret police are popular either in totalitarian societies, where they run the government more than the government runs them, or in free societies, where their activities are constrained by judges, who invoke procedural safeguards, by opposition politicians, who mobilize public opinion, and by traditions of law, which foster a demand for fairness. It is understandable that secret police who investigate, apprehend, and even judge suspects in secrecy, and who devote themselves unabashedly to the control of subversive thought as well as activity, are everywhere hated and feared. The Soviet OGPU ("united department of political police"), later the NKVD in the Ministry of Internal Affairs; the Nazi Gestapo and the SD (security service); and, before 1945, the Japanese "Thought Police"—these were hardly popular agencies and their chiefs never became national heroes.

In free societies, however, the idea of the policeman as hero is not entirely absent. The FBI as crime buster and protector against the Communist conspiracy, the "Mounty" as symbol of the Canadian nation and its frontier spirit, the cool secret agent of the British Secret Service as leading man in the spy thriller—all evoke considerable enthusiasm. But no nation except the United States has celebrated its internal security chief as a folk hero; the uncritical acclaim and adulation given J. Edgar Hoover may be unique.

[13] Shils.

Paradoxically, the publicity consciousness of American culture may enhance the power of secrecy, as I shall attempt to show in Chapter 7.

America's publicity consciousness mirrors more than the peculiarities of its political system and history, more than the central place of the mass media in daily leisure (see pp. 145–151); it is also linked to unusually weak mechanisms for maintaining distance in routine social interaction. Students of American "national character" since Tocqueville have noted the American's desire for quick, if superficial, intimacy (expressed in the urge to reach a first-name basis and in the general democratization of social relations); David Riesman has labeled it the "other-direction" of the "lonely crowd." The incidence of this phenomenon in diverse populations has yet to be ascertained, but it is probably more than mere sociological stereotype. Contrast the Frenchman's appreciation for reserve. Elaborate conventions of courtesy ritualize interpersonal relations and allow persons to keep their distance without being rude. The French sense of privacy—a compound of realism, skepticism, mistrust, individuality, and consciousness of rank—complicates initial contact with Frenchmen in social situations as well as in formal interviewing situations.[14] No such inhibitions keep the American pollster at bay or the American reporter from exposing the private life of any newsworthy figure.

Debates about variations in the balance between secrecy and publicity and its effects on recruitment, morale, and the conditions for intellectual work in various countries and organizations remain inconclusive. Have the American people, with their demand for publicity and their delight in the exposé, "imposed a veto upon the judgments of informed and responsible officials"?[15] Or have public officials and their staff experts acquired so much control over information, such skill in the use of secrecy and publicity, that they can shape public opinion and engineer consensus, in the manner of totalitarian regimes mobilizing enthusiasm in a plebiscite?[16] Does an American administrative leader trained to be suspicious of both

---

[14] Daniel Lerner, "Interviewing Frenchmen," *American Journal of Sociology,* LXII (September, 1956), 187–194; Michel Crozier, *The Bureaucratic Phenomenon* (Chicago: University of Chicago Press, 1964), pp. 214 ff.

[15] Walter Lippmann, *Essays in the Public Philosophy* (Boston: Little, Brown, and Company, 1955), p. 20.

[16] Rourke.

exposés and "secret" information acquire better or worse judgment in the use of intelligence than his counterpart in less publicity-conscious societies? Does a public exposed to the daily din of sensational inside dope acquire propaganditis—a strong, general distrust of the media? If so, is the effect to increase or decrease susceptibility to demagoguery—to enhance or block the development of an informed public opinion and its concomitant, a flow of critical opinion to the top? In the absence of comparative studies, extremely difficult to design in this area, we do not know what balance between privacy and publicity, what arrangements for organizing, processing, and protecting secret intelligence are most and least damaging to the quality of intelligence.

Questions about the effect of secrecy on scientific achievement, a base for high-quality intelligence, also require cross-national comparisons. Although verifiability through open debate is a central norm of science everywhere, we cannot assume that an accent on secrecy threatens good scientific work equally everywhere. The universal culture of science has national expression. If scientists in the Soviet Union are shackled relative to their counterparts in freer countries, they may be free relative to other Soviet citizens. With concomitant prestige and rewards they may suffer little loss from the secrecy consciousness of the regime.

Related to cultural variations in the incidence and effects of secrecy are variations in ethnocentrism among elites. All groups in conflict tend to regard themselves as wholly virtuous and admirable and their adversaries as evil and contemptible;[17] in the modern state ethnocentrism takes the form of national stereotypes which are occasionally a major source of intelligence failures.[18] Such stereotypes helped lead American statesmen to faulty interpretations of intelligence in the period before Pearl Harbor, when Far Eastern specialists were systematically kept from communicating accurate judgments not only because of their subordinate position but because they were believed to be too immersed in "the Oriental point of view."[19] Hitler's view of his opposition as a "Jewish world con-

[17] William Graham Sumner, *Folkways* (Boston: Ginn and Company, 1906), pp. 12 ff.
[18] Hilsman, pp. 103 ff.; Kendall, p. 543; Kautsky, p. 15; Ransom, p. 171; Wasserman, pp. 167–168.
[19] Wohlstetter, pp. 102, 395.

spiracy," the Western view of Hitler's actions as "calculated mad-
ness," the Soviet picture of "capitalist encirclement," American
images of the "Communist conspiracy" (run at first by clumsy
blacksmiths and then, after Sputnik, by technological supermen)—
these may be rationalizations for policies based on more substantial
grounds. But they were sufficiently self-convincing to weigh in
each nation's estimates of the power and intent of the others. If
American leaders in the early 1960's were having a difficult time
putting aside their delusions about a unitary "Sino-Soviet bloc,"
imagine the problem of the xenophobic men of Peking recognizing
the thaw in the Cold War. The example suggests that elites vary
in their ability to transcend ethnocentric molds. The sources,
amount, and effects of such variation would not be difficult to study,
but the task has not been attempted.

Insofar as national ideologies proscribe particular academic disciplines or encourage anti-expert or anti-intellectual fervor, they
shape the quality of intelligence at its source. During the period of
maximum Stalinist terror the Soviet regime wiped out genetics by
persecuting Mendelian deviationists, pronounced quantum me-
chanics inconsistent with dialectical materialism, and, directly
affecting the technical intelligence needed for economic planning,
labeled mathematical economics as bourgeois-idealist. It is difficult
to separate the ideological from the social conflicts here: objection
to particular intellectual perspectives may rationalize a general mistrust of troublesome experts and technicians, rooted in their indispensability, their love of autonomy, and the great social distance
between them and party rulers. Within free societies a similar
phenomenon is found in labor movements and labor parties.[20]
Perhaps the surest generalization is that national ideologies accenting either workers' control or the dictatorship of the proletariat
tend to subvert an effective organization of the intelligence function
by exacerbating universal cleavages between men of knowledge and
men of power.

A final determinant of the use and quality of intelligence that
might be called cultural-ideological is the time perspective of elites.
There may be differences among both nations and corporate bodies
in the extent of foresight typically employed by administrative

[20] Wilensky, *Intellectuals*, pp. 260–269.

leaders. Hans Speier offers some intriguing hypotheses.[21] Distinguishing between "utopian" plans (e.g., based on the belief that international conflict can be replaced by a harmony of interests) vs. non-utopian plans, short-range vs. long-range plans, and "reactive" moves ("muddling through" in response to a *fait accompli* of another power) vs. non-reactive moves, he suggests that (1) military weakness is associated either with long-range plans or with reactive moves, (2) political elites risen from the persecuted are more likely to plan far ahead than elites without a history of counter-elite action, and (3) democratic elites incline toward reactive, short-range, or utopian plans (unless experts with long tenure are very powerful), while elites recruited from a political class (e.g., an aristocracy) aim at longer-term objectives.

Speier's observations imply that the structural roots of variations in time perspective should be sought in the frequency and mechanism of succession. The frequent, routine succession of leaders in stable democracies, while encouraging continuity of past policy, may discourage long-range plans. For ardent planners, look to the Roman emperors more than to American presidents, to General de Gaulle more than to the series of successors to Churchill. The repeated succession crises of unstable totalitarian regimes may also permit little extended planning. If not too frequent, however, succession crises may open up opportunities for long-range planning by executives and staff with training and outlook vastly different from those of their predecessors. It is possible that Mussolini, who ruled for twenty-one years, and Stalin, who ruled for twenty-seven, had a longer time perspective than that of either their contemporary counterparts in modern democracies or the shaky military dictatorships of Latin America. In view of the common assumption that the other fellow has a plan—if not a plan for a Thousand-Year Reich, then at least one for next year—it is remarkable that the sociology of complex organizations has so little to say about the conditions that foster the failure of foresight.

If patterns of secrecy and publicity, ethnocentrism and ideology, and elite time perspective are to some extent "cultural" determinants of the uses and quality of intelligence, the place of interest groups in the political process is primarily a structural determinant.

[21] Hans Speier, *Social Order and the Risks of War* (New York: George W. Stewart, 1952), p. 448.

Among modern pluralist societies that encourage freedom of association, private associations proliferate. Converging on the executive and legislative branches of government, such associations always serve as a source of information, criticism, and support for government officials.[22] National variations here may be linked to the degree of central and regional planning (the more planning, the more essential the cooperation of groups affected by the plan) and to differences in the law affecting administrative use of group representation. But whatever the traditions of planning and the legal status of private advice, these groups everywhere specify policy alternatives and build a case for their preferences. The national variations are principally a matter of the efficiency and openness with which private associations and government officials consult one another and the degree to which the government delegates law-making and administrative functions to such groups. Too little is known about the effect of such differences on the quality of intelligence. However, if we compare West Germany, France, the United States, and Britain—countries with different political cultures—we get the impression that with respect to the role of interest groups in the flow of technical and political information, they do not differ greatly.

In their paradoxical combination of power and pliability, interest groups in Germany are perhaps unique. The power of "peak associations," federations of interest groups, has given a corporatist cast to the administrative life of successive German regimes. A contemporary expression of this is the formal requirement in manuals of procedure of the principal ministries of the Federal German Republic that the government consult the important private associations in the initial preparation of legislative proposals. At the same time, the German administrative system since Bismarck—an elite civil service that was compliant in ideological commitment and legalistic in mentality; a decentralized federal structure that necessitated the development of external controls such as administrative courts—facilitated quick control of local units of government by

22 Reinhard Bendix, *Nation-Building and Citizenship* (New York: John Wiley & Sons, 1964), pp. 131–142. Cf. Henry W. Ehrmann, ed., *Interest Groups on Four Continents* (Pittsburgh: University of Pittsburgh Press, 1958); and David B. Truman, *The Governmental Process: Political Interests and Public Opinion* (New York: Alfred A. Knopf, 1951).

Wilhelm II, Weimar, Hitler, and Adenauer alike.[23] Moreover, the very power of centralized private associations—their virtual incorporation into the administrative bureaucracy of the state—rendered them defenseless against totalitarian incursions; interest groups readily lost their independence. The paradox of power and pliability still remains.[24] The effect on intelligence may be a tendency to concentrate information at the top, as government officials communicate with one another and consult with top leaders of business, labor, the professions, and other interest groups; it may also create a greater gulf of understanding between interlocking elites and ordinary citizens.

Yet, the place of private associations as a source of intelligence is not so different elsewhere. France engages in more national economic planning and has nationalized a larger sector of the economy than West Germany, Britain, or the United States. Trade associations and, to a lesser degree, other voluntary associations have played a major role as sources of information essential to planning. Under the Fourth Republic, the power of interest groups

23 Cf. Herbert Jacob, *German Administration Since Bismarck* (New Haven: Yale University Press, 1963), pp. 200–215; Reinhard Bendix, *Max Weber: An Intellectual Portrait* (Garden City: Doubleday & Company, 1960).

24 In German industrial relations, for instance, we see, on the one hand, a complicated interlacing of employer associations, labor unions, works councils, and labor courts which together administer labor laws and apply regional and national collective agreements. The labor movement is stable, unified, and highly centralized. Union representatives are prominent in parliament, labor ministries, labor courts, and the social security administration. Under a unique scheme of "co-determination," labor representatives also serve on two of the three governing bodies of German firms in the iron, steel and coal industries— a board of supervisors and a managing board. The latter includes a labor director who, while he must be approved by a majority of the labor members of the supervisory board and he continues to hold union membership, is essentially a member of management. At the same time, the strike has withered away in postwar Germany more than in any other major European country. The labor movement remains weak at the local level. Works councils, apart from the unions, administer social welfare agencies of the plant and apply labor laws, thereby tying themselves to management and contributing to the atmosphere of paternalism in many German plants. This system is a natural outgrowth of the labor courts and works councils of previous regimes. For a sense of the continuity of German administrative systems, with special reference to labor problems, see Adolf Sturmthal, *Workers Councils: A Study of Workplace Organization on Both Sides of the Iron Curtain* (Cambridge: Harvard University Press, 1964), pp. 53–85. Cf. Franz L. Neumann, *Behemoth: The Structure and Practice of National Socialism* (New York: Oxford University Press, 1942); and Jacob.

in the face of a divided Parliament and a weak executive caused people to refer to them as "les féodalités"—the "feudal powers."[25] De Gaulle was going to change all that, and under the Fifth Republic the executive was strengthened at the expense of the French parliament, thereby curbing the covert, pervasive influence of *les groupes de pression*.[26] But French interest groups have developed even closer relationships with the bureaucracy. Because of the increased importance of planning and also because of the weakness of non-Gaullist political parties, some groups—especially those in agriculture and labor—have taken on new vitality.[27]

Although the United States relies less on central or regional planning than does France or even Germany, and although its legal framework for interest-group representation is quite different, lobbyists and other contact men serve as major channels of information between private associations and government, especially between competing staffs (see pp. 10ff., 19). Government agencies, no less than congressmen, use interested clientele as sources of intelligence as well as support. That much of this information is self-serving is a risk in all countries.

Several democracies have institutionalized the informational and advisory roles of interest groups in social and economic councils. The Netherlands, France, and Belgium require that the government consult these bodies on a great variety of public business; only in the Netherlands, however, has such a council fulfilled much of its protagonists' expectations. In Belgium, as in France, informal contacts between interest-group representatives and cabinet, bureaucracy, and parliament have been more important.[28]

The British have institutionalized the relationship between private interests and the government in various forms of the Royal Commission (see Chapter 7). Even when coping with the most

[25] Henry W. Ehrmann, *Organized Business in France* (Princeton: Princeton University Press, 1957); George Lavau, "Political Pressures by Interest Groups in France," in *Interest Groups on Four Continents,* ed. by Henry W. Ehrmann, pp. 60–95; and Val R. Lorwin, *The French Labor Movement* (Cambridge: Harvard University Press, 1954).

[26] Jean Meynaud, *Nouvelles études sur les groupes de pression en France* (Paris: Librairie Armand Colin, 1962), pp. 256–64.

[27] *Ibid.,* pp. 244–245.

[28] See the unpubl. paper (Center for Advanced Study in the Behavioral Sciences, 1962) by Val R. Lorwin, " 'All Collors But Red': Interest Groups and Political Parties in Belgium."

sensitive political issues, these commissions display an enviable impartiality. It has been argued that the "political culture" of Britain makes government by commission uniquely successful. Thus, where British parliamentary institutions operate in a more "Americanized" environment, they are somewhat weaker. Canada, for instance, relies on government commissions even more than does Britain. That adoption of British procedures does not always result in British practice is suggested by the partisanship of press and politicians surrounding both some of Canada's Royal Commissions (e.g., the Commission on Bilingualism and Biculturalism) and its Judicial Inquiries set up to investigate scandals such as the Rivard affair (drugs and bribery, 1964) and the Munsinger affair (sex and security, 1966). Designed to investigate the latter case, the Spence Inquiry focused on the romantic involvement of a former associate minister of defense with an alleged female spy, Gerda Munsinger. The Conservative leader of the opposition, Mr. Diefenbaker, whose past behavior as prime minister was under scrutiny, publicly denounced the Spence Inquiry as "errant Mc-Carthyism" and as an instrument of "political vengeance." He went on to repudiate the authority of Supreme Court Justice Spence, and to refuse to cooperate in any way with the inquiry—a reaction highly unlikely in Britain. But to attribute this constraint to British "political culture" is to miss its structural roots: Britain's population is more homogeneous and the status and authority of its elites— many of whose members share a common "Oxbridge" origin—are more secure. Canada is closer to the United States in its more heterogeneous population and in its fragmented, opportunistic, competitive elites. In such structural differences we can find deeper explanations of the relative objectivity, efficacy, and independence of British government commissions and of the occasional willingness of pressure groups to subordinate their private interests to the public interest. In any case, all modern democracies use commissions and similar administrative devices for expert advice, public enlightenment, and social reform. There are numerous adaptations that can make the same technique effective in diverse political settings. (See pp. 167ff.)

Similarly, as all democratic societies face the necessity of defending citizens against abuses of official power, they arrive at common solutions—procedural safeguards and outside checks, some of which are universally applicable and all of which involve a search for information as well as justice. Consider the Ombudsman—an official who investigates citizens' complaints against government bureaucracies and recommends a remedy if he finds the complaints justified (see p. 170 below). While this institution originated in Sweden, apparently analogous institutions have been or can be developed in common-law countries that have inherited the British parliamentary system (United Kingdom, Canada, New Zealand), in countries with federal forms that separate legislative and executive powers (the United States, the Philippines), and even in countries with a well-developed system of administrative courts providing easy access to judicial review (France, West Germany).[29] Problems of managing the welfare state are shared by all rich countries. Those concerned with justice for the citizen develop similar administrative devices for truthfinding and protection against abuse—various guides through the bureaucratic jungle, expediters to unsnarl the red tape and to speed the fair distribution of services.[30]

To recapitulate: In the analysis of intelligence, as in the study of other problems, much of what has been attributed to national character or culture on closer inspection is revealed as a product of variations in economic, political, or social organization. Nothing can be said with assurance in this area, but the following are plausible hypotheses:

    1. Economic organization shapes the types and quality of in-

[29] *The Ombudsman: Citizen's Defender*, ed. by Donald C. Rowat (London: George Allen & Unwin, 1965), p. 10. In the same volume, Fritz Morstein Marx cautions against the hasty "importation of foreign institutions." He emphasizes the difficulties of adapting the Ombudsman to the United States. *Ibid.*, pp. 255–263. These difficulties do not appear to be insurmountable (see pp. 167–172 below), although an American Ombudsman would obviously not solve all our problems of administrative justice and efficiency.

[30] Elsewhere I have argued that in the reluctant welfare state of America, a more aggressive matching of agency to clientele than that afforded by a grievance commissioner may be necessary. Doctrines of economic individualism reinforce structural barriers to the humane administration of health, education, and welfare services. An unusual accent on minimum government, private property, and the free market reinforces our decentralized federalism and our separation of powers, thereby making it difficult to finance public services and making it necessary to channel services obliquely through a labyrinth of local units, each more reluctant than its neighbor to yield a fraction of its autonomy. Wilensky and Lebeaux, 1965 edn., "The Problems and Prospects of the Welfare State," pp. v–lii and 33–44.

telligence. Insofar as market mechanisms, which simplify tasks of rational calculation, are displaced by central planning, planners' tension prevails; contact men who mediate between planners and performers are conspicuous; costs of information collection and processing soar; distortion of information increases.

2. Command economies and totalitarian political systems maximize the force of structural distortions of intelligence—hierarchy, inter-agency rivalry, ideological indoctrination, the passion for secrecy, and the demand for unitary loyalty. Thus, Hitler's Germany and Stalin's Russia epitomize information pathologies. Where the same organizational arrangements and practices appear in democracies, they have similar effects on intelligence.

3. The time perspective of elites and their penchant for rational planning vary, but cultural traditions (e.g., values and beliefs about utopias of world order or domination) explain this divergence less than the frequency and mechanism of succession. Frequent institutionalized succession encourages continuity of policy and discourages long-range plans. Infrequent succession by crisis opens up opportunities both for policy innovations and for long-range plans.

4. In pluralist societies, private associations ("interest groups") serve as a source of intelligence as well as a source of political support for government officials and for each other. Their role in the political process fluctuates with the degree of economic and social planning, and with their legal status in government decisions. While interest groups in West Germany may present a paradox of power and pliability, and while the expertise and independence of interest groups may be incorporated most effectively into government through Royal Commissions in Britain, the effect of such variations on the quality of intelligence does not appear to be as impressive as the contrasts between pluralist and totalitarian societies. If "political culture" shapes the uses of interest groups for intelligence it is in the efficiency and openness with which government taps private advice.

The more clearly "cultural" determinants of the uses and quality of intelligence include the following:

1. Among pluralist societies, patterns of publicity and secrecy—which affect what is said and how it is said in every context—vary greatly. The United States displays an ambivalent love-and-fear of secrecy and a unique degree of publicity consciousness. This cultural

pattern is symbolized by the unusual position of J. Edgar Hoover as folk hero and by the weakness of mechanisms for maintaining social distance in everyday life. Chapter 7 explores the interaction among secrecy, publicity, and the flow of intelligence in both organizations and society.

2. National elites diverge in their ability to transcend ethnocentric molds. Totalitarian elites whose power rests heavily on ideological indoctrination are typically most ethnocentric and xenophobic and thus most restricted in the range of intelligence they command.

3. National ideologies that accent either workers' control or the dictatorship of the proletariat exacerbate universal cleavages between intellectuals and men of power, thereby complicating intelligence problems.

Throughout this book, the richest stock of intelligence failures has come from government operations, especially in foreign policy and national security. This expresses more than mere availability of data (the spectacular miscalculations of foreign offices, the military, and intelligence agencies are spread on the record more often and more fully than the mistakes of industrial firms); it also reflects reality (in international relations modern nation-states are more likely to make costly blunders). All governments—totalitarian or free, parliamentary or not, with planned or less planned economies —are plagued by the pathologies of hierarchy, agency rivalry, and secrecy; all generate an urgent demand for "all the facts" and "short-run estimates." Further, the goals they seek are often vague and the feedback regarding achievement is difficult to interpret. The manufacturer of tricycles can gauge his potential market with reasonable accuracy, look to his sales and earnings as measures of performance; the head of state who chooses to intervene in Vietnam or Cuba is unlikely to be clear about goals, costs, or performance. Defenses of nations against structural and doctrinal roots of intelligence failures in the area of foreign policy are, therefore, universally weak and preconceptions are enduring.

National variations in the use of intelligence bearing on domestic policy may be greater than they are in foreign affairs because the effects of law and of political economy are greater. In the United States, the sharp separation of legislative from executive powers and the great prominence of market mechanisms and unconstrained bargaining among interest groups uncover struggles which in parliamentary democracies and totalitarian societies alike are confined within the executive; this disorderly openness at once sets limits on rational public action and reduces the power of preconceptions.

CHAPTER 7

Intelligence, Freedom, and Justice

I have concentrated so far on the structural and ideological determinants of the amount, kinds, and quality of intelligence. A summary of central themes appears in Chart 2 (p. 175). This chapter views the problem of intelligence in relation to basic tensions of a democratic society. What we think and do in the quest for useful knowledge affects the fate of such values as individual freedom, justice, and privacy. For instance, the intelligence doctrine of "all the facts" lends itself to the demand for publicity; the belief in "short-run estimates" and "inside dope" lends itself to the demand for secrecy. The tension between publicity and secrecy permeates administration, where the executive must deliberate in private at the same time that he keeps his employees informed, and politics, where the policy-maker must tap expert knowledge and protect secret sources at the same time that he briefs reporters and honors the public's "right to know."

The dilemmas of intelligence in a democratic society are most evident in three areas: the maintenance of democratic control of secret intelligence agencies and secret police; the effects of patterns of secrecy and publicity on the development of an enlightened public opinion; and the efficacy of alternative means for discovering truth in the administration of justice—adversary and inquisitorial procedures, the testimony of unchecked experts, and scientific methods. The ideal is to strike a balance in which constraints on the proliferation of secret police, secret agents, and secret files are matched by constraints on the spread of punishing publicity and, further, to devise procedural safeguards that insure the privacy and liberty of the individual confronting a bureaucratic world.

POLICE SECRECY

That the police—private or public, secret or open—are a potential threat to constitutional liberties and to the rule of law has been a strong feeling in the Anglo-American world, especially in early-nineteenth-century England and in twentieth-century America. Nevertheless, there has been in both countries a rise in the power and prestige of the police.[1]

London remained without a police force of any kind until 1829; the individual citizen was to maintain civic order and guard property. If carried out at all, police functions were performed by citizens acting as sheriffs, constables, or magistrates, or as members of militia, posses, watch-and-ward committees, or the Yeomanry (a cavalry force composed largely of small landowners). From the perspective of urban workers these citizen volunteers were particularly vicious in suppressing mobs, riots, and the "dangerous classes" (the poor) by means of volley-firing and saber-charging. Forming a common front with the leaders of the masses, London merchants, too, proclaimed that a police force would mean tyranny, espionage, destruction of individual liberty. In fact, they concerned themselves less about civil liberties than about protecting the mobs that they

[1] On British police see Charles Reith, *A Short History of the British Police* (London: Oxford University Press, 1948); Frederick C. Mather, *Public Order in the Age of the Chartists* (Manchester: University of Manchester Press, 1959), pp. 75–140, 182–225; and Jürgen Thorwald, *The Century of the Detective*, trans. by Richard and Clara Winston (New York: Harcourt, Brace and World, 1965), pp. 35–43. On the police in the United States, see Michael Banton, *The Policeman in the Community* (New York: Basic Books, 1964) and Charles Reith, *The Blind Eye of History: A Study of the Origins of the Present Era* (London: Faber and Faber, n.d. [1952]), pp. 54–129—two British students of law enforcement. Reith is plainly shocked by the American scene; his incredulous tone as he reports police practices underscores the differences between our armed, decentralized constabulary and the unarmed, centralized British police—differences more objectively analyzed by Banton. American police cope with a more heterogeneous, mobile population, operate in a context of weaker consensus regarding morals and laws, and have been more subject to outside political influence.

manipulated and incited to riot in order to embarrass the government when legislation inimical to commercial interests was proposed. Finally, the burgeoning urban industrialists, frightened by the rapid spread of crime, violence, and class conflict, nevertheless perceived that the Yeomanry and similar citizen police were exacerbating all three. (Parish constables were paying deputies to serve for them and the latter soon formed a confederacy in league with professional criminals.) However diverse the sources of hostility to the police, the appearance of the New Police in London in 1829 united all classes in near-universal demand that the Force be immediately disbanded. It is thus remarkable that the British eventually established a centralized efficient, metropolitan police, centered in New Scotland Yard. From a storm of criticism and hatred emerged the most respected police force in the world. Today —although some close observers note a slight deterioration in the relationship between police and public—it is still safe to say that the relatively benign, unarmed "bobby" is held in almost affectionate esteem.

The parish-constable police system was transferred to the American colonies. Although it failed in the mother country, it survived in the United States and can be seen today in the form of no less than 40,000 separate independent police forces. There is little evidence of public abhorrence of the police in nineteenth-century America to match that in Britain. Except for bursts of indignation at the use of private police, state police, and federal troops in strikes and riots, law enforcement officials were not generally objects of hatred. To respectable citizens in rural areas, the sheriff and his deputies— though lacking the omniscience bestowed by their television images —were often heroes. In cities where police were controlled by corrupt political machines, they were nevertheless often responsive to the needs of the immigrant masses—even providing prized careers for them. Hostility comparable to the early British response was delayed until racial minorities migrated to the big cities and, more recently, until the civil rights movement took hold. On the one hand, the police have become the symbol of white oppression of Negroes. On the other hand, the nineteenth-century British image of the "dangerous classes" is now being revived in the United States: anxiety about "crime in the streets" and the corresponding demand for public order and safety have risen, thereby strengthening the position of the police. This is evident in the successful 1966 campaign of white policemen in New York City against Mayor John Lindsay's civilian-dominated police review board. In general, professional police have become a larger fraction of the labor force, more trained in technique and demeanor, more skilled in accommodating themselves to legal constraints. The dramatic rise in their prestige and authority in Britain, the more modest rise in the United States, has paralleled the swift expansion in their command of modern technology. Systematic, scientific investigating machinery—from fingerprinting and ballistics to forensic medicine and toxicology—has proliferated in every society, whether free or not, and everywhere it has increased police capacity for surveillance and control.

In democratic societies, the growth of secret police and secret intelligence agencies has until very recently met with greater resistance or at least with greater dismay. Power, if invisible and therefore not effectively accountable, is generally considered subversive in a duly constituted government. From his experience with the German underground in World War II, Allen W. Dulles observed that "an intelligence service is the ideal vehicle for a conspiracy"[2]—a theme repeated in many attacks on the Central Intelligence Agency.[3] All students of totalitarian societies note that the secret police, drawing on secret dossiers on rulers and ruled alike, is a prime means of social control, at once a way of intimidating the underlying population and ferreting out dissenters within the ruling regime.

We have seen that the technology and manpower for developing a police state are widely available not only to external intelligence agencies such as the CIA and various military intelligence branches but to agencies mainly devoted to domestic intelligence or policing or both, and in government and industry—the Federal Bureau of Investigation (FBI), the Federal Narcotics Bureau, the Secret Service, the up-to-date metropolitan police department or industrial security consultant (see pp. 8ff. and 72ff.). Such organizations are becoming self-consciously "professionalized." Insofar as they

[2] Allen W. Dulles, *Germany's Underground* (New York: The Macmillan Company, 1947), p. 70.
[3] David Wise and Thomas B. Ross, *The Invisible Government* (New York: Random House, 1964).

find their definition of professionalism in efficient crime control, unmodified by a strong commitment to due process of law, they will subvert freedom and justice, or, at best, be indifferent to democratic values.

In the United States, the overcriminalization of the substantive law encourages abuses in the detection of crime. If we declare as crimes numerous acts that many or most citizens do not feel are morally wrong; if these acts do not harm others; and if few know about them or complain about them, we pose an intelligence problem for the police. In a case of murder or car theft the police have initial evidence that the act occurred; in a case of a Saturday-night poker game, they usually have no complaint to lead the way. Without a complainant the police are under pressure to seek out, if not provoke, the crime. Thus, the most frequent and spectacular instances of unconstitutional search and seizure, assembly-line arrest and screening, and advanced electronic eavesdropping occur in the pursuit of prostitutes, numbers runners, drug users, medical abortionists, homosexuals, chronic alcoholics, "vagrants and loiterers"— persons whose conduct, while offensive to the community-at-large, seldom evokes complaints from their purported victims.[4]

Illegal techniques of investigation are also prominent in the search for "subversives." Most important in the present context, the elaborate and typically covert intelligence machinery mobilized by federal detectives and metropolitan police, whatever it accomplishes in the control of professional criminals, is weak for discovering the truth about political crimes or vaguely defined misconduct. The FBI, in its celebrated pursuit of alleged spies and subversives, has stolen letters, tapped the phones of suspects and defense attorneys, protected perjurers, and relied heavily on the evidence of anonymous informers.[5] So faulty is the information it thus obtains that at

---

[4] Cf. Schur.

[5] Rourke, pp. 92 ff.; and Cook, pp. 239 ff., 248, 362, 366–381. Cook shows an insufficient appreciation of the character of the Communist Party when it functioned as an important force in American life; his account is burdened with liberal clichés (e.g., dark hints that Alger Hiss was framed are not persuasive in light of an earlier study—Herbert L. Packer, *Ex-Communist Witnesses: Four Studies in Fact Finding* [Stanford: Stanford University Press, 1962]). *The FBI Nobody Knows* is, nevertheless, a serious indictment of the FBI as a subverter of the law. A similar attack comes to the same conclusions for an earlier period: Max Lowenthal, *The Federal Bureau of Investigation* (New York: William Sloane Associates, 1950). For a more scholarly treatment, un-

the height of the McCarthy era in 1954—after years of FBI screening of hundreds of thousands of government workers and after sensational congressional exposés—only three of the "at least 75" federal employees formally accused of Communist activities from 1948 through 1953 by the House Un-American Activities Committee and the Senate Internal Security Committee had been brought to trial for any crime. Of the scores accused and subjected to trial by publicity, Alger Hiss, William Remington, and Judith Coplon were the only three who could be brought into court. Two others had died. Hiss and Remington were convicted of perjury. Miss Coplon's conviction on two counts of espionage was set aside because the FBI, at first vigorously denying wiretapping, was later forced to admit that some thirty agents had participated in a vast operation of electronic eavesdropping.[6] Even if we accept the argument that illegal means were justified for reasons of national security, the box score for those five years of hysteria does not inspire confidence in the truth of confidential dossiers on political beliefs and activities.

Belief in the informer's evidence, faith in the efficacy of undercover operations, and the weakness of outside criticism and control can sometimes produce absurd results. By the 1960's FBI undercover agents were so numerous in the Communist Party U.S.A. (one source claims that they were approaching a dominant position in the membership[7]) that they unwittingly began to inform on one another.

---

fortunately more restricted in scope, see Bontecou. Other sources provide little more than semi-official celebration of the FBI and its director since 1924, J. Edgar Hoover—e.g., Don Whitehead, *The FBI Story: A Report to the People* (New York: Random House, 1956). Besides using the investigative techniques described above, the FBI has apparently engaged in a good deal of informal intimidation of its critics in Congress and the press—which may account for the paucity of published analyses of its activities, in proportion to the record of responsible criticism of other government agencies, including the CIA. A prime reason that the FBI is so free to intimidate men of power is that it has no strong institutionalized competition. The CIA faces a sometimes resentful State Department and an equally resentful Defense Department. The FBI faces only local police who are unlikely sources of public criticism; the police depend on the FBI for its fingerprint collection, its laboratories for analyzing physical clues, and its training opportunities at the National Police Academy.

[6] Packer, *Ex-Communist Witness;* Cook, pp. 288, 358–362; and Lowenthal, pp. 434 ff.

[7] Cook, pp. 38–45.

The FBI is more than a repository of unevaluated "facts" on the political opinions and affiliations of ordinary citizens. As an operating agency it apprehends violators of federal laws within its jurisdiction (kidnappers, bank robbers) and cooperates with local, county, and state law enforcement agencies in crime control. As an intelligence agency it reports information on sabotage, subversion, and miscellaneous matters to other agencies of government. Not enough is known about the work of the FBI in record keeping, operations, or intelligence to judge its conformity to due process in any of these missions. It is likely that as an operating agency its interrogation procedures are at least as lawful, if not more so, than those of municipal police (see p. 143 below). The FBI's collection and use of unevaluated information is the mission that presents the greatest danger to the rule of law. The temptation to feed the files selectively to political friends in the executive and legislative branches must be very strong and, as we shall see, the use of these files is not always relevant to law enforcement.

In free societies and totalitarian societies alike, there is a general tendency for agencies charged with gathering intelligence on internal security to magnify the internal threat and for agencies responsible for external security to magnify the power of the outside enemy. Thus, the FBI has vigorously publicized a succession of menaces: white slavery beginning in 1910, spies in World War I, the Red Menace of the Palmer era, kidnapping and bank robbery during the 1930's, followed by the most glamorous menaces of all, sabotage and espionage in World War II and internal subversion in the Cold War. While these menaces were of course not fictional, the publicity given them was not closely related to their magnitude. In its sensational exaggerations, the FBI is like its counterparts elsewhere—intelligence agencies that try to persuade administrative leaders that they are imminently threatened by one conspiracy or another, one crime wave or another. What is perhaps unique is the FBI's success in publicizing its secret activities as a national cause beyond criticism and its chief as "Public Hero Number One."[8] In 1940, in the days when U.S. senators felt that it was politically safe to complain publicly of FBI activities, Senator Norris castigated J. Edgar Hoover as "the greatest hound for publicity on the Ameri-

[8] *Ibid.,* pp. 34–35, 163 ff.; Lowenthal, pp. 388–400.

can continent today."[9] Extralegal extensions of FBI power have plainly been enhanced by skillful press agents. And there is no question that this agency, spurred on by its fans on Capitol Hill, has intruded the police power into the realm of ideas.

EXECUTIVE SECRECY[10]

The demand for secrecy in administrative life has intensified everywhere, and the range of executive action shrouded in secrecy has widened. In an era of world wars, small wars, and cold wars, state secrets have become more important and more numerous. At the same time the vast expansion of executive power, evident in the multiplication of regulatory and investigative agencies, means that the government now collects information on the private business of millions of citizens and hundreds of organizations.[11]

[9] Whitehead, p. 177.

[10] The most sober treatment of this problem is Rourke.

[11] The problem of executive abuse of private information will be aggravated as electronic listening devices permit more efficient collection and as electronic data processing permits more efficient storage and retrieval. In an article from *Tape Recording*, February, 1965, "Is Big Brother Taping You?" Arthur Whitman claims that " 'in 1962, a House committee reported that at least 5,000 phones in Federal offices in Washington were bugged—not by Russians, but by American bureaucrats spying on each other. Not long ago, an official of the San Francisco Telephone Company estimated that 10,000 firms in Northern California alone monitor the calls of their executive employees without the executives' knowledge.

" 'Thus, the use of bugs and wiretaps has spread into other areas [beyond suspected spies and known criminals]:

" 'Classrooms in many school systems are bugged so that principals can flick a switch and listen to class discussions without the knowledge of teachers and pupils. Going the educators one better, students have, on many occasions, used hidden recorders, to "get the goods" on teachers suspected of liberal political views and other heresies.

" 'Business firms regularly bug the offices of key rivals to learn trade secrets or get inside knowledge about sales and other strategies.

" 'Corporations . . . monitor . . . conversations at spots where employees congregate; such as, timeclocks, locker rooms, cafeterias, and washrooms. One large company . . . installed bugs in the toilet paper containers in the ladies' "john."

" 'Politicians, each election season, tap phones and bug campaign headquarters to learn rivals' plans and strategies.' " Quoted in U.S. Senate, *Invasions of Privacy*, pp. 17–18. The extent of such activity is impossible to

In defense of executive secrecy, government officials generally invoke national security, the protection of their confidential informants, and the need to avoid tipping off criminals under investigation. We have seen that such secrecy can block the search for truth as well as facilitate it. A more important justification for executive secrecy is the clear need for confidential communications in executive deliberations. If men at the top feel vulnerable to attack for advice tentatively offered in private, they will keep quiet or avoid the strong expression of opinion; good intelligence will be lost. Passionate debate behind closed doors is as much a requirement of informed policy as the "right to know." The principle for a democracy is public accountability for decisions secretly arrived at, combined with offsetting public debate and court constraints on the executive use of secret information in the prosecution of individual citizens.

If secrecy sometimes serves truth, it can also serve the ends of justice. In fact secrecy is necessary to protect the individual from arbitrary and capricious use of official power. If the FBI, the Secret Service, and other law enforcement agencies reveal the malicious gossip and unchecked allegations in their confidential files, innocent men are harmed. If regulating agencies irresponsibly spread confidential economic intelligence, they harm businesses by revealing trade secrets and financial data to business rivals; they can also give their own regulating officials a chance at windfall benefits. If all organizations, whether public or private, disclose information in personnel files, they may damage the job applicant, by letting his employer know that he has applied for another job, by publicizing other embarrassing information that has no bearing upon the applicant's fitness for his work.[12]

While executive secrecy is sometimes necessary for truth, justice, and freedom, its costs to these same values are usually very high. The law of ascending secrecy in administrative behavior assures

estimate, but the testimony of government officials, business executives, and detectives before the Senate subcommittee suggests that it is increasing. Further, the technology employed is correspondingly more sophisticated. Telephone wiretaps, miniature tape recorders, and hidden microphones may become obsolete with the perfection of laser beams which when aimed at a distant room and converted into sound waves can tap a private conversation. *Ibid.*

[12] Rourke, pp. 33-35, 102 ff.

abuses that more than cancel the gains. Overclassifying information related to national defense is notorious. Two explanations apply to all classification systems.[13] First, penalties for release of state secrets are always more severe than those for over-classification. Second, by stamping it "top secret," the originator of a document advertises its importance and, hence, his own. In America, such motives for giving documents the highest possible security classification are rampant. An estimated million federal employees may classify executive records. Tons of trivial messages repose in the files in undeserved splendor.

Congress is a weak check on executive secrecy. The legislative branch makes much resentful noise about the hidden operations of bureaucrats and carries out innumerable investigations, but it has, in fact, tended to accept uncritically the need for secrecy in matters of national security—an expanding category.[14] The courts themselves provide a minimal check: they have given the government "what amounts to an absolute privilege against the disclosure of information related to matters of military or diplomatic significance."[15] They argue that the proper conduct of foreign relations demands restrictions and that effective law enforcement at home demands that the government be allowed to keep secret the names of those who supply information on illegal activities, even in criminal proceedings. The confidential information of informants, spies, stool pigeons, and *agents provocateurs,* must be revealed only where the government calls them to testify—a principle reaffirmed in the controversial case of *Jencks v. the United States.*[16] In general, the three branches of the American government, more publicity conscious than most governments (see pp. 116–118), are overwhelmingly on the side of secrecy.

[13] *Ibid.,* pp. 63–99, 107.
[14] *Ibid.,* p. 86.
[15] *Ibid.,* p. 88.
[16] 353 U.S. 657 (1957). Cf. Rourke, p. 97. In recent years the Supreme Court has cautiously moved toward modifying the government's privilege of hiding the identity of the informant. In *Roviaro v. United States,* 376 U.S. 53 (1957) and again in *Rugendorf v. United States,* 376 U.S. 528 (1964) the Court held that where disclosure of the informer's identity or of the contents of his communication is essential to a proper defense, the court may require such disclosure. If the government chooses to withhold the information because of the needs of official secrecy, the court may dismiss the action.

Secrecy designed to prevent the demoralization of the civil service can occasionally backfire; it can be manipulated by demagogues. When the late Senator McCarthy was asked for evidence to support his widely publicized accusation of disloyalty against eighty-one State Department employees, he said the evidence lay in the secret loyalty-security files of the Executive branch.[17] None of Senator McCarthy's charges was ever proved. One case almost came to trial, that of Val R. Lorwin. But just before it was due to be tried, the Assistant Attorney General in charge of the Criminal Division asked the Federal Court to dismiss the indictment because the Justice Department attorney, attempting to convince the Grand Jury to return the indictment, had made misstatements on two major points.[18]

In this, the only case on the famous list of eighty-one that even approached a courtroom, the "evidence" of the secret informer was both central and worthless. Lorwin's accuser, Harold W. Metz, insisted on remaining anonymous; he refused to confront his victim. Had the government not protected his anonymity, his accusations

[17] Rourke, pp. 71–72.
[18] The attorney, William A. Gallagher, incorrectly contended that two FBI agents could attest that Mr. Lorwin had "Communist connections" and that it was useless to bring Lorwin before the Grand Jury, since, "like all Communists," he would claim the Fifth Amendment. Both Lorwin and his wife had testified, under oath, vigorously and in detail, about their political beliefs and activities. Gallagher's statement to the Grand Jury that they might "take the Fifth" was therefore nonsense. Joseph C. Harsch speculates about the reasons for these misrepresentations: "Mr. Gallagher was a hold-over from the Truman Administration. He obtained the indictment on December 3, 1953 [under a statute punishing false statements to the government, whose requirements for conviction are less demanding than those under the perjury statute]. As a Truman hold-over, Mr. Gallagher's job security may have been in question. December of 1953 was in the wake of Attorney General Brownell's Chicago speech and the launching of the Harry Dexter White case against Mr. Truman. Around the Department of Justice it is suggested that perhaps Mr. Gallagher was trying to be more zealous than an Attorney General who was trying to be more zealous than the Senator." "State of the Nations, Case No. 64." *Christian Science Monitor*, May 27, 1954. Gallagher was dismissed. For details on the whole case, see *Departments of State and Justice, the Judiciary, and Related Agencies, Appropriations for 1956*. Hearings before the Subcommittee of the Committee on Appropriations, House of Representatives, 84th Congress, 1st Session (Washington: Government Printing Office, 1955), pp. 16–18, 85–96; Harsch, *op. cit.; The New York Times*, May 26, 1954; and Warren Unna, "Lorwin Vindication Followed 6-Year Fight to Clear Name of Connection with Reds," *Washington Post and Times Herald*, May 30, 1954.

would have been discredited more quickly, to the advantage not only of the accused but of the government.

Like so many now-forgotten episodes of the McCarthy period, this fantastic affair was reminiscent of Kafka's *The Trial*. In 1949, miscellaneous "derogatory material" in the Lorwin file had been thoroughly investigated and rejected by the burgeoning loyalty-security machinery. In 1950, when McCarthy unleashed his list, the administration reinvestigated all names on it. This reinvestigation turned up a statement by Metz.

The Metz accusation, the anonymous basis of Lorwin's travail for more than three and a half years, apparently grew out of a confused recollection in 1950 of something that Metz said had taken place fifteen years earlier. A former fellow-graduate student of Lorwin at Cornell University, Metz had briefly shared an apartment with the Lorwin couple in 1935. He now asserted that one evening, when he was a tenant of the Lorwins, Lorwin had told him that a group of people at the apartment were holding a Communist Party meeting, that he (Lorwin) was a Communist, and that he had then shown Metz his Communist Party card. Informed only that someone was ready to state that he had made these incriminating remarks, Lorwin had to list systematically everyone he had known in depression days and engage in a guessing game. The Metz affidavit, its contents surfaced but its source still anonymous,

. . . led to a lengthy series of investigations and hearings which ended on March 28, 1952, when Mr. Lorwin was given a complete clearance both for loyalty and for security. Ninety-seven witnesses had appeared on behalf of Mr. Lorwin during the proceedings. The Metz charge broke down on two grounds—first, evidence that Mr. Lorwin had been a militant anti-Communist who had helped defeat Communist efforts to secure control over several labor unions, and, second, the technical fact that Mr. Metz said the card he saw was red. Further evidence indicated that in 1935 the Socialist Party used a red card, whereas the Communist Party used a black-covered booklet. Mr. Lorwin's membership in the Socialist Party had been an open and acknowledged fact.[19]

Fifteen years after the alleged event, it took some digging to prove that black was black and red was red. Guessing that Metz was his accuser, Lorwin also gathered evidence to show that Metz was accustomed to using the label "Communist" not only for Com-

[19] Harsch, *op. cit.*

munists but for Socialists, New Dealers, and even liberal Republicans. In late 1953, at the height of the McCarthy era, the
Department of Justice resurrected the Metz allegation in order to
obtain an indictment charging Lorwin with making false statements
to the Loyalty-Security Board. At least the criminal indictment
ended the anonymity of Metz. In response to pretrial motions by
Lorwin's attorneys, the Federal District Court forced the Department of Justice to give Lorwin the Metz statement. Not until 1954
—after more than three years of fighting a shadow, after the
McCarthy attack, and after the Justice Department representative
had obtained his indictment from the grand jury—could Lorwin find
out that Metz was his accuser and exactly what Metz had told the
FBI.

Lorwin chose to suffer years of expense and diversion from his
normal scholarly interests to clear his name rather than to resign
quietly and to fade away as did many other victims of anonymous
informers.[20] Although fear is said to have pervaded liberal circles
in the McCarthy era, an impressive number of men and women had
shown their courage and principles by offering sworn testimony in
favor of Lorwin in the administrative hearings; many were even
eager to testify in his favor in the expected criminal trial. Most of
these people were then employees of the government, in the State
Department among other agencies, who knew what would happen
to their careers if they testified and a miscarriage of justice resulted
in Lorwin's conviction.

At the end, the Department of Justice may have sacrificed attorney Gallagher in order to protect accuser Metz; the latter had
good connections, having served in high research posts in the
Hoover Commission and the Republican National Committee. Not

[20] See Senator Kefauver's and Henning's remarks in praise of Lorwin. *Congressional Record,* Proceedings and Debates of the 83rd Congress, Vol. C,
Part 6, June 2, 1954, p. 7516, and Appendix, Vol. C, Part 20, June 30, 1954,
p. A4759. Another bizarre case where the victim successfully fought back is
described in Edward Lamb, *"Trial by Battle": The Case of a Washington
Witch-Hunt* (Santa Barbara: Center for the Study of Democratic Institutions,
Occasional Paper, April, 1964). A prominent Democrat and wealthy businessman, Lamb spent about $900,000 in a four-year campaign to prove that the
"derogatory information" in the files of Senator McCarthy, the FBI, and the
Federal Communications Commission about his "Communist associations" was
false and, further, that the FCC had hired, intimidated, and suborned witnesses
in hearings on Lamb's fitness as a broadcast licensee.

the smallest irony of the case was the fact that McCarthy had received the endorsement of the Communist Party when he was elected to the Senate, before he made a career of Communist-hunting, while his victim, Lorwin, was a "premature anti-Communist," known in the thirties as a vigorous opponent of the CP.

The Lorwin case is more than a vivid demonstration of the principle that the accuser should face the accused. It also shows the fallacy of the doctrine of "all the facts"—the idea that raw or unevaluated facts should be piled up in the files of intelligence agencies for possible use in some loosely defined emergency (see pp. 62–63). When the FBI engages in a search for physical evidence in specific crimes of kidnapping or car theft, its renowned technical efficiency is no myth, and its procedures of interrogation are often models of due process. Indeed, Chief Justice Warren complimented the Bureau for compiling over the years "an exemplary record of law enforcement while advising any suspect or arrested person, at the outset of an interview, that he is not required to make a statement, that any statement may be used against him in court, that the individual may obtain the services of an attorney of his own choice, and more recently, that he has the right to free counsel if he is unable to pay."[21]

But where the conduct under investigation concerns political opinions and affiliations—where there are no illegal acts spelled out in the statutes or the law books to predetermine the direction and limits of the inquiry—the police have no special competence and should not be made to bear responsibility for collecting information.[22] The problem of collecting "raw data" in such cases is illustrated in the remark of a hard-working FBI agent who was interviewing an experienced civil servant about the politics of a friend under investigation. After listening for hours to the patient and knowledgeable description of the New Dealish beliefs of the man he was investigating, the FBI agent held his head and said,

[21] *Miranda v. Arizona,* 384 U.S. 436 (1965), pp. 45–46. The Chief Justice was answering the contention that the restrictions of due process would hamper law enforcement. He referred to a letter from the Solicitor General outlining FBI interrogation procedures.

[22] For description of the training and techniques of FBI and other government agents engaged in this sort of work and analysis of the limitations of the material they collect and file, see Bontecou, pp. 75–100, 310–320—the most detailed and balanced treatment of this topic.

" 'Oh, all these ideas, I wish they'd put me back on straight criminal work.' "

All modern governments find discreet loyalty-security investigations by specialized intelligence agencies necessary in filling sensitive positions. If the informant is competent and the agent sophisticated, some gain in government security may result. Where neither party is up to the task—the agent not a student of politics, the informant not trustworthy—all that results is mischief. And where the effort reaches dragnet proportions—aiming at targets too numerous for competent investigation, indiscriminately embracing information from the sophisticated and the naïve, the dispassionate and the prejudiced, the sane and the insane—the mischief becomes monumental.

Executive secrecy used to protect professional gossips and liars is obviously costly for individual freedom and justice. An equally important cost is that executive secrecy obscures great issues of public policy and permits sustained masking of blunders.[23] It is a barrier to public appraisal of executive behavior. Public policy regarding national defense, foreign intervention, and arms control—more generally, the effectiveness of foreign policy—is concealed in a heavy mist of security. What was termed the "credibility gap" in the Johnson Administration's relations with the public is not peculiar to any one president; it is a growing problem for modern governments, as foreign policy becomes central to domestic politics and welfare, and the blanket of secrecy is spread wide.

Secrecy subverts not only an informed public opinion, but an informed academic community—both crucial to the solution of problems of intelligence. Scientists and academicians are typically opposed to executive secrecy because scholarship by nature is public not private; for good reason, academic norms hold that the truth is best approximated through open debate about evidence and the free interchange of ideas. That is why Harvard University has adopted a formal policy refusing classified research, and why in the mid-sixties faculties of other universities, among them Stanford University and the University of Pennsylvania, pressed for similar policies. Research on weapons systems and chemical-biological warfare presents especially sticky issues; the university community

---

[23] Cf. Aaron Wildavsky, *Dixon-Yates: A Study in Power Politics* (New Haven: Yale University Press, 1962).

argues that if it must be carried on in secret, the government should undertake the task itself, without subjecting universities to the pathologies of secrecy. When security-conscious governments restrict scholarly and scientific exchange, they block the progress of knowledge.

If national security more and more depends upon scientific achievement and if scientific achievement depends upon open communication among scientists working on related problems, security is best served by minimizing secrecy. In the long run, the practitioners of scientific secrecy conceal from themselves more than they hide from their enemies.

PUBLICITY

Too much publicity can be as great a threat to justice and truth as excessive secrecy. "A free society," Shils suggests, "can exist only when public spirit is balanced by an equal inclination of men to mind their own business."[24] How a nation resolves the tension between publicity and secrecy, between concern about the facts of public life and appreciation of privacy, affects the quality of daily life, of leisure, and of politics.

Insofar as public criticism of policy is a source of information in the formation of that policy, and insofar as public opinion shapes the selection and decisions of leaders in a democratic society, the focus of publicity—the issues emphasized and those blocked out— is a problem of intelligence. Insofar as sensational press coverage impairs judicial proceedings, publicity is a problem of justice.

Publicity and Justice

Courts have been impressed with the danger of Star Chamber proceedings. While in matters of national security they emphasize the government's privilege of secrecy, in more routine actions courts strive to protect defendants from secrecy, the traditional weapon of despotic government. Publicity, however, is just as devastating a weapon and the court is not the only place where

24 Shils, p. 21.

justice is administered. With the extension of government regulatory activity and congressional investigations into every area of political, economic, and social life—from alleged subversion to gambling, drugs, prices, and TV quiz shows—publicity is an increasingly powerful sanction, a pitiless punishment for individuals suspected of illegal deeds or merely of unpopular thoughts. The judge who "throws the book" at a prisoner to get his name in the paper, the legislator who launches an investigation into some easy symbol of evil (alleged Communists, racketeers, radical students, "welfare chiselers"), the government official who uses the threat of exposure to extend the range of law enforcement—all are engaged in the arbitrary administration of justice; all are undermining the rule of law.

Publicity particularly punishes an expanding segment of modern economies—large firms sensitive to public relations, such as manufacturers who compete by marginal product differentiation (autos, drugs, appliances, gasoline, razor blades) and advertising and consulting firms and brokerage houses that depend wholly on their reputation. In fields covered by the Security and Exchange Commission, the Food and Drug Administration, or the FEPC, the mere threat of exposure is enough to chasten many of these enterprises. Of course, publicity or the threat of it can also be benign: the Social Security Administration can inform beneficiaries of their rights; the FEPC can occasionally make a noncomplying employer stop discrimination through informal hearing with minimal fuss; the Food and Drug Administration can stop the consumer from using potentially harmful drugs until administrative suspicions are proven right or wrong. Moreover, not all firms exposed to publicity are entirely defenseless; when a Ralph Nader launches an auto safety campaign, General Motors does not lack resources for the counterattack.

The unjust use of publicity is a more urgent problem where the target is a defenseless individual and the publicist is a government official who, though not authorized to accomplish his aim through legal prosecution, yet achieves it through adverse publicity. There is little doubt that sensational legislative exposés stigmatizing expressions of unpopular views subject individuals to risks of insult, ostracism, and loss of employment.[25] Proof of innocence seldom

[25] Aside from the record of successful character assassination, we have a careful survey of a cross-section of the American people in 1954 that found

removes the scars of such public accusations and public "trials."[26] The late Senator Joseph McCarthy manipulated the mixture of secrecy and publicity by hearing witnesses in secret executive sessions and by then emerging with a press release on the day's lurid revelations. To say that this cuts both ways—that the publicity that launched Senator McCarthy's career also brought him down in the drama of the Army-McCarthy hearings[27]—is to ignore years of irreparable damage to individual reputations and careers, incalculable harm to government morale, a loss of talent in the Department of State and other sensitive agencies, a legacy of rigidity in foreign policy, the prolonged life of irrelevant doctrine. When men in the fifties are fired for advocating a more flexible policy toward China designed to reduce her isolation, men with similar views in the sixties do not press them with quite so much force. In this way the publicity that results in injustice to individuals reduces the quality of intelligence available to policy makers.

The courts have assumed that whatever its excesses, whatever the unwarranted injury to the innocent, publicity is essential for the proper flow of information to the electorate; they have, therefore, been very reluctant to recognize it as coercive and to restrict it. Until that recognition is widespread, there will be little substance to court condemnation of "exposure for exposure's sake"[28] and no effective measures to insure the accused access to defensive publicity.

Publicity, the Mass Media, and Public Opinion

Extravagant publicity injures innocent individuals and blocks intelligent public appraisal of policy. This is not only because of the expanding scope of investigative and quasi-judicial agencies but also because of the prominence of promotion in modern economies and the salience of the mass media in daily life and leisure. Two problems need to be separated here: first, the power of government publicity is greater on foreign than on domestic issues; and, second,

---

considerable intolerance not only of Communists but of Socialists, atheists, and suspected Communists who swear to their innocence. Samuel A. Stouffer, *Communism, Conformity, and Civil Liberties* (Garden City: Doubleday & Company, 1955).

[26] Cf. Bontecou, pp. 148–152.

[27] Rourke, p. 121.

[28] *Watkins v. United States,* 354 U.S. 178 (1957).

for foreign and domestic policy alike, the media emphasize crises over the routine truth.

In the promotional mania devoted to the private life and the goods and services that fill it, the government's voice is often lost. Today private outlays for advertising and public relations are almost equal to our current expenditures on public schools (elementary and secondary): each is about $18 billion annually.[29] The more abundance, the more activity to increase the desire for it. This is reflected in the way we spend our leisure time. The sheer arithmetic of media exposure (press, radio, film, television) is striking. Nine in ten American homes average five to six hours—over a third of each waking day—with the television set on. Additional time goes to reading newspapers and magazines.

The size of this frenzied promotion effort and the astonishing amount of exposure are well known. The impact on the quality of intelligence—on the information available both to the public and to responsible administrative leaders—is more difficult to judge.

Regarding domestic issues, we can agree with Professor Galbraith[30] that in the United States, perhaps to a unique degree, the promotional resources available to government are puny compared to those of the private sector—if we confine ourselves to the public civilian services. A sustained daily din whets our appetite for cars. Who whets the appetite for rapid transit, for the preservation of our natural resources, for more adequate hospitals? There is a big campaign to "put a tiger in your tank," only a small campaign to put more teachers in the schools. Basically what is seen, heard, and read is shaped by the promotional aims of the media—the desire to create wants in the private civilian sector. The occasional documentary or feature story on poverty or race, conservation or welfare, is typically confined to what television broadcasters call the "Sunday ghetto" or,

[29] In 1957–58 current expenditures on public schools were $11.7 billion; total advertising expenditures for all media were $10.3 billion. Machlup, pp. 104, 275. Business executive Harold S. Geneen estimates that the 1965 expenditure by business on advertising was $15.5 billion, with another $2 billion spent on PR. "Weak Spots in Communication," *San Francisco Chronicle*, May 13, 1966. The total outlay for 1964–65 elementary and secondary day schools was $18.6 billion. *Fall 1964 Statistics of Public Elementary and Secondary Day Schools*, U.S. Office of Education, Department of Health, Education, and Welfare (Washington: Government Printing Office, 1965).

[30] John Kenneth Galbraith, *The Affluent Society* (Boston: Houghton Mifflin, 1958).

if more favorably scheduled, it seldom penetrates the permeating noise. On the other hand, on issues of foreign or military policy, government-initiated publicity is typically overwhelming; and here the media, at least in the short run, tend to follow the official consensus.

There is a world of crisis journalism that has come to dominate the center of our political stage. This is a world where most of the "events" reported with an air of breathless urgency, do not happen at all in any spontaneous or natural sense; in the phrase of Daniel Boorstin,[31] they are "pseudo-events"—made to happen by journalists in order to satisfy the demand for sensational inside dope, by public relations men in order to build up their clients or knock down their enemies, or by government officials in order to sell or justify policy.

A dominant feature of crisis journalism is the failure to distinguish the trivial from the significant. If we take a hard look at the number of significant political crises since World War II, it comes down to a dozen or so: abroad, this would include Greece, Turkey, Israel, Korea, Hungary, Berlin, Suez, the Congo, Cuba, Vietnam, China; at home, the number could not be much larger. Yet hardly a week passes that some ephemeral pseudo-crisis does not scream from the headlines: the TFX contract is put on a par with arms control negotiations; every minor explosion on Cape Kennedy gets more coverage than the one that counts, the population explosion; the weekly big lies of a Joe McCarthy are solemnly reported on a par with a presidential message on the State of the Union; a bribe of a vicuña coat costing a few thousand gets as much attention as widespread price-fixing that costs hundreds of millions. The petty details of the operations of a vulnerable civilian agency such as the Office of Economic Opportunity are eagerly ferreted out; cries of "welfare scandals" and corruption in the war on poverty are as common as they are exaggerated. Public scrutiny of military expenditures ten or twenty times as large as the cost of the entire skirmish with poverty is both more cautious and less penetrating.

When the media present an appropriate balance of attention, when they cover real crises extensively, they tend to honor the claims of secrecy, and to adopt a semi-official consensus, especially in international affairs, until the real world intrudes forcibly in the

[31] Daniel Boorstin, *The Image or What Happened to the American Dream* (New York: Atheneum, 1962).

form of visible resources committed, dramatic attacks by friendly statesmen, and other signs that things are not quite what the government has claimed. In the Vietnam affair, the television networks, which have otherwise done an impressive job of covering distant events, hewed close to the official rhetoric until late 1965; it was a crisis not a war; it was an invasion by the unified forces of Communism, not a complicated civil war with successive foreign interventions; there was a Vietnamese government with a wide base of popular support, not a shaky despotism; and America was reconstructing the country, not destroying it. Only when a few courageous senators went against the tide and began to advise and dissent did the media come through with some balanced coverage.[32]

We do not know whether media crises and real-life crises alike are becoming part of an undifferentiated world of mass entertainment and promotion—in which selling soap is like selling a candidate image, exposing Communists is like exposing General Motors. We can guess, though, that there is a strain toward the depoliticization of political life. Their preoccupation with sales promotion gives the broadcast media a bland, often fuzzy tone. For instance, the necessity of not offending anyone, of emphasizing what everyone can accept, makes the television networks choose heroes who are strangely apolitical. Think of the most popular TV shows of recent years—Westerns. The heroes are frontiersmen—rural, self-reliant, anarchic, unconstrained. An impatient, simple-minded irresponsibility pervades the performance of these characters—and maybe it is not too much to suppose that the Good Guys–Bad Guys mentality they encourage spills over into domestic and international politics. Ronald Reagan's ride across the political scene in 1966, like Barry Goldwater's in 1964, had the earmarks of the "adult" Western— whose hero is also above politics and who promises to clean up the mess with one quick draw.

Finally, it is possible that the revival of World War II movies on the Late Late Show, the glorification of the joys of hand-to-hand

---

[32] The strength of the network consensus was evident as late as December 14, 1965, when CBS risked a debate on a special program, "Where We Stand on Vietnam." Six network correspondents, released from the network's ban on the expression of personal opinion, agreed that there was no realistic alternative to the existing American policy. The only unmuted voice of criticism was that of James Cameron, a British journalist. Neil Compton, "TV Chronicle," *Commentary*, XLI (April, 1966), 84–86.

combat on the prime-time shows, condition us for the daily dose of real-life slaughter—our sensibilities so atrophied that all we see on the six-o'clock news is just another Bad Guy biting the dust.

Even the sensational investigations by publicity-hungry congressmen are placed within this oversimplified allegorical frame of Good Guy vs. Bad Guy. I was struck by the confusion displayed by some Detroit citizens we interviewed in 1960 when we asked them to recall the late Senator Joseph McCarthy. " 'Did you ever watch him on TV or follow him in the press?' " " 'Yes,' " they said. " 'And at that time, how did you feel about Senator McCarthy?' " " 'Oh, he really put Costello on the spot,' " or " 'He was a fine man—it's too bad he didn't make Vice President.' " In their world, the media world, one investigation is like another; McCarthy as prosecutor is no different from Kefauver—or, for that matter, Perry Mason.[33]

It is these intangible effects that lead critics of the media to use such words as "trivialize" and "vulgarize" in describing the values the media communicate and, in general, to label press, radio, and television the "mass media of distraction." The media impact on the quality of public opinion and the effect of the latter on government policy are elusive problems, difficult to study; they are nonetheless significant for an understanding of modern society.

ADMINISTRATIVE DEVICES FOR TRUTH-FINDING

That the excesses of unwarranted secrecy and punishing publicity at once obstruct justice for individuals and stifle the criticism necessary for enlightened public opinion; that government officials, however limited in their promotion of domestic civilian programs, can dominate debate on national security; that the media vacillate between silence in honor of security and competitive screaming about un-

33 These few interviews are merely suggestive; of 678 lower-middle-class and upper-working-class men interviewed, only a dozen mistook the McCarthy show for another. The overwhelming majority of the 1354 men interviewed in various samples had roughly accurate recollections. Twenty-two per cent of the total and 31 per cent of the middle mass recalled McCarthy with enthusiasm—this in 1960, several years after his death. See Harold L. Wilensky, "Measures and Effects of Social Mobility," in *Social Structure and Mobility in Economic Development,* ed. by Neil J. Smelser and Seymour Martin Lipset (Chicago: Aldine Publishing Company, 1966), pp. 98–140, 16n, and 35n.

differentiated crises and pseudo-events—these developments unmistakably affect the quality of intelligence. Less dramatic is the erosion of devices for truth-finding in everyday administrative life. The adversary principle, in courts and administrative agencies alike, for instance, is slowly losing its pre-eminent place—a tendency related to the elaboration of the intelligence function.

Informal adjudication and fact-finding are becoming more prominent in all modern societies. Overloaded with work and information, modern governments are moved to settle things expertly and informally; the regulated parties, in turn, want to avoid the expense, uncertainty, and publicity of formal litigation and to cultivate the good will of regulatory officials. To the extent that quasi-judicial procedures are pivotal to administration, it is vital to learn more about them. The relative merits of various devices for symbolizing justice and fairness (the consumer counsel, the Ombudsman) and for discovering "facts" (reliance on technical experts, legislative investigations, public commissions, and courts) are little understood.

Because legal contexts illuminate more general problems in truth-finding, consider first the adversary process typified by a jury trial. Through partisan contest conducted according to rules each counsel makes the strongest case he can before an impartial judge and jury. The deficiencies of adversary procedure are obvious. A circus atmosphere may develop as attorneys become preoccupied with press releases rather than legal briefs, with courtroom histrionics rather than reasoned argument ("When you can't win a case, jaw it"). Further, adversary procedure, because it rests on partisan initiative, limits the kind of evidence presented; the contending parties define the issue and say what is relevant. Finally, the procedure is limited for resolving technical issues; a trial ". . . is not well adapted to the intelligible sequential ordering of complex factual data. . . . Either it leaves out too much to be informative or it includes too much to be orderly."[34] It may bog down in well-established, trivial detail. But these limitations, not inevitable, are offset by the overriding advantages of partisan advocacy, including the opportunity to test the credibility of witnesses through cross-examination. In or out of court, the adversary process is the best way to assure that assertions are exposed to systematic scrutiny by men with countervailing interests who are motivated to press hard.

[34] Packer, *Ex-Communist Witnesses*, p. 230.

In the popular view, science is a more disinterested and, therefore, better institution for uncovering truth. But major advances in scientific theory often come from men insisting on opposing models of physical or social nature. They are often polemical; their debate is sometimes carried on in the spirit of armies at war, as Priestley's holding action against Lavoisier's theory of chemical elements, Marx's invective about German idealism, and Weber's insistence on the role of religious ethics in economic life all illustrate.[35] Three characteristics of science, however, mark it as different from adversary procedure and limit its use in everyday administrative life as well as in the court. First, although individual scientists may be contentious, they are oriented more toward truth than power. The judge or the official must give some weight to political consequences of decisions; the scientist is ideally oblivious of such considerations. Second, differences in science are settled by colleagues; scientific truths rest ultimately on the consensus of the competent. It is thus too technical for many administrative purposes; the capacity to assess scientific truth is well developed only among those immersed in its traditions and techniques. Finally, because scientific propositions take a long time to establish, science is not an ideal procedure for urgent organizational and judicial decisions. In short, although adversary proceedings do not involve critical experimental tests, they resemble science in their systematic regulation of the clash of views, and they have the additional advantage of sensitivity to political interests, greater availability to non-expert officials and judges, and speed.

Despite their considerable merit for truth-finding, and even greater merit for justice, adversary systems are being weakened or eliminated in several areas of modern life. This is evident in four developments: the bypassing of courts; the movement to incorporate vague social and moral purposes in specialized courts; the use of nonlegal knowledge and processes; and the substitution of inquisitorial for adversary methods in many contexts.

The first problem is rooted in shortages of judicial manpower and budget. Sheer crowding of the court calendar has forced litigants with urgent problems to turn to other tribunals. Commercial arbitration is neither as fair nor as accurate as court procedure, but

[35] Cf. Kuhn, pp. 150, 158, 165–171, *passim*.

it is quicker and cheaper; business finds it expedient for settling a huge volume of controversy. Similarly, legislators unhappy about slow-moving justice have set up scores of quasi-judicial agencies.[36] Some of these arrangements reduce adversariness; others, like arbitration, retain it.

Remaining controversies still overload the courts, evoking pressures to find substitutes for adversariness. The case for substitutes is strong—for example, in personal injury and accident cases, which constitute the core of the court calendar. In a perceptive examination of the traffic safety problem, Moynihan[37] argues that it is not merely that the auto industry's venality has assured that an estimated one out of every three automobiles manufactured in Detroit ends up with blood on it; not merely that the public is ambivalent about the dangers of driving and the question of safety; nor even that until 1966 the government evaded the problem by substituting exhortation for the collection of data on accidents and safety design and for money and experts to devise serious programs. The root of the difficulty is that we have never applied the necessary standards of evidence and self-criticism; we have instead treated the automobile as a source of taxes and, with the rise of the State Police and the spread of insurance company doctrines of individual liability, as an issue of criminal law enforcement. The result is an intense concentration on the guilt of individual drivers, a futile effort to punish the violator, and a paralyzing overcrowding of court calendars. Great gains are possible if we ". . . put to an end the present idiocies of armed police arresting and often imprisoning hordes of citizens who are then hauled before courts incompetent to judge a problem that is in any event impossible to define in legal terms."[38] In many, perhaps in most cases we simply cannot ascertain just how an acci-

[36] E. Eugene Davis, "Legal Structures in a Changing Society," in *Society and the Law,* ed. by F. James Davis *et al.* (New York: The Free Press, 1962), p. 220. Occasionally legislators create new tribunals that bypass the court because they hope to produce more favorable decisions. The impetus behind workmen's compensation boards and commissions, for instance, was the hope of progressive law-makers and their constituents that such agencies would take the worker's side. See the unpubl. diss. (University of California, Berkeley, 1966) by Philippe Nonet, "Administrative Justice: A Sociological Study of the California Industrial Accidents Commission."

[37] Daniel P. Moynihan, "The War Against the Automobile," *The Public Interest,* No. 3 (Spring, 1966), pp. 10–26.

[38] *Ibid.,* p. 26.

dent occurs, much less apportion the blame among the manufacturer, the victim, the accused, and a host of poorly understood and sometimes unavoidable mechanical, chemical, thermal, and electrical causes. The best principle is to seek the truth only where there is a reasonable chance of finding it. It might be desirable to set up a compensation system for victims of accidents which does not depend on determination of fault—a system already in effect in the province of Saskatchewan.

Excluding traffic safety, an increasing part of the criminal law system is being removed from the safeguards of adversary procedures—notably the time after arrest and before trial when the police and the district attorney decide whether the suspect will go to court or not. That more than 80 per cent of suspects plead guilty suggests considerable pressure to "cop a plea"—that is, accept informal promises of lesser charges and lighter penalties in exchange for reducing the workload of the DA and the courts.[39] To explain his heavier sentence on the one of five defendants who refused to plead guilty, a federal judge remarked: ". . . if in one year, 248 judges are to deal with 35,517 defendants, the district courts must encourage pleas of guilty. One way to encourage pleas of guilty is to establish or announce a policy that, in the ordinary case, leniency will not be granted to a defendant who stands trial."[40] That some innocent men are thus persuaded to plead guilty is plain.[41]

Another threat to adversariness is the need of the courts to incorporate nonlegal knowledge into the process of decision. Part of

[39] Donald J. Newman, "Pleading Guilty for Considerations: A Study of Bargain Justice," in *The Sociology of Punishment and Correction,* ed. by Norman Johnson, *et al.* (New York: John Wiley & Sons, 1962), pp. 24–32; Skolnick, pp. 13–14.

[40] *United States v. Wiley,* 184 F. Supp. 679 (N. D. Ill., 1960). This decision was reversed on appeal.

[41] In 1959, again in response to overcrowding of the court calendar, a special committee of the American Bar Association suggested ten remedies, three of which would reduce adversariness: (1) encouragement of jury waivers; (2) use of pretrial conferences; and (3) disposition of some cases by lawyers acting as referees, commissioners, auditors, or arbitrators. E. Eugene Davis, p. 221. For the case against such measures see the data and arguments in Hans Zeisel, Harry Kalven, Jr., and Bernard Buchholz, *Delay in the Courts* (Boston: Little, Brown, and Company, 1959). They claim that the time that would be saved is grossly exaggerated and, in any case, the gain would not offset the erosion of the ideal that litigants should have free access to courts and qualified judges.

the humanitarian trend of the twentieth century has been the infusion of social and moral purposes, particularly the rehabilitative ideal, into judicial and police procedures. This is evident in juvenile courts, in family courts, and in the occasional use of psychiatric-clinical knowledge and social science in all courts. The danger lies in an increasing reliance on unchecked experts.

Now that we have set up children's courts with the ideology of treatment and rehabilitation rather than punishment and revenge, we face a new dilemma. Even in the well-run, well-staffed court for children, there is a conflict of values between paternalism and justice, linked to a conflict between two approaches to the truth—the clinical therapeutic truth of the psychological sciences and the adversary truth of the lawyer. An enlightened juvenile court judge in Pittsburgh sums up the distinctive philosophy of the juvenile court in a way that highlights the problem. He points to the difference between the question, " 'Did you or did you not?' " and the quite different question of the juvenile court, " 'Why, under what circumstances, and what can be done to help?' "[42] The conflict in functions is not hard to see, though it is extremely difficult to resolve. Should the court assume that the delinquent act is a symptom of underlying psychological or family maladjustment, take jurisdiction over an increasing variety of cases, and seek to operate as a sympathetic substitute parent, with adjustment of any youngster who comes before it as the aim? Should it, in short, be a generalized social agency? Or should it instead be primarily a dispenser of justice, giving careful attention to whether it has a right to intervene in the first place and, if so, respecting the rules of evidence. Are not the facts of delinquent behavior often in dispute? By virtue of its authority and the training of its functionaries, is not the court on firmer ground when it sticks to the legal questions (what is the legal status of the child, who shall have custody, does the community have the right to intervene in his life, and so on), leaving social services to agencies specially equipped to diagnose and plan treatment?[43]

[42] Gustav L. Schramm, "Philosophy of the Juvenile Court," *Annals of the American Academy of Political and Social Science,* CCLVI (January, 1949), 107.

[43] H. L. Wilensky and C. N. Lebeaux, *Industrial Society and Social Welfare* (New York: Russell Sage Foundation, 1958), pp. 220–222. For an extended,

Most critics of the children's court feel that some balance between the conflicting goals of due process and rehabilitation of the young is possible and desirable. They suggest the following procedural reforms: "regulate detention practices, advise parents and children of the right to counsel, circumscribe the use of questionable evidence, separate out determination of jurisdiction from treatment, protect the confidentiality of records, and at the same time maintain an informal and private atmosphere consistent with the best protection of children."[44]

Family courts present similar problems. Under restrictive divorce laws, the application of the adversary principle in a search for the guilty party is misplaced. More liberal divorce laws recognize the large number of non-contending parties for whom separation or divorce is desirable for everyone involved, for parents and for children for whom the continued marriage is also a punishment. Even under the most liberal divorce laws, however, there are numerous cases in which conflicts between husbands and wives over the desirability of divorce, over custody of children, or over alimony are severe and where the best interests of the spouses and children are difficult to determine. If these cases are not to be dealt with as just another form of litigation but as social-clinical problems, whose values shall prevail, what knowledge is relevant, and what safeguards for justice shall be used? The marriage counseling and reconciliation procedures now gaining ground—on the surface a civilized approach to family breakup—depend entirely on the availability of well-trained personnel, which does not now exist and which legislators would be reluctant to pay for if it did exist.[45]

The need to avoid premature confidence in "scientific" testimony is even more apparent in the use of psychiatrists in commitment proceedings or in the determination of criminal insanity, and in the

---

recent statement of the conflict between due process of law and individualized treatment, see David Matza, *Delinquency and Drift* (New York: John Wiley & Sons, 1964), ch. 4. Cf. Alfred J. Kahn, *A Court for Children: A Study of the New York City Children's Court* (New York: Columbia University Press, 1953), especially chs. 10 and 11; and Paul W. Tappan, *Juvenile Delinquency.* (New York: McGraw-Hill Book Co., 1949).

[44] Alex Elson, "Juvenile Courts and Due Process," in *Justice for the Child: The Juvenile Court in Transition,* ed. by Margaret K. Rosenheim (New York: The Free Press, 1962), p. 99.

[45] W. Friedmann, *Law in a Changing Society* (Berkeley and Los Angeles: University of California Press, 1959), p. 228.

use of social workers and criminologists in the administration of probation and parole. At the heart of the controversy regarding psychiatric testimony is the fact that the psychiatrist is attempting to get the community to accept a highly tentative theory of behavior and behavior change. Like the advocates of children's courts, psychiatrists focus attention on the criminal not the crime, seek to rehabilitate rather than punish, and want to replace prisons with hospitals. They despair of the legal definitions of insanity because they are obsolete, because legal rules are posited on the theory of free will and responsibility rather than on a theory of psychological determinism, and because they are forced to testify in legal rather than psychiatric terms.[46]

At the other extreme, critics like Dr. Thomas S. Szasz discount psychiatric claims. They argue that there is no evidence that mental disease causes criminal behavior; that there is no evidence that traditional psychiatry can reform criminals or noncriminals.[47] Further, they think that the law should not attempt to abrogate its own responsibility by shifting the burden of proof onto the expert.

Courts maintain a position short of full acceptance of psychiatric testimony.[48] And it is likely that jurors who hear insanity cases, while they pay careful attention to psychiatric testimony, decide whether or not the person is sane primarily on their own assessment of whether the defendant was able to act rationally in the commission of legally proscribed acts. Jurors tend to think that the psychiatrist has an investment in finding something wrong with everybody.[49] Where the judge acts without a jury, as in commitment hearings, there may be greater willingness to accept the psychiatrist or other physician's opinion as conclusive. In 1965 over 13,000 Californians were committed to mental hospitals. Commitment generally progresses through four stages. First, the person is brought to

[46] C. Ray Jeffrey, "Criminal Justice and Social Change," in Davis et al., Society and the Law, pp. 290–298. See cases and comments in Monrad G. Paulsen and Sanford H. Kadish, Criminal Law and Its Processes (Boston: Little, Brown, and Company, 1962), pp. 312–353.

[47] Thomas S. Szasz, Law, Liberty, and Psychiatry (New York: The Macmillan Company, 1963), especially pp. 91–190. See also George Dession, "Psychiatry and the Conditioning of Criminal Justice," Yale Law Review, XLVII (January, 1938), 319–340.

[48] Friedmann, pp. 166–177.

[49] Rita M. James, "Jurors' Assessment of Criminal Responsibility," Social Problems, VII (Summer, 1959), 58–69.

a hospital observation ward for seventy-two hours. Next, two medical examiners diagnose and make recommendations to the court. They need not be psychiatrists, but "may be drawn from a panel of local physicians, staff doctors from a mental hospital, private psychiatrists, or any combination of these and others, including retired general practitioners."[50] It is necessary only that they be medical doctors. These examinations frequently take place on an assembly-line basis, and in general they average less than ten minutes.[51]

Third, the examiner makes a recommendation to the court. The California Assembly Subcommittee on Mental Health Services noted that the criteria for commitment are vague and that there is a presumption of mental illness and a tendency to recommend commitment. "In the subcommittee's Survey of Commitment Courts, observers reported that in 78 per cent of the cases the examining physicians recommended commitment. In only 11 per cent of the hearings were alternatives even discussed by the examining physicians. In contrast, the observers administering the Subcommittee's questionnaire stated a belief that alternatives to commitment would have been desirable in 47 per cent of the cases."[52]

The final step is the court hearing. The survey found that the average length of commitment hearings in California was 4.7 minutes; one-third took less than two minutes each.[53] Judges are inclined to accept the examiners' recommendation, because, among other things, those committed are generally too poor to hire contending lawyers, and the public defender is overworked.[54] Thus an average professional assessment of less than fifteen minutes may result in a lifetime incarceration in a mental institution.

Similarly, in post-conviction dispositional proceedings—when probation as an alternative to imprisonment is granted or revoked or when a prisoner is released on parole—the administrative agen-

---

[50] *The Dilemma of Mental Commitments in California: A Background Document*. Subcommittee on Mental Health Services, California Assembly (Sacramento: Department of General Services, Documents Section, 1966), p. 27.

[51] *Ibid.*, pp. 29–31. See also Thomas J. Scheff, "The Societal Reaction to Deviance: Ascriptive Elements in the Psychiatric Screening of Mental Patients in a Midwestern State," *Social Problems*, XI (Spring, 1964), 401–413.

[52] California Assembly, *The Dilemma*, pp. 42–43.

[53] *Ibid.*, p. 43.

[54] *Ibid.*, pp. 43–50.

cies often use no adversary procedure. They rely on probation officers with varying degrees of training whose reports are largely beyond the challenge of the defendant.[55]

A final kind of expert knowledge that would diminish the adversary quality of the trial is that provided by social science. The Supreme Court's attention to the "Brandeis Brief" set the precedent that judges may take notice of nonauthoritative, extra-legal sources of social information—"all matters of general knowledge."[56] The Brandeis Brief was designed to establish that a legislative act was reasonable, as shown by the fact that responsible persons held opinions and made assertions which supported its judgments. In principle, however, social-science evidence could go as well to the truth of the facts asserted, and increasingly is admitted for that purpose. Nevertheless the influence of social science on legal decision-making is still limited. Lawyers generally object to the use of social-science data in court on the grounds that the judge has neither the time nor the skill to make an independent investigation of the data he notes and, more important, when data are submitted in a brief and not as evidence presented for the record, they cannot be impeached nor can countervailing data be offered.[57] Social scientists who have written on this issue tend to feel that the courts should take more cognizance of social-science expertise than they do. They argue that the rules of evidence lag far behind scientific standards of evidence and that adversary procedure is better for discovering values than for discovering matters of fact.[58]

[55] For an excellent analysis of the tension between a system of individualized disposition and a fair hearing in an adversary proceeding, see Sanford H. Kadish, "The Advocate and the Expert: Counsel in the Peno-Correctional Process," *Minnesota Law Review*, XLVII (January, 1961), 803–841. For discussion of the legal problems, see Ernst W. Puttkammer, *Administration of Criminal Law* (Chicago: University of Chicago Press, 1953), pp. 220–230; and Paulsen and Kadish, pp. 168–181, 198–209.

[56] *Muller v. Oregon*, 208 U.S. 412 (1908). The case involved a law on hours of work for women. Brandeis, as a consulting attorney to the state of Oregon, cited reports of public investigating committees, books and articles by medical authorities and social workers.

[57] Paul Freund, "The Brandeis Brief," *On Understanding the Supreme Court* (Boston: Little, Brown, and Company, 1951), pp. 86–92. Anon. note, "Social and Economic Facts—Appraisal of Suggested Techniques for Presenting Them to the Courts," *Harvard Law Review*, LXI (February, 1948), 692–702.

[58] Edward W. Cleary, "Evidence as a Problem in Communicating," *Vanderbilt Law Review*, V (April, 1952), 277–281. Cf. Arnold M. Rose, "The Social

The issues in the use of data from psychiatry and social science are not fundamentally different from issues in the use of any expert testimony; they are difficult questions of the state of knowledge in the relevant discipline and the degree of consensus among the competent. Toxicologists can disagree about the effects of a poison as much as sociologists might disagree about the meaning of a survey of prejudice. Indeed, the court might on some issues place more confidence in expert social-science data that it now excludes and reject some of the opinions of leading citizens that it now admits. For instance, in 1952 the NAACP asked the Elmo Roper organization to undertake an objective survey of public sentiment in Marion County, Florida, the scene of a pending retrial of Walter Irvin, a Negro accused of raping a white woman.[59] The survey aimed to provide a basis for concluding either that Irvin could obtain a fair trial in Marion County or that the community had so prejudged guilt or innocence that a fair trial would be impossible. The survey also included adjoining Lake County (the scene both of the alleged crime and of the first trial) and two counties in northern Florida (Gadsden and Jackson) far from the action. In the context of an interview on national and state issues, a cross-section of whites in each county was asked questions about the rape case and about the contrast case of Sheriff Sullivan, a white man accused of taking bribes in Dade County. A small cross-section of Negro adults (N = 151) was interviewed in Marion County only. Selected results revealed that prejudgment among whites in the Irvin case was significantly higher in Lake and Marion counties (43 and 63 per cent said, " 'I feel sure he is guilty' ") than in Jackson County (17 per cent) and Gadsden County (25 per cent). Prejudgment in the Sullivan case did not exceed 18 per cent in any county and within each county was lower than prejudgment in the rape case. Negroes were more worried about what might happen to a juror in both cases than were whites, but Negro fears were very much higher in the Irvin case than in the Sheriff Sullivan case (e.g., in answer to the question " 'Do you think anybody on the jury in the Irvin case

---

Scientist as an Expert Witness," *Minnesota Law Review,* XL (February, 1956), 205–218.

[59] Julian L. Woodward, "A Scientific Attempt to Provide Evidence for a Decision on Change of Venue," *American Sociological Review,* XVII (August, 1952), 447–452.

would get away with it if they voted "not guilty" or do you think something might happen to them if they did?' " 84 per cent of the Negroes vs. 16 per cent of the whites expressed fear that something might happen). In general, the pattern of response for a variety of questions was consistent with the argument of the defense for a change in venue. The judge allowed the survey director and field supervisor to describe their methods in court, but when the findings were to be introduced, he sustained the district attorney's objection: since the interviews were anonymous, no respondent could be connected with opinions recorded on the questionnaire, and therefore no cross-examination was possible. The survey results were ruled out as hearsay evidence. Later a parade of leading citizens testified that the state of opinion in the county was such that a fair trial could definitely be had. Change of venue was denied; Irvin received his "fair trial" and was convicted.

My argument, then, is not that social science provides weaker evidence than that commonly admitted into court. Nor is it that social research is necessarily "softer" than physical science, sample surveys always less rigorous than forensic ballistics, the clinical insight of a psychiatrist less valuable than the practiced eye of a handwriting expert. It is instead that in all the examples discussed above —in juvenile court and in family court, in psychiatry, social work, and social science alike—there is danger that the claims of experts will be accepted uncritically. Where inquisitorial procedures replace adversary procedures—that is, where the judge himself takes responsibility for eliciting truth—it is important that the inquisitor be expert enough to evaluate the uses and limits of the knowledge he extracts. There is the further need to find equivalents to adversary procedures so that experts do not remain unchallenged. .

The question of court use of nonlegal knowledge in nonadversary proceedings is part of a broader problem in public administration: what institutional arrangements will improve the quasi-judicial and fact-finding operations of all branches of government?

The ultimate assurance that experts will be questioned fruitfully lies in a pattern of political pluralism: a diversity of strong, independent interest groups representing a significant division of values and engaged in open conflict and competition. Perhaps the epitome is labor-management relations. A great many officials, flanked by their experts, undertake visible confrontations, using techniques of private negotiation, conciliation, and arbitration, as well as public propaganda and persuasion. Clashing goals are rather well defined; adversary methods of truth-finding are dominant.

Two radical contrasts to this pluralist pattern are most dangerous for the purposes of intelligence and justice. In the first case an organization has or seems to have a monopoly of information and relies on its own unchecked expertise. We see this in the making of foreign policy and in such agencies as the CIA and the FBI; the pathologies of secrecy combine with excessive reliance on specialized house intelligence to maximize the power of preconceptions (see pp. 24ff. and 48ff.). In the second case, the public interest is diffuse, and a purported expertise is given heavy weight, not because there is a monopoly of information—real or fancied—but because no contending groups provide diverse versions of the truth. Into the void pour the most parochial pressures. For instance, the public interest in highways is mixed and vaguely defined. Everyone wants them but not if they sweep through one's backyard. The downtown businessman is pleased that automobiles have access to his business, but suspicious that they might have better access to some suburban shopping center; in any case, he is unhappy about the rush-hour crush and the parking scramble. The average American is delighted by the $47 billion plan to build nonstop, limited-access, high-speed freeways. But his dream of going anywhere quickly and conveniently at the touch of an accelerator is shattered when too many others have the same idea at the same time; the psychological wear and tear of the journey to work is oppressive. City officials and urban planners favor roads, too, but they are concerned when highway programs eat up valuable land and displace people without providing new sources of city tax revenues. They are also vaguely uneasy about air pollution. In such situations, it is imperative to devise administrative structures that invite the clash of expert opinion and include an adversary system to dramatize issues and define the public interest. In the absence of such safeguards, a potent nationwide lobby in 1956 was able to mobilize public sentiment for the Interstate Highway System embracing both urban and rural areas. The lobby included auto manufacturers and their 64,000 local car dealers, gasoline companies, tire producers, the state motor clubs, highway contractors and highway department officials in city halls and state capitols, the trucking industry, the cement and asphalt companies, and the many businesses and industries that profit from cars and roads. Described as "old-fashioned" were plans to rebuild rapid transit facilities; ignored was the unwritten law that added roads demand added parking space and the two together merely invite a new overflow of automobiles.

That highway engineers became so powerful during the subsequent decade can be attributed in part to the vacuum of intelligence and power created by the typical state highway commission as well as by the continued failure to formulate broad national and state transportation policies. In California, the Highway Commission, a group of laymen appointed by the governor, has final responsibility for route locations. Although in the mid-sixties this Commission was one of the more independent-minded in the nation and although the San Francisco Bay Area was the scene of a lively highway revolt, the technical people of the Division of Highways continued to dominate the decisions. As in many other states, the Commissioners have no staff of their own to develop critical evaluations of proposals from the highway engineers who, left to their own devices, would put a highway through the Washington Monument.[60]

In official fact-finding for public enlightenment the problem is not merely to open up a wide range of policy alternatives but to create incentives for persistent criticism of evidentiary value. None of the major administrative alternatives is perfect; each has some advantages.

A legislative investigation has two advantages over a court: first, because it is nonadversary, it is broader in scope; second, it more effectively engages public attention. Theoretically, winning or losing is not the immediate problem. So witnesses speak more freely; what appears to be a coherent narrative is recorded. But politics and publicity and the occasional temptation to use unverifiable information

[60] For discussion of the effects of the technical nature of decisions on the quality of intelligence, see above, pp. 79–81. For an excellent case study of the role of engineers, planners, and private interests in the location and design of an intercity freeway in and around St. Paul, see Alan A. Altshuler, *The City Planning Process: A Political Analysis* (Ithaca: Cornell University Press, 1965), pp. 17–83. The apparent clarity of technical standards of the engineers (traffic service and cost) and their sense of rectitude overwhelmed less-focused and less-coordinated interests and beliefs.

from unidentified witnesses are crippling disadvantages.[61] Preparation by legislators and their staff is typically casual and unsystematic. The proceedings are too often free-ranging but fuzzy, free-wheeling but incompetent, public but unfair, effective but irresponsible.

The advantage of an agency hearing over a jury trial is its expertise. Instead of a group of twelve people assembled for one case, it is a continuing body whose cumulative experience presumably gives it competence. If the issue is complex and technical, as in rate and route proceedings in regulated industries—indeed, as in all government decisions regarding the allocation of economic resources—and the aim is to arrive at guidelines for future behavior rather than to judge past behavior in the individual case, administrative hearings are a good compromise between the trial and the legislative investigation. Even here, however, if the administrative agency is removed from the general constraints of political pluralism (the CIA, the FBI) or lacks enough independence to render a critical judgment (the ICC, the FCC and other government commissions staffed by the industries they regulate), it is a weak source of justice in individual cases and only moderately useful for public enlightenment.

For official fact-finding and public education, a more meaningful compromise is to move out of conventional channels of investigation and communication toward men of independent mind and stature—a strategy commonly used to overcome the pathologies of hierarchy and specialization (see pp. 45–53 above). The British provide two models: the Tribunal of Inquiry and the Royal Commission of Inquiry. The United States has used a variety of government commissions, with varying composition, function, and result. And, although its scope is narrow, the review boards set up by a few American labor unions deserve attention as sources of organizational intelligence and justice.

The British use commissions to find facts rather than to apply sanctions; they keep such bodies more or less free of political pressures. A Tribunal of Inquiry is the device for investigating serious government scandals. It is typically chaired by a Justice of the High Court; its members are in effect appointed by the Cabinet. Its fact-finding, mainly adjudicative, aims to provide an orderly account of

[61] Cf. Packer, *Ex-Communist Witnesses*, pp. 221–231.

what happened. Facing quasi-political issues, these Tribunals adopt methods of procedure somewhat more flexible than those of the courts. But they almost always observe such normal safeguards for witnesses as the right of cross-examination by counsel. At the end, they issue public reports of their findings. Their record of thoroughness, objectivity, and respect for the rights of the accused has excited the admiration of a number of students of government.[62] The British seldom resort to the device of the Tribunal; in recent years one investigated an allegation that public officials had accepted gifts in return for favorable official action, another investigated the improper disclosure of financial information.

An older and more common investigatory instrument is the Royal Commission of Inquiry, used chiefly to investigate social problems or new problems of policy and to prepare the way for major legislative innovations.[63] It may exist for a few months or several years. Its members are drawn from all segments of the British elite outside Parliament; they are sophisticated experts or persons of eminence in the judiciary, universities, government, labor unions, business, the professions, and welfare.[64] Where there are strong conflicts of interest on the issue, the members are likely to be representative—the Commission on Liquor Licensing included representatives of unions, temperance societies, the liquor industry, and social workers, as well as government experts—but even in such cases they see service more as a civic duty than as a means to fight traditional battles. The Royal

[62] Lindsay Rogers, "Congressional Investigations: The Problem and Its Solution." *University of Chicago Law Review*, XVIII (Spring, 1951), 464–477; Herman Finer, "Congressional Investigations: The British System." *University of Chicago Law Review*, XVIII (Spring, 1951), 564, 568–570; Telford Taylor, *Grand Inquest: The Story of Congressional Investigations* (New York: Simon and Schuster, 1955), pp. 292–294; and Packer, *Ex-Communist Witnesses*, pp. 236–237.

[63] Charles J. Hanser, *Guide to Decision: The Royal Commission* (Totowa, New Jersey: The Bedminster Press, 1965); and Hugh M. Clokie and J. W. Robinson, *Royal Commissions of Inquiry: The Significance of Investigations in British Politics* (Stanford: Stanford University Press, 1937). Cf. Finer, p. 554; Taylor, pp. 290–291. Among other issues, Commissions have dealt with national health insurance (1924), awards to inventors (1946), control and ownership of the press (1947), capital punishment (1949), taxation (1951), marriage and divorce (1951), the law relating to mental illness and mental deficiency (1954), and doctors' and dentists' remuneration (1957).

[64] Hanser, pp. 182, 258–259.

Commission is designed to bring disinterested common sense, data, and good judgment to bear on major social issues. Its fact-finding, mainly educative and legislative, aims to provide a basis for public policy. Reinforcing its independence, it usually employs its own staff and counsel.

The typical Royal Commission transcends current "political realities"; it is years ahead of what is currently acceptable. Although a few Commissions may have been diversionary—using studies as a way to avoid action—many have stimulated major social reforms. Two impressive recent examples are the Wolfenden Report on sexual deviance, whose recommendations touched off eight years of public debate culminating in legislation that abolished all penalties for homosexual behavior between consenting adults, and the report of Lord Robbins in British universities, which questioned traditional elitist assumptions and became the basis for a marked expansion of British higher education.[65]

A combination of expertise, independence, and access to the highest councils of state makes the Royal Commission an indispensable source of intelligence for both the public and the government. Several observers note, however, that the adaptation of British experience to American needs would be difficult.[66] Rivalry between the White House and Congress means that an investigation set up by one is viewed as a threat to the other. And Congress zealously guards its traditional investigatory powers. In the absence of a parliamentary form of government to mitigate conflict between legislative and executive branches, dispassionate fact-finding is politically dangerous.[67] Yet many American government commissions have

[65] Martin Trow, "Second Thoughts on Robbins: A Question of Size and Shape," *Universities Quarterly*, XVIII (March, 1964), 136–152. The Robbins Committee was not technically a "Royal Commission" officially appointed by the Crown, which cannot be discharged by a succeeding Government. It was the second level in the ranking of advisory bodies; in this instance, the government felt no need for the prestige of "Royal" origin. But such special committees have the same high-caliber, unpaid membership, independence, and standards as the Royal Commission. The several kinds of British commissions are alike in their broad functions. Cf. Hanser, pp. 35 ff., 51–53, 86.

[66] Telford Taylor, pp. 285–287; Packer, *Ex-Communist Witnesses*, pp. 241–246.

[67] Packer suggests a system of *ad hoc* tribunals that permits initiation by either branch subject to a speedy check by the other (e.g., a veto within a fixed time). To reduce conflict and increase independence, members

been able to perform impressive services. In the early decades of
this century, the findings of numerous Industrial Commissions study-
ing labor conditions led to significant reforms. In recent years, such
commissions have provided continuous expert advice (the President's Science Advisory Committee, a statutory body with fixed-term
memberships), evaluation of government operations (the committee headed by Emanuel Piore of IBM to assess the work of government science laboratories), and fact-finding (presidential boards
established to deal with emergency strikes).[68] Perhaps the closest
approximation to the British Royal Commission is the "blue-ribbon"
study commission that confronts a big social problem and makes
policy recommendations. One of the best of these in recent years
was the national Commission on Technology, Automation, and
Economic Progress. Despite its mixed labor-management-public
composition (members included Walter P. Reuther of the United
Autoworkers, Thomas J. Watson, Jr., of the IBM Corporation, and
Whitney M. Young, Jr., of the National Urban League), it issued
a trenchant statement of domestic economic problems.[69] Sociology
Professor Daniel Bell, a member of this commission, describes its
operations and lists some general functions of all such study groups,
which cannot be adequately performed by other government agencies or by Congress. First, the study commission provides a means

---

would be drawn from a standing panel of one or two hundred persons
from private life, designated in equal numbers by the President, a Senate
leader, and the Speaker of the House; each tribunal would have its own
staff and counsel and "the power to subpoena witnesses and documents,
to take testimony under oath, to compel testimony as to which the privilege
against self-incrimination is invoked by granting immunity from criminal
prosecution, and to obtain such material from the files of the FBI and
other Government agencies as it may deem pertinent to the subject of inquiry
and to the testimony of witnesses called before the tribunal" (p. 245). Procedures would depend on whether the purpose is to investigate alleged mis-
deeds of individuals or to analyze a social issue. Presumably each purpose would
require a different approach to the facts. Where damage may be inflicted on the
individual, he must be accorded the opportunity to participate in the process
meaningfully and effectively by presenting evidence concerning his particular
case; where legislative rules are to be formulated, it is appropriate to rely on
more general knowledge, statements of probability, and representative cases. Cf.
Kenneth Culp Davis, *Administrative Law Treatise,* Vol. II (St. Paul: West
Publishing Company, 1958), pp. 353–363.

[68] Daniel Bell, "Government by Commission," *The Public Interest,* No. 3
(Spring, 1966), p. 6.

[69] *Technology and the American Economy,* I, February, 1966 (Washington:
Government Printing Office, 1966).

for direct representation of "functional constituencies," increasingly important in the power structure of modern society. Second, it permits the government to explore the limits and possibilities of action with groups that can prevent or facilitate change. Third, it focuses public attention on certain issues and mobilizes support for particular policies without closing off discussion and hardening positions. Finally, it involves nongovernmental elites in the formulation of public policy.[70]

These functions are more difficult to execute but also more essential in a decentralized political system characterized by a strong division of powers and by erratic swings between excessive secrecy and excessive publicity. Illustrating the difficulties is the controversial Gaither Committee, a group of distinguished citizens who in 1957 presented to the President and the National Security Council a classified report on American defense requirements.[71] The report differed sharply from government policy in its estimate of the Soviet threat and the appropriate size of the defense budget. Drawing upon RAND's research on the effectiveness and vulnerability of air bases (see pp. 36–37 above) and upon other data, the Gaither Report forcefully urged that American missile sites be hardened and dispersed and that our limited-war capacity be increased, thereby indirectly challenging Secretary Dulles's policy of massive retaliation. The Eisenhower administration tried to keep the report secret. Operating agencies saw the civilian outsiders as too far out of touch with their problems and resented their interference. Although the Gaither Report significantly influenced the analysis of strategy by defense intellectuals, although its new interpretation of the facts may have encouraged the administration to take a fresh look at our defense posture, it naturally did not have an instantaneous impact on administration policy. Instead, the Report was used by the pro-spending groups within the administration against the more powerful anti-spending groups and by the opposition Democrats in Congress against the executive. Adopting the typical American counterbalance to secrecy, the losing faction leaked the Report to the newspapers and to critics of administration policy. In a system characterized by the ambivalent love-and-fear of secrecy and the

70 Bell, p. 7. Cf. Hanser, p. 144.
71 For a shrewd account of the Gaither episode see Morton H. Halperin, "The Gaither Committee and the Policy Process," *World Politics*, XIII (April, 1961), 360–384.

ready resort to publicity, in circumstances where top leadership is weak and consequently unwilling to use the results of independent thought to overcome internal bureaucratic opposition by means of appeals to the public—in such a situation the effectiveness of blue-ribbon study commissions is reduced and the response to their findings is unpredictable.

It is a plausible hypothesis that administrative leaders with the best experts on the payroll make the best use of external sources of intelligence—partly because such leaders are already exposed to professionally independent staff and partly because that staff is a recruitment link to sophisticated outsiders. The point is evident in the strong academic ties of the U.S. government's Council of Economic Advisers—analyzed at length above (see pp. 94–109). And it can be seen indirectly in a new development in the American labor movement. One of America's best-staffed unions, the UAW-AFL-CIO, has exposed itself systematically to outside criticism of its internal operations by a public review board.[72] Established by labor leaders unusually anxious to protect the rights of union members, this board of independent labor relations experts provides a final "court of appeals" in rights cases. Through its decisions, annual reports, and contacts with the union's own staff, the Board has made officials at every level aware of constitutional provisions, of decisions of the international executive board, and of procedural lapses within the union hierarchy. By acting to remove threats to members' rights, top UAW leaders not only promote internal democracy and their own reputation among members and the public; they learn more of what goes on inside their union. At least two other unions—the Upholsterers' International Union and the United Packinghouse Workers' Union—have established review boards.

The principle underlying the government commission and the review board—to go outside the established bureaucracy for truth on a social issue or for justice in an individual case—is the basis for an institution now spreading throughout the Western world, the Ombudsman.[73] In Scandinavia, the Ombudsman is an officer of

72 Jack Stieber, Walter E. Oberer, and Michael Harrington, *Democracy and Public Review: An Analysis of the UAW Public Review Board* (Santa Barbara: Center for the Study of Democratic Institutions, 1960).

73 A long-needed survey of experience with various versions of this idea has recently been published. *The Ombudsman: Citizen's Defender,* ed. by

Parliament who investigates citizens' complaints about unfair treatment by government departments or officials and who seeks a remedy, if he finds a complaint justified. His powers are confined to investigation and recommendation. Hearings are private; decisions, public. Although the Ombudsman can bring cases of administrative abuse to public attention and although questions of the confidentiality of files are variously resolved, the use of publicity as punishment is minimal.[74] In Scandinavia the Ombudsman is exclusively an agent of the legislature, but this is not an essential feature of the system. What counts in its success is a unique blend of expertise, political independence, the power to investigate, easy access for citizens, and speedy disposition of cases. In general, as a close observer of the impact of government on the individual, the Ombudsman is both an outside check on administrative negligence or abuse and an invaluable source of intelligence for executive agencies and the legislature. In the United States somewhat similar functions are served by the Inspector General of the Army. Even grievancemen or shop stewards in labor unions, despite their partisan roles, often serve as a channel of upward communication ("information feedback") for management as well as processors of complaints. But they lack the independence of an Ombudsman. Non-judicial civilian review boards for citizens' grievances against the police also perform similar functions. But they single out a polarized conflict between one occupational group and one minority; they lack the generality of a municipal grievance commissioner with authority to examine any complaint by any citizen against any agency, the police along with everyone else.

In sum, the possible administrative devices for approaching the truth are as diverse as they are important. Whatever its political risks, as a means to counter the expanding influence of unchecked experts, to preserve open discussion of complex issues, and to mobilize elite support for innovations, the independent government com-

Donald C. Rowat (London: George Allen & Unwin, 1965). The institution originated in Sweden in 1809; it later developed in Finland, was adopted by Denmark in 1955, and spread to Norway and New Zealand in 1962. By 1966, proposals to establish the Ombudsman system were being discussed in Canada, Britain, the Netherlands, India, Ireland, and the United States.

[74] Even in Sweden and Finland, where there is free access to most official documents, information on security matters, trade secrets, and the treatment of alcoholics or the mentally ill is kept secret. *Ibid.*, pp. 7, 49–50, 84, 103–105.

mission has no peer. We need to institutionalize the use of such commissions. At the same time we must make a greater attempt to preserve adversary safeguards in quasi-judicial decision-making as well as in courts—or to find approximations that assure intelligent inquiry. Commissions, *ad hoc* tribunals, administrative courts, Ombudsmen—none of these are panaceas for any problem in public administration, but all can help make the values of truth, freedom, and justice less precarious.

CHAPTER 8

Conclusion

A managerial revolution has taken place but its form is less dramatic than that envisaged by Max Weber and Thorstein Veblen and popularized by James Burnham.[1] Instead of scientists, engineers, and other technical staff coming to power by virtue of their indispensability, there is a shift in power to administrative leaders—in the economy, to coalitions of top managers and experts, each

[1] Weber explicitly rules out the assumption that indispensable occupational function leads to political power, but in some of his writings he pictures the expert, epitome of the bureaucratic trend, as overtowering. (Wilensky, *Intellectuals*, pp. 15 ff. Cf. Bendix, *Max Weber*, pp. 451 ff., on Weber's anticipation of "a dictatorship of the bureaucrats.") Theorists of the managerial revolution vary in their precise specifications of the new men of power—ranging from Veblen's "engineers" (*The Engineers and the Price System* [New York: The Viking Press, 1921]), Laski's "experts" (*op. cit.*), or Burnham's "managers" (*The Managerial Revolution* [New York: John Day, 1941]) to Lasswell's "propagandists," allied with or identical to lawyers (H. D. Lasswell, *The Analysis of Political Behavior* [London: Routledge and Kegan Paul, 1948], pp. 176, 26–27, 143; cf. H. D. Lasswell, "World Politics and Personal Insecurity," in *A Study of Power*, ed. by H. D. Lasswell, Charles E. Merriam, and T. V. Smith [Glencoe: The Free Press, 1950], pp. 6–7). More recently the Lasswell group has interpreted the revolution of our time as a shift in influence from "specialists in bargaining" to intellectuals ("symbol specialists" or "masters of persuasion"), to "specialists in violence," or to those with "administrative and police skills." These rather loose distinctions confuse the problem of locating the ruling groups with the problem of analyzing the means of control and styles of leadership available to any ruling group. (H. D. Lasswell, Daniel Lerner, and C. E. Rothwell, *The Comparative Study of Elites* [Stanford: Stanford University Press, 1952], esp. pp. 16–18, 31 ff.) While these writers identify the main actors and their depiction of the generating forces variously, they have two things in common: (1) they all point to a group or groups of functionaries in complex organizations who possess specialized knowledge and skills as the indispensables in the modern world; (2) they all assume some correspondence of indispensability and power.

acquiring some of the skills of the other; in government, to the Executive branch, gaining at the expense of the legislature. Information is now, as before, a source of power, but it is increasingly a source of confusion. The proliferation of both technical and political-ideological information and a chronic condition of information overload have exacerbated the classic problem of intelligence. An increasing share of organizational resources goes to the intelligence function; structural sources of intelligence failures become more prominent; doctrines of intelligence—ideas about how knowledge should be tapped and staff services organized—become more fateful.

At the same time that problems become more complicated and technical, available information technology and expert staff present more possibilities for solutions. Whatever the national variations in ideologies justifying economic activity, whatever the degree of pluralism in political life, there is a universal increase in information-consciousness at the top; elites in every rich country are moved to break through mere slogans and grasp reality. Their success in understanding internal operations and external environment is affected by the shape of the organizations they command and by their defenses against information pathologies.

Throughout this book I have traced the implications of my analysis for sociological research. Instead of reviewing these themes here, I have briefly outlined in Chart 2 hypotheses about the major sources of intelligence failures and typical organizational strategies for reducing failures. In this chapter I will discuss two implications for administrative practice which are also leads for the student of organization: (1) Some gains in the quality of intelligence are possible from a reorganization of the intelligence function; but (2) much of an organization's defense against information pathologies lies in (a) the top executive's attitude toward knowledge—a product of his own education and orientation, his exposure to independent sources, his capacity to break through the wall of conventional wisdom, and (b) the intelligence specialist's capacity to affect the general tone of policy discourse.

An approach based on reorganization of formal structure has a deceptive simplicity. If the hierarchy is too tall, flatten it; give more experts more autonomy by having them report to fewer bosses. If departmental rivalry blocks communication, set interdepartmental

ROOTS OF FAILURE	MAIN EFFECTS ON INTELLIGENCE	ORGANIZATIONAL DEFENSES AGAINST INFORMATION PATHOLOGIES
Structural attributes that maximize distortion and blockage		
Many ranks in hierarchy, emphasis on rank in style and symbolism. A tall pyramid narrowing sharply at the top, providing long promotion ladders for a few.	Blocks upward communication. More effort to create organization men via loyalty criteria in recruitment, indoctrination, etc. Keeps experts in their "place" (subordinate, isolated). [But hierarchy eases internal control, motivates hard work.]	Team or project organization. Investigation and inspection machinery. Communicate out of channels. Rely on informed outsiders. Diversify channels. Develop general advisors at the top. Accent persuasion, manipulation in administrative style.
Great specialization and interdepartmental rivalry. A large number of organizational units involved. Specialization on geographical basis.	Parochialism—much irrelevant or misleading information. Expert too distant from policy. Agreed-on estimates conceal strong dissent, obscure issues and alternatives. [But specialization increases efficiency in knowledge production and if problem of upward communication can be solved (see hierarchy), rivalry makes top alert to diverse perspectives.]	Recruit managers from staff. Rotation. Conferences of diverse specialists (but avoid consensual judgments or agreement by exhaustion). Career lines from field to headquarters. Examine multiple sources firsthand. Encourage constructive rivalry. Create liaison groups (e.g., between research and development).
"Overcentralized" intelligence.	Top out of touch, too overloaded, too scattered, the intelligence is scattered, the dysfunctions of hierarchy and specialization are maximized.] Expert with data too distant from policy use. After move away from decentralization, unified consensual judgment fosters intelligence fantasies, gives illusion of reliable information.	Develop interpretive skills, integrate collection and evaluation at every point where important decisions are made. Strike balance, depending on purpose.

[continued on next page]

175

ROOTS OF FAILURE	MAIN EFFECTS ON INTELLIGENCE	ORGANIZATIONAL DEFENSES AGAINST INFORMATION PATHOLOGIES
Doctrines that maximize distortion and blockage (e.g., misleading dichotomies)		
"Facts" to "fill in gaps" vs. "evaluated facts" or "interpretation."	Collection kept subordinate and separate from interpretation. Experts excluded from policy deliberations. Pathologies of specialization and hierarchy maximized. More recruits who are raw empiricists, or conventional "backstoppers." More anti-intellectualism (resistance to new ideas, unfamiliar questions, outsiders plus exaggerated belief in practical experience).	Develop interpretive skills and staff. Set up study commissions (e.g., Royal Commissions), review boards, with men of independent mind and stature.
"Intelligence" ("information gathering" or "research") vs. "operations" (clandestine operations).	Fact-gathering attracts naïve realists with weak interpretive abilities. Secret operations attract adventurers—unreliable, hard to control.	Integrate research and operations. Accent research. Rotation. Make secret agencies accountable to competent (strong, independent) authority. Restrict clandestine action.
"Overt" vs. "covert" intelligence. The notion that secret sources are superior. The "right to know" (vs. execu-	Accent on secrecy (1) necessitates loyalty-security systems (recruit cautious mediocrities) and segregation of operations from research (breakdown in	Make full use of overt sources. Minimize loyalty-security criteria, use only for very sensitive positions, when clear danger, with due process.

tive privacy in decision process and accountability for effects).	communication); (2) impairs critical judgment, dulls sense of relevance, blinds executive to superior open sources; (3) creates poor conditions for intellectual work, blocks recruitment of independent-minded experts, top scholars; (4) can demoralize an organization. Even good information if gathered by secret means is treacherous or unusable; could be enemy plant or work of double agent. Debilitating, punishing publicity and crisis journalism. Blocks private expression of unpopular views.	Avoid invasion of employee privacy. Use institutionalized adversary procedures or equivalents. Perform competitively (spying on rivals unnecessary); with efficient innovation, loss of secrets not costly. Insure media competition and diversity. Individual access to defensive publicity.
Prediction or estimate vs. analysis and orientation.	Prediction inappropriate where identity of enemy is unclear, organizational goals ambiguous or conflicting, policy alternatives poorly defined. Boss asks the impossible, expert wastes time. Demand for short, speedy journalistic estimates of future diverts experts from proper work. Failure of short-run predictions reinforces anti-intellectualism. "Cry wolf syndrome."	Train executives in uses and limits of experts in various fields. Recruit better-trained experts, who will limit claims and maintain professional autonomy. Invest more in general orienting analyses.

[continued on next page]

ROOTS OF FAILURE	MAIN EFFECTS ON INTELLIGENCE	ORGANIZATIONAL DEFENSES AGAINST INFORMATION PATHOLOGIES
Types of problems and processes that maximize distortion and blockage		
Decision is not urgent, but involves heavy costs, great risks or uncertainty, and significant changes in goals and methods.	More time and motive to search for information but more weight for established policy and vested interests. Policy discussion is more formal, rank-oriented. (I.e., distortions of hierarchy, rivalry more prominent; doctrine accenting "facts to fill in gaps" more salient.) More chance for paralyzing delays? More chance for building case to confirm mistaken in-group preconceptions?	See defenses against structural and doctrinal roots of failure, above.
Problems are those of established organization with slow growth rate, "stable" environment.	Policy discussion is more formal, rank-oriented.	See above
Frequent, institutionalized succession (i.e., no succession crises).	Bias toward continuity of established policy, official prejudice. Short time perspective.	See above

178

task forces in motion. If experts and executives are parochial, move them about from job to job, agency to agency; send them back to school to stretch their minds; seek new sources of manpower. If secrecy and security regulations prevent the recruitment of skillful interpreters of data—men with scholarly imagination—then change the regulations, use secrecy only where it is functionally necessary, apply loyalty criteria only in posts of extraordinary sensitivity in time of clear and present danger.

Such redesign of structure, however, meets its limits where it entails large losses of efficiency, coordination, and control, and where structural resistances to change are strong. If anything is clear from this book, it is that intelligence failures are built into complex organizations. On the one hand, the most readily accomplished revamping of structure turns out to be mere organizational tinkering. Establishing an interdepartmental committee makes formal what was unofficial before—the selective sharing of inside information, the public restatement of fixed departmental positions. On the other hand, even when the reorganization of formal structure is pushed to its limit, the basic sources of distortion remain in some degree: insofar as the proper mastery of the task calls for specialization and the need to motivate and control personnel necessitates hierarchy; insofar as coordination demands centralization; insofar as the exigencies of decision seem to require direct answers, if not short-run predictions of the future; insofar as internal security and outside competition necessitate secrecy—to the extent that these other organizational interests must be protected—a singleminded attention to administrative reforms that facilitate the flow of accurate information is inappropriate. And, finally, many sources of intelligence failures are natural to the state of the organization's development and are therefore substantially beyond its control; if swiftly growing organizations in contact with a fluid environment and facing urgent problems are less vulnerable to structural and doctrinal distortions of information, that is no help to a more established, slower-growing organization coping with more routine crises.

Thus, the alert executive is everywhere forced to bypass the regular machinery and seek firsthand exposure to intelligence sources in and out of the organization. In matters delicate and urgent, more imaginative administrative leaders typically move to points along the organization's boundaries: looking toward the bottom, they rely on internal communications specialists such as education directors and auditors; looking outward, they rely on contact men such as press officers, technical salesmen, foreign service officers, lobbyists, mediators. They talk to reporters and researchers investigating their organizations; they establish study commissions or review boards comprised entirely of outsiders, like the members of British Royal Commissions; they institutionalize complaints procedures and thereby subject themselves to systematic, independent criticism from below, as in the case of the Ombudsman; they assemble *ad hoc* committees, kitchen cabinets, general advisors, personal representatives. These unofficial intelligence agents, some of them defined as peripheral, may constitute the most important and reliable source of organizational intelligence. They are sufficiently sensitive to the culture of the executive to communicate, independent enough to provide detached judgment; they bring to bear the multiple perspectives of marginal men.

For these reasons there is some truth to the common assumption that a sophisticated reporter working with open sources is better than an agent working with top-secret information. On the key question of whether an invasion of Cuba would touch off an organized insurrection against Castro by the Cuban resistance, reporters such as Joseph Newman of the New York *Herald Tribune,* fresh from the scene, had better estimates than Allan Dulles and Richard Bissell of the CIA, whose thoughts suffered from the burden of secrecy.[2] The only systematic treatment we have of press coverage and intelligence estimates in a crisis situation, however, is a close study of the Pearl Harbor case: "Comparing top secret Intelligence evaluations of enemy intentions with estimates in the contemporary press," it concludes, "one is struck by the relative soundness of the less privileged judgments." In complex political predictions "the knowledgeability of a good news reporter is more helpful than access to a few top-secret cables. A reporter will usually have available a multiplicity of public evidences of the secrets contained in the cables themselves, since it is only in the last days of crisis that a government will attempt total censorship."[3] Obviously,

[2] Schlesinger, *A Thousand Days,* pp. 247–248.
[3] Wohlstetter, pp. 169, 130. Cf. pp. 122, 124–125.

though, not all reporters are "sophisticated" and not all knowledgeable reporters agree on issues of policy. Reporters typically share the anti-intellectual spirit and crude empiricism of intelligence specialists. We cannot settle the question without comparisons of both good and bad estimates among larger populations of outsiders (e.g., columnists in all the prestige papers) and insiders (e.g., top staff in all the major intelligence agencies) on several issues—comparisons that do not yet exist.

More general research implications are apparent. We need studies that compare the performance of organizations or governments that rely most and least on (1) unofficial sources and (2) various types of outside sources, both official (study commissions, grievance commissioners, management consultants, advisory corporations, task forces) and unofficial (journalists, scholars, other marginal men). Estimates of the costs and gains for intelligence of various strategies for bypassing or diversifying official channels might be feasible.

An equally difficult but crucial area for research is the effect of the new information technology and of related managerial techniques on the problem of intelligence. Glib talk about the computer taking over executive functions runs rampant. It is said that systems researchers, bemused by their mathematical models, are taking all the creativity out of decision, and presumably the joy out of living. If we combine the rapid handling of information by computers, the application of mathematics and statistics to administrative problems (linear programming, simulation, operations research, and systems analysis), and the recruitment of better-educated managers who are smart enough to use the staff to put these methods to work, then we have a formula for revolution in administrative leadership. The speculation is that it will mean greater centralization of authority, clearer accountability of subordinates, a sharper distinction between top management and staff, and the rest of the organization, and eventually a transformation of the planning and innovating functions.[4] It is not at all clear, however, that

[4] Cf. M. Philipson, ed., *Automation: Implications for the Future* (New York: Vintage Books, 1962); Herbert A. Simon, *The New Science of Management Decision* (New York: Harper & Brothers, 1960); George P. Shultz and Thomas L. Whisler, eds., *Management Organization and the Computer* (New York: The Free Press, 1960); and Thomas L. Whisler and Harold J. Leavitt, "Management in the 1980's," *Harvard Business Review,* XXXVI (November–December, 1958), 41–48.

these changes, if they do spread widely, will weaken the roots of intelligence failure. No one argues that in these highly programmed systems there will be less specialization, less accent on hierarchy and command, although there is considerable question about the degree and forms of centralization.[5] It is likely, too, that the new flood of information will not make the doctrines of "all the facts" and "short-run estimates" less attractive.

From our previous discussion of the growing demand for experts who can supply a blend of technical and political intelligence, however, we can infer one fact of the matter: whatever the uses of electronic data processing (EDP) in routinizing decisions involving large-scale repetitive operations (as in accounting, inventory control, production scheduling and control) and whatever the expansion of applied research on narrow technical problems, there remains a great shortage of generalized policy advice. The systems analyst, symbol of the new "Whiz Kids," reflects one of many

[5] One sales finance company computerized its information system, including data on repayments of individual loans and analysis of the impact of delinquencies on the portfolio of each local office. Managers of local offices all over the country soon discovered that their bosses at central headquarters, where the computer was located, had this information before it arrived at the local office. (Reports could immediately be walked down the hall to the top manager but were mailed less swiftly to the distant local offices.) Further, central headquarters did not hesitate to phone local managers about either particular delinquencies or trends. ("What are you doing about Mrs. Jones, case #578?") Several results are worth noting. A number of local managers became demoralized because they perceived loss of control. Some actually quit and other less able men took their places; others created "under the table" information systems to protect themselves, thus negating the efficiency introduced by the computer. Exacerbating the problem of status was the tendency of low-level professionals in the controller's department to exert pressure directly on headquarters executives, who then passed it down the line. It can be argued that such problems are transitional, slated to give way as new men are trained and real-time systems introduced. In this case, the finance company hopes to find an economical way to give local managers immediate access to centralized computer memories. That would solve the problem of slow mails, but not the endemic problems of complex organization—among them, the natural tendency of top managers with information about off-standard performance to swarm all over the culprits and the latter to retaliate by restricting or distorting information and by other means. As Myers suggests, information technology may be neutral in its effects on centralization. It merely presents more possibilities of either centralizing or decentralizing information sources, authority, and other aspects of organizational structure. Charles A. Myers, "Some Implications of Computers for Management," unpubl. paper, Annual Meeting of the Industrial Relations Research Association, San Francisco, December 28, 1966. See above, pp. 58–62.

efforts to meet that shortage. No doubt, lower-level technical experts are susceptible to technicism; they sometimes exaggerate the importance of their methods, substituting means for ends. But this phenomenon is not new; dedicated specialists have always pushed their specialties. More important, the graphic horror of directionless machinery taking over denies the main functions of both top staff experts and executives. Experts who move into policy circles typically provide analytical advice defining major alternatives in a situation of great uncertainty. Top executives typically incorporate analytical judgments, value judgments, practical experience, and intuition into policy decisions.[6] Neither the expert nor his boss can long remain preoccupied with means and methods; both strain toward a synoptic view. With the diffusion of more efficient information technology, the good sense of the questions asked, the relevance of the categories used for analysis, and the reliability of the data become even more important. Proper respect for the GIGO principle becomes the law of administrative survival.[7]

I do not wish to minimize the dangers of technicism. The question of the conditions under which the tyranny of technique prevails deserves serious attention, but to talk about the age of "technological idiots" and "cheerful robots" clouds the issues. Consider the problems of the United States Defense Department, symbol of the new managerial revolution. There are few major weapons systems today that can be developed for less than a billion dollars; investment and operating costs are far higher than that. Nowhere is the price of irrational decision or poor judgment greater, and nowhere has the apparatus of modern management been more aggressively and skillfully applied. To evaluate the claims for these techniques is premature because they have prevailed in Defense only a few years and have spread to such agencies as the Office of Economic Opportunity only recently. It was not until May, 1966, that all departments and most agencies of the United States government were required to use the Planning-Programming Budgeting System (see p. 18 above and the discussion of RAND,

6 Cf. Bruce L. R. Smith, "Strategic Expertise," pp. 71–72; Price, pp. 124 ff.; Wilensky, *Intellectuals,* pp. 209 ff.

7 The GIGO principle holds that, in using computers, if you put *Garbage In* you get *Garbage Out.*

pp. 36ff.).[8] Moreover, data on the impact of information technology and of such related ideas as "cost-benefit analysis" or "systems analysis" are either nonexistent or not publicly available. Using
the Defense Department as a model, however, we can glimpse the
broadest implications of the new managerial revolution for government and industry. The most likely outcomes are the following:

1. At every level there will be increased pressure to explicate
assumptions and goals more clearly and to subject them to
quantitative analysis. There is no doubt that the techniques of
systems analysis have made choices among weapons more conscious and rational, sometimes resulting in the liquidation of
glamorous hardware preferred by bellicose congressmen. The
controversy about Secretary McNamara's decision to move from
bombers to missiles provides several examples. At one point Air
Force enthusiasts in Congress demanded the continued development and procurement of the Skybolt air-to-surface ballistic
missile (which would have cost about $3 billion, not counting
the cost of additional warheads) and the purchase of a fifteenth
wing of B-52 bombers. McNamara's cost-effectiveness studies
gave him strength to resist such demands.[9] Strangelovian phi-

losophers in the Air Force and elsewhere found the Secretary a formidable opponent.

2. Insofar as top managers know what questions to ask, and can elicit good data (i.e., overcome the structural and doctrinal roots of intelligence failure), their decisions will be more efficient. More data bearing on more alternatives will be explored, longer chains of causation analyzed, the consequences of a policy decision for a whole organizational system more often grasped.[10] Whatever one thinks of American foreign policy, it would be difficult to argue that the shift from "massive retaliation" to "graduated response" and "flexible, balanced defense," carried out during the administration of Secretary McNamara, decreased the range of options.

3. Insofar as top managers ask the wrong questions and muster poor intelligence, wrong decisions will be more efficiently arrived at, and poor judgment, now buttressed by awesome statistics, will be made more effective. Wherever the new tools and perspectives are institutionalized, more weight will attach to data and systems analyses, whatever their quality. The chance is increased that information errors will ricochet at high speed throughout the system.

4. The number and influence of information technologists will increase and the power of executives in charge of such staffs will be enhanced, at least in the short run. The most significant fact about the Defense Department story is that with far less formal reorganization than that attempted by his predecessors, Secretary McNamara succeeded in shifting the locus of authority to central civilian management; he revolutionized the processes of decision-making. PPBS gave him the ability to cut across organizational lines and particularly to integrate both complementary and competitive functions of rival services—an effective substitute for unification, a goal that had eluded everyone else.

5. As executives who are well equipped with information

---

have systems like Polaris whose missiles can be withheld for days, if desired, and used at times and against targets chosen by the President.' " *Ibid.*, p. 218.

[10] In some ways, a systems approach is congenial to the perspective of sociology. Both accent the interdependence and interaction of parts of a social system. Instead of "cutting a problem down to size," systems researchers at their best enlarge it by uncovering and methodically gauging the effect of consequences unanticipated by specialized groups.

technologists expand their influence, competing executives, not so well equipped, find that they have lost room for maneuver and bargaining. For instance, when an organization adopts PPBS and gives a planning and analysis group review powers, the budget proposals that are skillfully cast in formal cost-benefit terms receive preferential treatment; others lose out. In a university budget scramble, a library unit that shows how an $80,000 expenditure for additional staff will permit a better schedule of hours, which in turn will increase the circulation of books and the use of reference services by X amount and decrease student waiting time by Y amount, and, further, that this small cost will yield greater gains than equivalent investment in any other library services—that library unit will outpace competitors who use traditional methods of budget justification. In such situations, executives who lose are moved to resist. Either they fight fire with fire, assemble and train the staff and master the techniques (which results in a general, competitive upgrading of manpower), or they resist implementation of policies based on the new techniques (which increases dysfunctional conflict between departments and ranks), or, having resisted unsuccessfully, they are forced to leave.

6. The gulf between top executives and the information technologists, on the one hand, and men whose work is more programmed, on the other, will widen. One troublesome expression of this gulf is the issue of how much information about goals and conflicts of goals and about priorities in the allocation of scarce resources can or should be shared, once goals and means have become more explicit and quantitative at central headquarters. The problem is partly technical. It is difficult to compare different preferences within similar categories of activity (library service measured by book circulation rates versus classroom service measured by teacher-pupil ratio, the circulation of Mickey Spillane versus that of Plato), let alone preferences in contrasting categories (library services versus research on air pollution). The problem is also partly political and moral. If the Department of Agriculture gives top priority to shifting a million people out of farming, should it advertise this aim? If the university using systems analysis gives priority to applied research product over teaching and to the professional schools over the

liberal arts, should those interested in scholarship and general education be informed? Early in its history the Office of Economic Opportunity carried on cost-benefit evaluations of some of its anti-poverty program, but the results were kept in-house. If all value conflicts, all clashes of interest, are made explicit every year, so that administrators can compare every item in a budget with every other and eliminate those that contribute little to an explicit value scheme, two consequences follow: (1) latent conflicts become manifest and positions become more polarized; (2) the administrator is tempted to keep a larger fraction of what he knows to himself; he avoids explaining the relative insignificance of powerful programs (public information policies become more manipulative, credibility gaps widen). In short, information technology may aggravate the "honesty problem."[11] It is like the familiar dilemma of central planners everywhere: the target plan is announced, the real plan is kept quiet, but word creeps around (see p. 111).

The most difficult claim to assess is that information technologists, oriented to the measurement of gains and costs, inevitably drive out the "soft" in favor of the "hard" variables, that instead of wisdom and good sense the tyranny of technique prevails. Information technologists argue that there is nothing intrinsic to their methods that prevents proper respect for qualitative variables and judgments. To quantify what it makes sense to quantify and to avoid quantifying what cannot be quantified is not to give the easily measured variables undue weight. Moreover, even the most "technical" of experts are valued primarily for their interpretive skills and creative judgment. The controller who introduced the Planning-Programming Budgeting System into the Office of the Secretary of Defense observes that the techniques are actually rather simple. "What distinguishes the useful and productive analyst," he says, "is his ability to formulate (or design) the problem; to choose appropriate objectives; to define the relevant, important environments or situations in which to test the alternatives; to judge the reliability of his cost and other data; and, finally, and not least, his ingenuity in inventing new systems or alternatives to evaluate."[12]

[11] Virginia Held, "PPBS Comes to Washington," *The Public Interest*, No. 4 (Summer, 1966), pp. 102–115.
[12] Hitch, p. 54.

In the absence of studies of the influence of information technologists in diverse settings, we cannot assess these claims. In order to bring the issues into focus, however, consider two hypothetical examples—one, the realistic case of the Defense Department's role in the continuation of the Vietnam war; the other, an even more speculative case of a systems analyst confronting the problem of outdoor recreation.

In the mid-1960's the Defense Department displayed a remarkable taste for ghoulish statistics—body counts and kill ratios in Vietnam villages.[13] One can argue that this was not the result of systems analysis or any other modern method of management. Nor was the Vietnam intervention a case of evaluation techniques molding the objective—that is, technicism. Rather, the statistics resulted from a desperate effort to find a substitute for the old-fashioned battle line that told the warring nation whether it was ahead or behind. And the policy resulted from political leaders being seized by specious analogies—Vietnam is seen as Munich, as Greece, as Czechoslovakia; Southeast Asia, with per capita incomes in the range of $100, becomes Europe with incomes twenty to thirty times as large; the 1930's and 1940's are the 1960's; civil wars accompanied by multiple outside interventions are simple wars of aggression; unpopular military dictatorships are the same as popular legitimate governments; wholesale destruction of property and life and corruption on a grand scale are called "saving our allies from Communism" and "maintaining world order."

But it is equally plausible—and it follows more directly from our analysis of the obstacles to gathering reliable data on such matters—to argue that the statistics are full of error, and that even if they were accurate, analysis of the easy-to-measure variables (casualties suffered by the Viet Cong and the South Vietnamese) was driving out consideration of the hard-to-measure variables and long-run costs (the nature of popular support for a South Vietnam

[13] These were the measures of progress receiving most publicity. Other measures analyzed by Defense included the percentage of territory controlled by the two sides, the relative rates of defection, the number of incidents initiated by the Viet Cong per month, and comparative losses of weapons. Nonmilitary indices included "the number of applications for licenses to start new businesses, the movement of goods and food by road and water, loans to farmers and fishermen, and the number of students in rural areas." W. W. Kaufmann, p. 260.

government, the effect of the war on the Western Alliance and on domestic civility, the effect of bombing on the will to resist). It is even possible that cost-benefit approaches tend to rivet the attention on relative outcomes (if the enemy continues to lose more than we lose, relative to resources, he will give up) while the absolute level of current investment (are the high costs in money and blood and in hard-to-measure losses worth the effort?) fades into the background. In any case, if in assessing our policy in Vietnam in the 1960's top decision-makers were taking their data seriously—perhaps because kill ratios and the like represent a touch of spurious certainty in a highly uncertain world—the availability of the data and of the analysis techniques must be counted a determinant of foreign policy.

The example of the planning of outdoor recreation suggests again that systems analysis is applicable to more benign purposes, too, and that the insight, imagination, and values of the systems analyzer are relevant whatever the purpose. A cost-benefit approach to government expenditures on outdoor recreation might take this form:[14] Calculate benefits on the basis of "merit-weighted user-days," a measure of various sorts of recreation for various sorts of people under various conditions. Weight the simple measure of "user days"—a function of the numbers of persons expected to use a park and of the lengths of time of their stays—to take account of evaluations that some user days are better than others. Perhaps you would judge that a day spent by a child in the wilderness, absorbing the visual, tactile, and aural delights of nature, has more lasting value than an adult's picnicking in a crowded, noisy, fly-ridden, garbage-strewn park; "that the marginal utility of additional recreation declines as larger amounts are made available; that equity requires government to provide more recreational opportunities to those who most need them and can least afford private alternatives," and so on. Now evaluate expenditures on alternative parks and their expected number of users in terms of the "merit-rated user days" each can provide. The calculations would be complex, but information technologists could work out an optimal budget for outdoor recreation that fits any explicit value scheme and any level of expenditure.

[14] Held, p. 110, citing a paper by Ruth P. Mack and Sumner Myers.

There is no problem that cannot be approached in this rational way. Assuming the availability of accurate data and a continued decline in data processing costs, the crucial limitation is not that information technologists are necessarily restricted in their intellectual perspectives by the techniques of their job. Rather, it is that on average their training does not overcome their limited political and social sensitivities. The integration of values, theory, and practice nowhere depends more on the supply of talent. The danger of technicism is in direct proportion to the shortage of educated men. Too often the new technologists are methodical and exact in their specialized fields, but impressionable, naïve, and opinionated on broader issues of policy. Like the executives they advise, they lack a sense of relevance and analogy—the critical common sense and trained judgment that mark an educated man.

That breadth of view combined with technical skill is a requisite for effective policy advice is especially true when social science is to be incorporated into decision-making. Insofar as the users of social research mainly demand short-run predictions—forecasts of the demand for soap, estimates of whether internal dissension in Peking will make the Chinese more or less likely to greet a bombing escalation with a troop commitment—they deprive themselves of the main contributions of social science. Although there have been many successes in prediction, notably in demography, in economics, and in polls of voting intentions (where the question is simple and the forecast is very short), the specific data of social sciences are typically outdated in the short run. They are far more useful for constructing comprehensive pictures of social reality and for understanding extended social trends. They are a primary source of political and ideological intelligence.

Given the institutional roots of intelligence failures, scattered about like land mines, given the urgency of so many big decisions, what counts is the top executive's preconceptions—what he has in mind when he enters the room and must act. The role of experts and intellectuals in shaping these preconceptions, in and out of the organization, is little understood. For example, in college and in training programs on the job, business executives and government officials are increasingly exposed to the perspectives of economics, sociology, psychology, and anthropology, sometimes in the form of that brand of history and political science which is infused with "the behavioral sciences." If education in social science does not yield direct answers to immediate questions, perhaps it does break through executives' cruder stereotypes, enhance their understanding of themselves and their organizations, alert them to the range of relevant variables, and make them more skillful in the use of experts.

Similarly, the symbols that surround the executive in his daily life shape his orientation. Experts and intellectuals who can write, speak, and present ideas quickly and easily have a major influence on speeches and resolutions, by-laws and contracts, press releases and house organs, legal, economic, or scientific briefs and testimony. In private conference and committee meeting they set the tone of policy discourse. No one who examines the history of such doctrines as "strategic bombing" and "massive retaliation," or the sad tale of foreign intervention in such places as Cuba and Vietnam, can be impressed with "the end of ideology," if by that we mean the end of illusions that systematically conceal social reality. And in all these cases, intellectuals have played their part in creating and sustaining the symbolic atmosphere within which men calculate. Many a brittle slogan has perpetuated a policy long outmoded.

To read the history of modern intelligence failures is to get the nagging feeling that men at the top are often out of touch, that good intelligence is difficult to come by and enormously difficult to listen to; that big decisions are very delicate but not necessarily deliberative; that sustained good judgment is rare. Bemoaning the decline of meaningful action, T. S. Eliot once spoke of a world that ends "not with a bang but a whimper." What we have to fear is that the bang will come, preceded by the contemporary equivalent of the whimper—a faint rustle of paper as some self-convinced chief of state, reviewing a secret memo full of comfortable rationalizations just repeated at the final conference, fails to muster the necessary intelligence and wit and miscalculates the power and the intent of his adversaries.

Bibliography

Abel, Elie. *The Missile Crisis.* Paperback edn. New York: Bantam Books, 1966.

Adams, Sherman. *Firsthand Report.* New York: Popular Library, 1962.

Altshuler, Alan. *The City Planning Process: A Political Analysis.* Ithaca: Cornell University Press, 1965.

Argyris, Chris. *Organization of a Bank.* New Haven: Labor and Management Center, Yale University, 1954.

Aron, Raymond. *On War.* New York: Doubleday Anchor Books, 1959.

Bailey, Stephen K. *Congress Makes a Law: The Story Behind the Employment Act of 1946.* New York: Columbia University Press, 1950.

Banton, Michael. *The Policeman in the Community.* New York: Basic Books, 1964.

Barber, Bernard. *Science and the Social Order.* Rev. edn. New York: Collier Books, 1962.

Baritz, Loren. *The Servants of Power: A History of the Use of Social Science in American Industry.* Middletown: Wesleyan University Press, 1960.

Barnard, Chester I. "Functions and Pathology of Status Systems in Formal Organizations," in *Industry and Society.* Ed. by William Foote Whyte. New York: McGraw-Hill Book Co., 1946. Pp. 46–83.

Barth, Alan. *The Price of Liberty.* New York: The Viking Press, 1961.

Bauer, Raymond A., Ithiel de Sola Pool, and Lewis Anthony Dexter. *American Business and Public Policy: The Politics of Foreign Trade.* New York: Atherton Press of Prentice-Hall, 1963.

Bell, Daniel. "Government by Commission," *The Public Interest,* No. 3 (Spring, 1966), pp. 3–9.

Bendix, Reinhard. *Max Weber: An Intellectual Portrait.* Garden City: Doubleday & Company, 1960.

Bendix Reinhard. "The Age of Ideology: Persistent and Changing" in *Ideology and Discontent.* Ed. by David E. Apter. New York: The Free Press, 1964. Pp. 294–327.

Bendix, Reinhard. *Nation-building and Citizenship: Studies of Our Changing Social Order.* New York: John Wiley & Sons, 1964.

Berliner, Joseph S. *Factory and Manager in the U.S.S.R.* Cambridge: Harvard University Press, 1957.

Blau, Peter M., and Richard W. Scott. *Formal Organizations: A Comparative Approach.* San Francisco: Chandler Publishing Company, 1962.

Bontecou, Eleanor. *The Federal Loyalty-Security Program.* Ithaca: Cornell University Press, 1953.

Boorstin, Daniel J. *The Image or What Happened to the American Dream.* New York: Atheneum, 1962.

Brooks, John. *The Fate of the Edsel and Other Business Adventures.* New York: Harper & Row, 1959.

Burnham, James. *The Managerial Revolution.* New York: John Day, 1941.

Burns, James MacGregor. *Roosevelt: The Lion and the Fox.* Harvest paperback edn. New York: Harcourt, Brace and World, 1956.

Burns, Tom, and G. M. Stalker. *The Management of Innovation.* London: Tavistock Publications, 1961.

Butow, Robert J. C. *Japan's Decision to Surrender.* Stanford: Stanford University Press, 1954.

Butterfield, Herbert. *The Statecraft of Machiavelli.* 1st edn., Collier paperback. New York: Collier Books, 1962.

California Assembly, *The Dilemma of Mental Commitments in California: A Background Document.* Subcommittee on Mental Health Services. Sacramento: Department of General Services, Documents Section, 1966.

Churchill, Winston S. *Their Finest Hour.* Vol. II: *The Second World War.* 6 vols. Boston: Houghton Mifflin, 1949.

Cleary, Edward W. "Evidence as a Problem in Communicating," *Vanderbilt Law Review,* V (April, 1952), 277–281.

Clokie, H. M., and J. W. Robinson. *Royal Commissions of Inquiry: The Significance of Investigations in British Politics.* Stanford: Stanford University Press, 1937.

Compton, Neil. "TV Chronicle," *Commentary,* XLI (April, 1966), 84–86.

Cook, Fred J. *The FBI Nobody Knows.* New York: Pyramid Publications, 1965.

Craven, Wesley F., and James L. Cate, eds. *The Army Air Forces in World War II.* 7 vols. Chicago: University of Chicago Press, 1948–1958.

Crozier, Michel. *The Bureaucratic Phenomenon.* Chicago: University of Chicago Press, 1964.

Cyert, Richard, and James March. *A Behavioral Theory of the Firm.* Englewood Cliffs: Prentice-Hall, 1963.

Dahl, Robert A., and Charles E. Lindblom. *Politics, Economics, and Welfare: Planning and Politico-Economic Systems Resolved into Basic Social Processes.* New York: Harper & Brothers, 1953.

Dale, Ernest. *Planning and Developing the Company Organization Structure,* Research Report No. 20. New York: American Management Association, 1952.

Dale, Jerry. "Bill of Rights Violated—by Company Snoopers," *UAW-Solidarity,* IX (March, 1965), 4–5.

Dalton, Melville. *Men Who Manage: Fusions of Feeling and Theory in Administration.* New York: John Wiley & Sons, 1959.

Davey, Harold W. "The Experience of Other Countries," in "Formulating the Federal Government's Economic Program: A Symposium," *American Political Science Review* XLII (April, 1948), 295–307.

Davis, E. Eugene. "Legal Structures in a Changing Society," in F. James Davis, *et al. Society and the Law.* New York: The Free Press, 1962. Pp. 196–226.

Davis, F. James, Henry H. Foster, Jr., C. Ray Jeffery, and E. Eugene Davis. *Society and the Law.* New York: The Free Press, 1962.

Davis, Kenneth Culp. *Administrative Law Treatise.* Vol. II. St. Paul: West Publishing, 1958.

de Huszar, George B., ed. *The Intellectuals: A Controversial Portrait.* Glencoe: The Free Press, 1960.

Dession, George. "Psychiatry and the Conditioning of Criminal Justice," *Yale Law Review,* XLVII (January, 1938), 319–340.

Devons, Ely. *Planning in Practice: Essays in Aircraft Planning in Wartime.* Cambridge, Eng.: At the University Press, 1950.

Draper, Jean, and George Strother. "Testing a Model for Organizational Growth," *Human Organization* XXII (Summer, 1963), 180–194.

Drucker, Peter. *The Practice of Management.* New York: Harper & Brothers, 1954.

Dubin, Robert. *The World of Work: Industrial Society and Human Relations.* Englewood Cliffs: Prentice-Hall, 1958.

Dulles, Allen W. *Germany's Underground.* New York: The Macmillan Company, 1947.

Dulles, Allen W. *The Craft of Intelligence.* New York: Harper & Row, 1963.

Ehrmann, Henry W. *Organized Business in France.* Princeton: Princeton University Press, 1957.

Ehrmann, Henry W., ed. *Interest Groups on Four Continents.* Pittsburgh: University of Pittsburgh Press, 1958.

Elder, Robert Ellsworth. *The Policy Machine: The Department of State and American Foreign Policy.* Syracuse: University Press, 1960.

Elson, Alex. "Juvenile Courts and Due Process," in *Justice for the Child: The Juventile Court in Transition.* Ed. by Margaret K. Rosenheim. New York: The Free Press, 1962. Pp. 95–117.

Etzioni, Amitai. *Modern Organizations.* Englewood Cliffs: Prentice-Hall, 1964.

Evans, Allan. "Intelligence and Policy Formation," *World Politics,* XII (October, 1959), 84–91.

Fagen, Richard R. "Calculation and Emotion in Foreign Policy: The Cuban Case," *Journal of Conflict Resolution,* VI (September, 1962), 214–221.

Fesler, James W. "Field Organization" in *Elements of Public Administration.* Ed. by Fritz Morstein Marx. 2nd edn. Englewood Cliffs: Prentice-Hall, 1959. Pp. 246–273.

Festinger, Leon, Henry W. Riecken, and Stanley Schachter. *When Prophecy Fails.* New York: Harper & Row, 1956.

Finer, Herman. "Congressional Investigations: The British System," *University of Chicago Law Review,* XVIII (Spring, 1951), 521–570.

Flash, Edward S., Jr. *Economic Advice and Presidential Leadership: The Council of Economic Advisers.* New York: Columbia University Press, 1965.

Freund, Paul. "The Brandeis Brief," *On Understanding the Supreme Court.* Boston: Little, Brown, and Company, 1951. Pp. 86–92.

Fried, Robert C. *The Italian Prefects: A Study in Administrative Politics.* New Haven: Yale University Press, 1963.

Friedmann, Wolfgang G. *Law in a Changing Society.* Berkeley and Los Angeles: University of California Press, 1959.

Galbraith, John Kenneth, *The Affluent Society.* Boston: Houghton Mifflin, 1958.

George, Alexander L. *Propaganda Analysis: A Study of Inferences Made from Nazi Propaganda in World War II.* Evanston: Row, Peterson & Co., 1959.

Giovannitti, Len, and Fred Freed. *The Decision to Drop the Bomb.* New York: Coward-McCann, 1965.

Goffman, Erving. *Asylums: Essays on the Social Situation of Mental Patients and Other Inmates.* New York: Doubleday Anchor Books, 1961.

Goldner, Fred H. "Going Down in the World," *Trans-action*, I (November, 1963), 2–4.

Goldner, Fred H. "Demotion in Industrial Management," *American Sociological Review*, XXX (October, 1965), 714–724.

Gordon, Margaret S. *Retraining and Labor Market Adjustment in Western Europe*. United States Department of Labor, Manpower Automation Research Monograph, No. 4. Berkeley: Institute of Industrial Relations, 1965.

Gouldner, Alvin W., and S. M. Miller. *Applied Sociology: Opportunities and Problems*. New York: The Free Press, 1965.

Hagstrom, Warren O. *The Scientific Community*. New York: Basic Books, 1965.

Haire, Mason. "Biological Models and Empirical Histories of the Growth of Organizations," in *Modern Organization Theory*. Ed. by Mason Haire. New York: John Wiley & Sons, 1959. Pp. 272–306.

Halperin, Morton H. "The Gaither Committee and the Policy Process," *World Politics*, XIII (April, 1961), 360–384.

Hamilton, Capt. James. "LEIU—Its Objects and Operations," *Yearbook, 1961*. International Association of Chiefs of Police, 1961, 119–122.

Hammond, Paul Y. *Organizing for Defense: The American Military Establishment in the Twentieth Century*. Princeton: Princeton University Press, 1961.

Hanser, Charles J. *Guide to Decision: The Royal Commission*. Totowa, N.J.: The Bedminster Press, 1965.

Harney, Malachi L., and John C. Cross. *The Informer in Law Enforcement*. Springfield: Charles C Thomas, 1960.

Harris, Seymour E. *Economics of the Kennedy Years*. New York: Harper & Row, 1964.

Held, Virginia. "PPBS Comes to Washington," *The Public Interest*, No. 4 (Summer, 1966), pp. 102–115.

Hilsman, Roger. *Strategic Intelligence and National Decisions*. Glencoe: The Free Press, 1956.

Hitch, Charles J. *Decision-Making for Defense*. Berkeley and Los Angeles: University of California Press, 1965.

Hobbs, Edward H. *Behind the President: A Study of Executive Office Agencies*. Washington: Public Affairs Press, 1954.

Horelick, Arnold L. "The Cuban Missile Crisis: An Analysis of Soviet Calculations and Behavior," *World Politics*, XVI (April, 1964), 363–389.

Horowitz, Irving Louis. "The Life and Death of Project Camelot." *Trans-action*, III (November–December, 1965), 3–7, 44–49.

Huntington, Samuel P. *The Common Defense: Strategic Programs in National Politics.* New York: Columbia University Press, 1961.

Huntington, Samuel P. *The Soldier and the State: The Theory and Politics of Civil-military Relations.* Cambridge: The Belknap Press of Harvard University Press, 1964.

Iklé, Fred Charles. *The Social Impact of Bomb Destruction.* Norman: University of Oklahoma Press, 1958.

Jacob, Herbert. *German Administration Since Bismarck.* New Haven: Yale University Press, 1963.

James, Rita M. "Jurors' Assessment of Criminal Responsibility," *Social Problems,* VII (Summer, 1959), 58–69.

Janowitz, Morris. *The Professional Soldier: A Social and Political Portrait.* Glencoe: The Free Press, 1960.

Jasinsky, Frank J. "Use and Misuse of Efficiency Controls," *Harvard Business Review,* XXXIV (July–August, 1956), 105–112.

Jeffrey, C. Ray. "Criminal Justice and Social Change," in F. James Davis *et al. Society and the Law.* New York: The Free Press, 1962. Pp. 290–298.

Jones, R. V. "Scientific Intelligence," *Journal of the Royal United Service Institution,* XCII (August, 1947), 352–369.

Kadish, Sanford H. "The Advocate and the Expert: Counsel in the Peno-Correctional Process," *Minnesota Law Review,* XLVII (January, 1961), 803–841.

Kahn, Alfred J. *A Court for Children: A Study of the New York City Children's Court.* New York: Columbia University Press, 1953.

Kaufman, Herbert. *The Forest Ranger: A Study in Administrative Behavior.* Baltimore: Johns Hopkins Press, 1960.

Kaufmann, William W. *The McNamara Strategy.* New York: Harper & Row, 1964.

Kautsky, John H. "Myth, Self-fulfilling Prophecy, and Symbolic Reassurance in the East-West Conflict," *The Journal of Conflict Resolution,* IX (March, 1965), 1–17.

Kendall, Willmoore. "The Function of Intelligence," *World Politics,* I (July, 1949), 542–552.

Kent, Sherman. *Strategic Intelligence.* Princeton: Princeton University Press, 1949.

Knorr, Klaus. "Failures in National Intelligence Estimates: The Case of the Cuban Missiles," *World Politics,* XVI (April, 1964), 455–467.

Kornhauser, William. *Scientists in Industry: Conflict and Accommodation.* Berkeley and Los Angeles: University of California Press, 1962.

Kuhn, Thomas S. *The Structure of Scientific Revolutions*. 1st Phoenix edn. Chicago: University of Chicago Press, 1962.

Lamb, Edward. *"Trial by Battle": The Case of a Washington Witch-Hunt*. Santa Barbara: Center for the Study of Democratic Institutions, Occasional Paper, April, 1964.

Lane, Robert E. "The Decline of Politics and Ideology in a Knowledgeable Society," *American Sociological Review*, XXXI (October, 1966), 649–662.

Laski, Harold J. *The Limitations of the Expert*. London: The Fabian Society, 1931.

Lasswell, Harold D. "The Garrison State," *American Journal of Sociology* XLVI (January, 1941), 455–468.

Lasswell, Harold D. *The Analysis of Political Behavior*. London: Routledge and Kegan Paul, 1948.

Lasswell, Harold D. "World Politics and Personal Insecurity" in *A Study of Power*. Ed. by H. D. Lasswell, Charles E. Merriam, and T. V. Smith. Glencoe: The Free Press, 1950. Pp. 3–307.

Lasswell, Harold D., Daniel Lerner, and C. E. Rothwell. *The Comparative Study of Elites*. Stanford: Stanford University Press, 1952.

Lavau, George. "Political Pressures by Interest Groups in France," in *Interest Groups on Four Continents*. Ed. by Henry W. Ehrmann. Pittsburgh: University of Pittsburgh Press, 1958. Pp. 60–95.

Lazarsfeld, Paul F. "Reflections on Business," *The American Journal of Sociology*, LXV (July, 1959), 1–31.

Lazarsfeld, Paul F., William H. Sewell, and Harold L. Wilensky, eds. *The Uses of Sociology*. New York: Basic Books, 1967.

LeMay, General Curtis E., with M. Kantor. *Mission with LeMay*. Garden City: Doubleday & Company, 1965.

Lerner, Daniel. "Interviewing Frenchmen," *American Journal of Sociology*, LXII (September, 1956), 187–194.

Lippmann, Walter. *Essays in the Public Philosophy*. Boston: Little, Brown, and Company, 1955.

Lorwin, Val R. *The French Labor Movement*. Cambridge: Harvard University Press, 1954.

Lorwin, Val R. "'All Colors But Red': Interest Groups and Political Parties in Belgium." Unpublished paper. Center for Advanced Study in the Behavioral Sciences, 1962.

Lowenthal, Max. *The Federal Bureau of Investigation*. New York: William Sloane Associates, 1950.

Machlup, Fritz. *The Production and Distribution of Knowledge in the United States*. Princeton: Princeton University Press, 1962.

Macmahon, Arthur W. "Congressional Oversight of Administration:

The Power of the Purse," in *New Perspectives on the House of Representatives*. Ed. by Robert L Peabody and Nelson W. Polsby. Chicago: Rand McNally & Company, 1963. Pp. 325–381.

Macmahon, Arthur W., John D. Millett, and Gladys Ogden. *The Administration of Federal Work Relief*. Chicago: Public Administration Service, 1941. (Published for the Committee on Public Administration of the Social Science Research Council.)

March, James G., and Herbert A. Simon. *Organizations*. New York: John Wiley & Sons, 1958.

Marshall, S. L. A. *The River and the Gauntlet: Defeat of the Eighth Army by the Chinese Communist Forces, November, 1950, in the Battle of the Congchon River, Korea*. New York: William Morrow & Co., 1953.

Marx, Fritz Morstein, ed. "Formulating the Federal Government's Economic Program: A Symposium," *The American Political Science Review*, XLII (April, 1948), 272–336.

Mather, Frederick C. *Public Order in the Age of the Chartists*. Manchester: University of Manchester Press, 1959.

Matthews, Herbert Lionel. *The Cuban Story*. New York: G. Braziller, 1961.

Matza, David. *Delinquency and Drift*. New York: John Wiley & Sons, 1964.

McWhinney, W. H. "On the Geometry of Organizations," *Administrative Science Quarterly*, X (December, 1965), 347–363.

Merton, Robert K. "The Unanticipated Consequences of Purposive Social Action," *American Sociological Review*, I (December, 1936), 894–904.

Merton, Robert K. "The Role of Applied Social Science in the Formation of Policy: A Research Memorandum," *Philosophy of Science*, XVI (July, 1949), 161–181.

Merton, Robert K. "Priorities in Scientific Discovery" in *The Sociology of Science*. Ed. by Bernard Barber and Walter Hirsch. New York: The Free Press, 1962. Pp. 447–485.

Meyerson, Martin, and E. C. Banfield. *Politics, Planning, and the Public Interest*. Glencoe: The Free Press, 1955.

Meynaud, Jean. *Nouvelles études sur les groupes de pression en France*. Paris: Librairie Armand Colin, 1962.

Milbrath, Lester W. *The Washington Lobbyists*. Chicago: Rand McNally & Company, 1963.

Milburn, T. W., and J. F. Milburn. "Predictions of Threats and Beliefs about How to Meet Them," *American Behavioral Scientist*, IX (March, 1966), 3–7.

Miller, Delbert C., and William H. Form. *Industrial Sociology: The*

Sociology of Work Organizations. 2nd edn. New York: Harper & Row, 1964.

Miller, Norman C. *The Great Salad Oil Swindle*. New York: Coward-McCann, 1965.

Millikan, Max F. "Inquiry and Policy: The Relation of Knowledge to Action" in *The Human Meaning of the Social Sciences*. Ed. by Daniel Lerner. New York: World Publishing Company, 1959. Pp. 158–182.

Moore, David G. "Managerial Strategies and Organization Dynamics in Sears Retailing." Unpublished doctoral dissertation. Chicago: University of Chicago, 1954.

Moore, Wilbert E., and Melvin M. Tumin. "Some Social Functions of Ignorance," *American Sociological Review*, XIV (December, 1949), 787–795.

Moynihan, Daniel P. "The War Against the Automobile," *The Public Interest*, No. 3 (Spring, 1966), pp. 10–26.

Moyzisch, L. C. *Operation Cicero*. New York: Coward-McCann, 1950.

Municipal Police Administration. 5th edn. Chicago: International City Managers' Association, 1961. Pp. 114–116.

Myers, Charles A. "Some Implications of Computers for Management." Unpublished paper. Annual Meeting of Industrial Relations Research Association. San Francisco, December 28, 1966.

Myers, Charles A., and John G. Turnbull. "Line and Staff in Industrial Relations," *Harvard Business Review*, XXXIV (July–August, 1956), 113–124.

Neumann, Franz L. *Behemoth: The Structure and Practice of National Socialism*. New York: Oxford University Press, 1942.

Neustadt, Richard E. *Presidential Power: The Politics of Leadership*. New York: John Wiley & Sons, 1960.

Newman, Donald J. "Pleading Guilty for Considerations: A Study of Bargain Justice," in *The Sociology of Punishment and Correction*. Ed. by Norman Johnson, Leonard Savity, and Marvin E. Wolfgang. New York: John Wiley & Sons, 1962. Pp. 24–32.

New York State, Office of the Counsel. *Combatting Organized Crime*. Report of the 1965 Oyster Bay, New York, Conference. Albany, 1966.

Nisbet, Robert A. "Project Camelot: An Autopsy," *The Public Interest*, No. 5 (Fall, 1966), pp. 45–69.

Nonet, Philippe. "Administrative Justice: A Sociological Study of the California Industrial Accidents Commission." Unpublished doctoral dissertation. Berkeley: University of California, 1966.

Nourse, Edwin G., and Bertram M. Gross. "The Role of the Council of

Economic Advisers," *American Political Science Review*, XLII (April, 1948), 283–295.

Novick, David, ed. *Program Budgeting: Program Analysis and the Federal Budget.* Cambridge: Harvard University Press, 1965.

Packer, Herbert L. *Ex-Communist Witnesses: Four Studies in Fact Finding.* Stanford: Stanford University Press, 1962.

Paulsen, Monrad G., and Sanford H. Kadish. *Criminal Law and Its Processes.* Boston: Little, Brown, and Company, 1962.

Perkins, Frances. *The Roosevelt I Knew.* New York: The Viking Press, 1946.

Pettee, George S. *The Future of American Secret Intelligence.* Washington: Infantry Journal Press, 1946.

Philipson, Morris, ed. *Automation: Implications for the Future.* New York: Vintage Books, 1962.

Platt, Washington. *Strategic Intelligence Production: Basic Principles.* New York: Frederick A. Praeger, 1957.

Possony, Stefan T. "Organized Intelligence: The Problem of the French General Staff," *Social Research*, VIII (May, 1941), 213–237.

Price, Don K. *Government and Science: Their Dynamic Relation in American Democracy.* New York: New York University Press, 1954.

Puttkammer, Ernst W. *Administration of Criminal Law.* Chicago: University of Chicago Press, 1953.

Ransom, Harry Howe. *Central Intelligence and National Security.* Cambridge: Harvard University Press, 1958.

Read, W. "Factors Affecting Upward Communication at Middle Management Levels in Industrial Organizations." Unpublished doctoral dissertation. Ann Arbor: University of Michigan, 1959.

Reith, Charles. *A Short History of the British Police.* London: Oxford University Press, 1948.

Reith, Charles. *The Blind Eye of History: A Study of the Origins of the Present Era.* London: Faber and Faber, n.d. [1952].

Rogers, Lindsay. "Congressional Investigations: The Problem and Its Solution," *University of Chicago Law Review*, XVIII (Spring, 1951), 464–477.

Rose, Arnold M. "Voluntary Associations in France," in A. M. Rose, *Theory and Method in the Social Sciences.* Minneapolis: University of Minnesota Press, 1954. Pp. 72–115.

Rose, Arnold M. "The Social Scientist as an Expert Witness," *Minnesota Law Review*, XL (February, 1956), 205–218.

Roskill, Captain S. W. *The War at Sea, 1939–1945.* 3 vols. London: H.M.S.O., 1956.

Rourke, Francis E. *Secrecy and Publicity: Dilemmas of Democracy.* Baltimore: Johns Hopkins Press, 1961.

Rowat, Donald C., ed. *The Ombudsman: Citizen's Defender.* London: George Allen & Unwin, 1965.

Sayles, Leonard R. *Behavior of Industrial Work Groups: Prediction and Control.* New York: John Wiley & Sons, 1958.

Schattschneider, Elmer E. *Politics, Pressures and the Tariff: A Study of Free Private Enterprise in Pressure Politics, as Shown in the 1929–1930 Revision of the Tariff.* Englewood Cliffs: Prentice-Hall, 1935.

Scheff, Thomas J. "The Societal Reaction to Deviance: Ascriptive Elements in the Psychiatric Screening of Mental Patients in a Midwestern State," *Social Problems,* XI (Spring, 1964), 401–413.

Schilling, Warner R., Paul Y. Hammond, and Glenn H. Snyder. *Strategy, Politics, and Defense Budgets.* New York: Columbia University Press, 1962.

Schlesinger, Arthur M., Jr. *The Age of Roosevelt,* Vol. II: *The Coming of the New Deal.* Boston: Houghton Mifflin, 1959.

Schlesinger, Arthur M., Jr. *A Thousand Days: John F. Kennedy in the White House.* Boston: Houghton Mifflin, 1965.

Schramm, Gustav L. "Philosophy of the Juvenile Court," *Annals of the American Academy of Political and Social Science,* CCLVI (January, 1949), 101–108.

Schumpeter, Joseph A. *Capitalism, Socialism and Democracy.* 2nd edn. New York: Harper & Brothers, 1947.

Schur, Edwin M. *Crimes without Victims: Deviant Behavior and Public Policy—Abortion, Homosexuality, Drug Addiction.* Englewood Cliffs: Prentice-Hall, 1965.

Seabury, Paul. *The Wilhelmstrasse: A Study of German Diplomats under the Nazi Regime.* Berkeley and Los Angeles: University of California Press, 1954.

Selznick, Philip. *TVA and the Grass Roots: A Study in the Sociology of Formal Organization.* Berkeley and Los Angeles: University of California Press, 1949.

Selznick, Philip. *Leadership in Administration: A Sociological Interpretation.* Evanston: Row, Peterson & Co., 1957.

Shanley, John F. "Objectives of the Police Intelligence Unit," *The Police Chief,* XXXI (May, 1964), 10–11, 50.

Shepard, Herbert A. "Nine Dilemmas in Industrial Research," *Administrative Science Quarterly,* I (December, 1956), 295–309.

Sherwood, Robert E. *Roosevelt and Hopkins.* Bantam edn., revised and enlarged. 2 vols. New York: Harper & Brothers, 1948.

Shils, Edward A. *The Torment of Secrecy: The Background and Conse-
    quences of American Security Policies.* Glencoe: The Free Press,
    1956.
Shultz, George P., and Thomas L. Whisler. eds. *Management Organiza-
    tion and the Computer.* New York: The Free Press, 1960.
Silverman, Corinne. *The President's Economic Advisers,* Interuniversity
    Case Program Case Series, Number 48. Alabama: University of
    Alabama Press, 1959.
Simon, Herbert A. *The New Science of Management Decision.* New
    York: Harper & Brothers, 1960.
Simon, Herbert A., Harold Guetzkow, George Kozmetsky, and Gordon
    Tyndall. *Centralization vs. Decentralization in Organizing the
    Controller's Department.* New York: American Book–Stratford
    Press, 1954. (A Research Study and Report prepared for Con-
    trollership Foundation, Inc.)
Simon, Herbert A., Donald W. Smithburg, and Victor A. Thompson.
    Public Administration. New York: Alfred A. Knopf, 1950.
Skolnick, Jerome. *Justice without Trial.* New York: John Wiley &
    Sons, 1966.
Smith, Bruce L. R. "Strategic Expertise and National Security Policy:
    A Case Study" in *Public Policy.* Ed. by John D. Montgomery and
    Arthur Smithies. Cambridge: Graduate School of Public Ad-
    ministration, Harvard University, 1964. Pp. 69–106.
Smith, Bruce L. R. *The RAND Corporation: Case Study of a Non-
    profit Advisory Corporation.* Cambridge: Harvard University
    Press, 1966.
Smith, Richard Austin. "Business Espionage," *Fortune,* LIII (May,
    1956), 118–121, 190, 192, 194.
Snow, C. P. *Science and Government.* Rev. with new appendix. New
    York: New American Library, 1962. (Prepared for Godkin Lec-
    tures, Harvard University, 1960.)
Snyder, Richard C., and Glenn D. Paige. "The United States Decision
    to Resist Aggression in Korea" in *Foreign Policy Decision-Making:
    An Approach to the Study of International Politics.* Ed. by Richard
    C. Snyder, H. W. Bruck, and Burton Sapin. New York: The Free
    Press, 1962. Pp. 206–249.
"Social and Economic Facts—Appraisal of Suggested Techniques for
    Presenting Them to the Courts." Anon. note, *Harvard Law Re-
    view,* LXI (February, 1948), 692–702.
Sorensen, Theodore C. *Decision-making in the White House.* New
    York: Columbia University Press, 1963.
Sorensen, Theodore C. *Kennedy.* New York: Harper & Row, 1965.

Speier, Hans. *Social Order and the Risks of War.* New York: George W. Stewart, 1952.

Stieber, Jack, Walter E. Oberer, and Michael Harrington. *Democracy and Public Review: An Analysis of the UAW Public Review Board.* Santa Barbara: Center for the Study of Democratic Institutions, 1960.

Stouffer, Samuel A. *Communism, Conformity, and Civil Liberties: A Cross-section of the Nation Speaks Its Mind.* Garden City: Doubleday & Company, 1955.

Street, David, Robert D. Vinter, and Charles Perrow. *Organization for Treatment.* Glencoe: The Free Press, 1966.

Sturmthal, Adolf. *Workers Councils: A Study of Workplace Organization on Both Sides of the Iron Curtain.* Cambridge: Harvard University Press, 1964.

Sumner, William Graham. *Folkways: A Study of the Sociological Importance of Usages, Manners, Customs, Mores, and Morals.* Boston: Ginn and Company, 1906.

Szasz, Thomas S. *Law, Liberty, and Psychiatry.* New York: The Macmillan Company, 1963.

Tappan, Paul W. *Juvenile Delinquency.* New York: McGraw-Hill Book Co., 1949.

Taylor, A. J. P. *English History 1914–1945.* New York and Oxford: Oxford University Press, 1965.

Taylor, Telford. *Grand Inquest: The Story of Congressional Investigations.* New York: Simon and Schuster, 1955.

Technology and the American Economy. National Commission on Technology, Automation, and Economic Progress. Washington: Government Printing Office, 1966. I (February, 1966).

Teeters, Negley K., and John O. Reinemann. *The Challenge of Delinquency.* New York: Prentice-Hall, 1950.

Thompson, Victor A. *The Regulatory Process in OPA Gas Rationing.* New York: Columbia University, King's Crown Press, 1950.

Thorwald, Jürgen. *The Century of the Detective.* Trans. by Richard and Clara Winston. New York: Harcourt, Brace and World, 1965.

Treml, Vladimir G. "Input-Output Analysis and Soviet Planning," in *Mathematical Techniques and Soviet Planning.* McLean, Va.: Research Analysis Corporation, 1965, mimeo. Pp. 1–61.

Trow, Martin. "Second Thoughts on Robbins: A Question of Size and Shape." *Universities Quarterly,* XVIII (March, 1964), 136–152.

Truman, David B. *The Governmental Process: Political Interests and Public Opinion.* New York: Alfred A. Knopf, 1951.

Tuchman, Barbara, *The Guns of August.* Dell paperback edn. New York: Dell Publishing Co., 1963.

United Automobile, Aerospace and Agricultural Implement Workers of America (UAW). *Proceedings of the Nineteenth Constitutional Convention, March 20–27, 1964.* Atlantic City, N.J.

U.S. House of Representatives. *Departments of State and Justice, the Judiciary, and Related Agencies, Appropriations for 1956.* Hearings before the Subcommittee of the Committee on Appropriations, House of Representatives, 84th Congress, 1st Session. Washington: Government Printing Office, 1955.

U.S. Office of Education, Department of Health, Education, and Welfare. *Fall 1964 Statistics of Public Elementary and Secondary Day Schools.* Washington: Government Printing Office, 1965.

U.S. Senate. *Invasions of Privacy.* Hearings before the Subcommittee on Administrative Practice and Procedure of the Committee on the Judiciary, United States Senate. 89th Congress, 1st Session. Washington: Government Printing Office, 1965. Part I: February 18, 23, 24, and March 2, 3, 1965; part II: April 13, 27, 28, 29, May 5, 6, and June 7, 1965; part III: July 13, 14, 15, 19, 20, 21, 27, and August 9, 1965.

U.S. Strategic Bombing Survey. 316 volumes. Washington: Government Printing Office, 1945–1947.

Urwick, L. "Organization as a Technical Problem," in *Papers on the Science of Administration.* Ed. by Luther Gulick and L. Urwick. New York: Columbia University, Institute of Public Administration, 1937. Pp. 49–88.

Vagts, Alfred. *Defense and Diplomacy: The Soldier and the Conduct of Foreign Relations.* New York: King's Crown Press, 1956.

Veblen, Thorstein. *The Engineers and the Price System.* New York: The Viking Press, 1921.

Ward, Benjamin. *The Socialist Economy: A Study of Organizational Alternatives.* New York: Random House, 1967.

Wasserman, Benno. "The Failure of Intelligence Prediction," *Political Studies,* VIII (June, 1960), 156–169.

Webster, Sir Charles, and Noble Frankland. *The Strategic Air Offensive Against Germany 1939–1945.* 4 vols. London: H.M.S.O., 1961.

Westley, William A. "Secrecy and the Police," *Social Forces,* XXXIV (March, 1956), 254–257.

Whisler, Thomas L., and Harold J. Leavitt. "Management in the 1980's," *Harvard Business Review,* XXXVI (November–December, 1958), 41–48.

Whitehead, Don. *The FBI Story: A Report to the People*. New York: Random House, 1956.

Whyte, William F. *Money and Motivation*. New York: Harper & Brothers, 1955.

Wildavsky, Aaron. *Dixon-Yates: A Study in Power Politics*. New Haven: Yale University Press, 1962.

Wildavsky, Aaron. *The Politics of the Budgetary Process*. Boston: Little, Brown, and Company, 1964.

Wildavsky, Aaron, and Arthur Hammond. "Comprehensive Versus Incremental Budgeting in the Department of Agriculture," *Administrative Science Quarterly*, X (December, 1965), 321–346.

Wilensky, Harold L. *Intellectuals in Labor Unions: Organizational Pressures on Professional Roles*. Glencoe: The Free Press, 1956.

Wilensky, Harold L. "Work, Careers, and Social Integration," *International Social Science Journal*, XII (Fall, 1960), 543–560.

Wilensky, Harold L. "The Professionalization of Everyone?" *The American Journal of Sociology*, LXX (September, 1964) 137–158.

Wilensky, Harold L. "Measures and Effects of Social Mobility," in *Social Structure and Mobility in Economic Development*. Ed. by Neil J. Smelser and Seymour Martin Lipset. Chicago: Aldine Publishing Company, 1966. Pp. 98–140.

Wilensky, Harold L. "Work as a Social Problem," in *Social Problems*. Ed. by Howard S. Becker. New York: John Wiley & Sons, 1966. Pp. 117–166.

Wilensky, Harold L., and Charles N. Lebeaux, *Industrial Society and Social Welfare*. Paperbound edn. with new intro. (New York: The Free Press, 1965). New York: Russell Sage Foundation, 1958.

Wiles, P. J. D. *The Political Economy of Communism*. Cambridge: Harvard University Press, 1962.

Wilson, O. W. *Police Administration*. New York: McGraw-Hill Book Co., 1958.

Wise, David, and Thomas B. Ross. *The Invisible Government*. New York: Random House, 1964.

Wohlstetter, Roberta. *Pearl Harbor: Warning and Decision*. Stanford: Stanford University Press, 1962.

Woodward, Julian L. "A Scientific Attempt to Provide Evidence for a Decision on Change of Venue," *American Sociological Review*, XVII (August, 1952), 447–452.

Zeisel, Hans, Harry Kalven, Jr., and Bernard Buchholz. *Delay in the Courts*. Boston: Little, Brown, and Company, 1959.

Index